'02 25+

ᄂ²⁵ᶜ

Lone Patriot

Lone Patriot

The Short Career of an American Militiaman

JANE KRAMER

PANTHEON BOOKS   NEW YORK

All rights reserved under International and Pan-American
Copyright Conventions. Published in the United States by
Pantheon Books, a division of Random House, Inc.,
New York, and simultaneously in Canada by
Random House of Canada Limited, Toronto.

Pantheon Books and colophon are registered
trademarks of Random House, Inc.

Portions of this work previously appeared in *The New Yorker*.

A Cataloging-in-Publication record has been established
for this title by the Library of Congress.

www.pantheonbooks.com

Book design by Cassandra J. Pappas

Printed in the United States of America

FIRST EDITION
2   4   6   8   9   7   5   3   1

In memory of
Louis I. Kramer

Acknowledgments

THIS BOOK IS about one moment in an ongoing American story that some people devote their lives to documenting—something I remember whenever I clear a new shelf for the books and articles those people have written or open my e-mail to more evidence of their immense commitment. By now, I must have read forty or fifty books that in one way or another deal with the history of the movement that has come, grotesquely, to be called the Patriot movement, and it is in large part because of that work that I was able to proceed with any certainty or confidence through my own small portrait of the militiaman named John Pitner. Two books I would like to acknowledge in particular: Kenneth Stern's *A Force Upon the Plain,* which appeared the year John Pitner was arrested, and which was national, even international, in its scope; and a book I've referred to countless times in the two years since its publication, David Neiwert's *In God's Country,* a remarkably comprehensive study of the Patriots of the Pacific Northwest (including some of the Patriots in this book).

I began the research for *Lone Patriot* in 1996 and the writing in the fall of 1997, the year John Pitner's trial ended. Early in 1998, still waiting for various appeals to be decided and for a much-delayed second trial to start, I put the project aside. That trial finally took place in the early winter of 2000, and when Pitner himself got out of prison—which he did in January last year—I was able to finish the book. I am indebted to *The New Yorker* for giving me the leave of absence in which to do this. And to the American Academy in Berlin, for giving me the support (and distance) that made it possible.

So many people have helped me in the course of this long wait, keeping me up to date on what was happening in Whatcom County, Washington, while I was back in Europe working. I am grateful to them all. First and foremost, to Jared Hohlt and Luiza Chwialkowska, who worked with me during the first two years; officially, they were my research interns, but it's much more accurate to call them my colleagues and collaborators, since this is what they quickly became. To my Washington colleagues Cathy Logg, Rachel Prentice, Paul de Armond, Scott North, and David Neiwert, who were themselves following the armed right and were incredibly generous with their time and their own research. To every one of the more than ninety people I interviewed in the year I was traveling to Whatcom County and Seattle, including, certainly, John Pitner and his family. And to the friends I made there—especially to David Brewster, then editor of the *Seattle Weekly,* who offered me not only an office away from home but also the imprimatur of his own good name. The list of people who helped, welcomed, and advised me, and are now my friends, is long; I hope they like this book, but I won't burden them with it here.

I want to thank my editor and good friend, Shelley Wanger, not only for her unfailing editorial clarity, but for her inexhaustible kindness and nearly inexhaustible patience. Shelley's assistant, Rahel Lerner, for her feats of down-to-the-wire checking. My agent and old friend, Ed Victor, for fielding for me so wisely and so gracefully. My husband, Vincent, and my daughter and son-in-law, Aleksandra and John, for all the above and much more. And finally, my dog, Pico, who wore a hole in the rug, sitting by my desk.

New York, March 2002

Lone Patriot

One

THE ENEMY TOOK John Pitner by subterfuge and surprise, on a hot midsummer Saturday when no one could really have been expected to stand and fight, and the result was that John lost his liberty before he had a chance to save America. The date was July 27, 1996, the time was five in the afternoon, and the place was a low, gray, pre-fabricated house—the prosecutor said "trailer" and the papers said "mobile home," but the company that made it said "*manufactured* home"—hidden in a small riverine clearing in the woods of Whatcom County, Washington, about eighteen miles inland from Bellingham Bay, and not much farther than that from the Canadian border. In Bellingham, at five, people were already shaking off the day—getting into their cars and heading down to the harbor to watch the kayaks come in and then, maybe, stop for a drink and dinner while the sun melted into a pink line over the San Juan Islands. But out in the county, in the tangled scrub and wayward ash woods that a few very old Whatcom loggers could still remember as breathing forest, the air was heavy, and people were sitting around watching reruns, too listless to enjoy the liberty they had. John himself wasn't watching anything. He was thinking about the real estate agent who had called twice to tell him she was on her way, and, of course, he was also thinking about the invasion of the New World Order, wondering whether, given the imminence of the invasion, it was worth his while to put a second coat of gray paint on the wooden deck of a house that was up for sale anyway. John was very concerned about his liberty. He believed that liberty was something God had guaranteed to men like him, men who were Patriots, and that now the New World Order was chipping it away, like the deck paint on his own porch.

When John was out pitching Armageddon, in his official capacity as founder, promoter, banker, quartermaster, and commander in chief of a Patriot army he called the Washington State Militia, he would sometimes raise his right hand and swear to die fighting to preserve his liberty and yours. "Yup, that's me, give me liberty or give me death," he'd say, after a thoughtful pause which seemed to suggest that, whatever you might have heard to the contrary, the phrase, along with the sentiment, was his. John was armed, he was ready for the big battle, and he never intended to get stopped in his hero's tracks—stopped, much less, in a pair of old pants and a T-shirt, in his own house, at the end of a summer day, by a small woman with a 9 mm Glock, a pair of handcuffs, and an ID from the Federal Bureau of Investigation—but that was what in fact happened. He heard the noise of a car bumping down the dirt road to his clearing and got up to look out the window, expecting to see the realtor and, with any luck, the client she had asked to bring. No one else knew he was home that afternoon, or was even in Whatcom County. His wife, Deborah Sue, had left him that spring and was living in town. His daughter, Rachel, who had driven out earlier for a swim, was certainly back in town, too—though for a moment he wondered if it *was* Rachel, coming to retrieve something she'd forgotten, like her bathing suit or her best lipstick. But just then he spotted the woman, walking toward him with her jacket open in the heat and the Glock poking out of her shoulder holster and what looked to be two companions moving through the trees behind her, hanging back to cover her as she made the short trip across the clearing and up a couple of wooden steps to his front door. John claimed later, and probably still claims, that Special Agent Catherine Fahey of the Bellingham office of the Federal Bureau of Investigation was so nervous coming through the door of the leader of the Washington State Militia that she followed him through the house, cornered him in the bathroom, and held her gun to his temple while one of the people he'd spotted in the trees a minute earlier pulled his arms behind him and snapped the cuffs on for her, whereas Fahey testified that it wasn't the bathroom, it was the bedroom, and that her gun was pointed at the floor. The result, in any event, was the same. John never made his last stand against the New World Order; he was arrested instead, and by all accounts he surrendered quietly, though not without warning Fahey that if he was out of phone contact with the Patriot world for more than twenty-four hours, militias all over the country would go on "tac-4 alert" and his own militiamen—seven thousand of them, he told her—would be deployed. He called it a declaration of war. That night he slept in a holding cell near Seattle, and on Monday, in the resentful company of three other Whatcom County militiamen, three Seattle Freemen, and one of the Freemen's wives, he was formally charged before a magistrate of the U.S. District Court for Western Washington. The charge against him was "conspiracy"—"conspiracy to make and possess destructive devices"—and the purpose of those devices was "an eventual confrontation" with the federal government or the United Nations. The case became known as *United States v. John Irvin Pitner et al.*

WHEN I INTERVIEWED John Pitner for the first time, four months before his arrest and about three months after I had started talking to people on the Patriot fringe of the American right, there were thought to be as many as eight hundred militias in the country—even as many as nine hundred, given the strong likelihood that the most seriously armed militias were going to be the ones nobody outside the Patriot underground had ever heard of. Today, there are fewer than two hundred known militias, which is to say active, identifiable, self-designated, paramilitary, citizens' reserves teetering aboveground on the perch of their First Amendment right to speak freely and assemble peaceably and their Second Amendment license to buy arms and organize. Some people claim the militia movement is over. Some claim it was never much of a movement anyway, since, at least in theory, all you ever really needed to make a militia was one like-minded friend and the loan of a hunting rifle. But even today, with so many watch groups committed to tracking activity on the armed right, there is no consensus on the number of people actually *in* militias. The FBI last put it at forty thousand, but other estimates I've seen run from an improbably modest five or ten thousand to an improbably cautionary four hundred thousand. And, this being pretty much what they ran five years ago, it could also be true that the number of men in armed, unknown, underground, Patriot hate groups, if not the groups themselves, has simply increased accordingly (an assumption that at least helps to explain the discovery of huge caches of machine guns and explosives seized in the trailer of one Montana militiaman late this winter, along with thirty thousand rounds of ammunition and a hit list that included most of the county's law enforcement personnel).

My colleague Cathy Logg, an ex-Marine and Bellingham grandmother who at the time of John's arrest was covering crime for the *Bellingham Herald,* told me that after John's trial ended, in 1997, she had fought to keep the story of the Washington State Militia open, and lost. "My boss kind of thought, 'They've arrested these guys, and the rattlesnake is dead,' and I said, 'Noooo, they've just cut off the rattle,' " was the way she put it, and of course she was right. For one thing, it's harder to stay rattling aboveground than it once was. Militias that court attention—militias with leaders like John who go public with their names and numbers and what John used to call their "Good Samaritan" faces, and talk to reporters, and make speeches—are, almost by definition, the easiest ones to infiltrate (and so many undercover cops and agents were fed into the militia movement in 1995, after the Oklahoma City bombing, that it's likely all of them *were* infiltrated). For another, a good argument can be made that, with the right in the White House, a few militiamen, at least, have started sleeping better and, by extension, that any militiaman who isn't sleeping better was probably headed underground all along. Norman Olson, who once ran the Michigan Milita (and was so eager for attention himself that he called to confirm the connection between his own Michigan Militia and Terry Nichols, the Oklahoma City conspirator now in prison on a life sentence, before anyone even knew about a connection) disbanded his latest militia a few months after George W. Bush's inauguration, telling reporters, with some disgust, that "across the nation, there is a satisfaction among Patriots with the way things are going." The difference, of course, is that in the mid-nineties Bill Clinton was still in the first term of a two-term presidency, the Senate was still in Democratic hands, and the radical right was represented by Newt Gingrich, the new Speaker of the House and, as it turned out, a man who could have been bought off with a short ride in *Air Force One.* Today, the country has a war on terror that is not homegrown, a born-again president, an attorney general more highly regarded on the Patriot Web sites than in the *New York Times,* and a House whip who sounds as if John Pitner drafts his stump speeches. The Good Samaritan faces are what you see in Congress, though right now their preoccupation has shifted from the Wall Street conspiracy to the conspiracy called Al Qaeda that tried to destroy Wall Street on September 11, 2001. The problem for militias today is less the tedium of satisfaction than it is a kind of ideological conflict of interest, since Osama bin Laden's followers seem to have precisely the same enemies they do—with the notable distinction that Al Qaeda's enemies list includes white American Christians, people like *them,* while theirs has always included foreigners, or, you could say, people who are not white, American, and Christian. Some of the supremacist groups have managed to get around this the way one American neo-Nazi did when he posted a note of congratulations to the terrorists of September 11th, praising them for "testicular" courage while reminding them not even to think about "marrying our daughters." But it was not the sort of thing a Good Samaritan would say.

It has to be said that, in 1996, my idea of the American mainstream was exceptionally limited. I had grown up in the McCarthy years and had long since accepted that what Richard Hofstadter so famously described as "the paranoid style in American politics" might also be our most enduring style. I had even produced a book about a cowboy, hoping to discover what happened to an American archetype when his own myths of liberty failed. But after twenty years of living between New York and Paris, and of reporting almost entirely from Europe, nothing, not even my own experience writing about the kinds of nationalism that were surfacing (and resurfacing) there in the eighties and nineties, really prepared me for the ideology of Oklahoma City, or for the peculiarly American rhetoric of the militiamen I started meeting, or—and maybe it was this, more than anything—for the evidence of danger to people like me in what was after all *my* country. Certainly, nothing prepared me for how unfamiliar the West would seem, with its militias and Freemen and Patriot tribes all gathering for the big fight—which I imagine is why I ended up in Whatcom County, with my back to the Pacific, talking to John Pitner. John believed that the fight for America was going to start in Whatcom County, and, short of Alaska, Whatcom County was just about as far west as you could go in the continental United States. John didn't credit anyone

who tried to dissuade him, not even his sheriff, Dale Brandland, who was the only lawman in Whatcom County whose
authority John recognized, the only one with what he called
the "constitutional right" even to *be* in the county. The sheriff
wanted everyone to believe that war in Whatcom County was
impossible, if for no reason other than that the government
was incapable of organizing anything as complicated as a war
in Whatcom County. ("Not without screwing up," as he explained it to me.) But John told me what he had told his men
in the Washington State Militia: that the enemy they called
the New World Order—the president and the United States
Army and the United Nations troops and the FBI SWAT
teams and the Earth First! terrorists and all the other conspirators who took their orders from David Rockefeller and the
rest of the Marxist elite on the Council on Foreign Relations
and the Trilateral Commission and got their weapons from
the eight Jewish bankers who owned the Federal Reserve—
was going to cross the Canadian border just below Vancouver,
and fan out off the Interstate 5 to start the battle for America
on the very road where John and Debbie Pitner had put their
house. John never said, not precisely, that the masterminds of
the New World Order had chosen Valley Highway 9 because a
Patriot by the name of John Pitner lived there. He liked to
present himself as a modest man, just an honest citizen doing
what he could to alert his neighbors to the great conspiracy
against them. He wanted to enlighten, not frighten, the farmers and loggers and born-again dropouts who lived near him
on Valley Highway, which wasn't a highway at all—not for
moving tanks and armies—but a country road, winding beside the south fork of the Nooksack River, up from the little
town of Deming and east through Van Zandt and Acme and

Sedro Woolley and a couple of other villages so small they had simply kept the name of the first settler to stay long enough to need a tombstone. It wasn't John's fault if some of his neighbors looked at the documents, theirs for such a small price, thought things over, and came to the conclusion that John Pitner was the reason the enemy was going to launch its assault on freedom on a stretch of back-country road in the woods of the northwest corner of the state of Washington, instead of, say, marching right down the Interstate 5 to Seattle, or even to Los Angeles—or for that matter crossing from the east of Canada and knocking out Wall Street on the way to the town they always referred to, shaking their heads or rolling their eyes and sighing, as "*that* Washington." Not even the sheriff thought it was John's fault. "It's not like they're stupid," Brandland told me, when I was in Bellingham for the first time and asking everyone I met to describe the kind of people who believed in John. "They select their information. If it doesn't fit their paradigm, it's out. I try to keep an open mind. I just don't write them off as being nuts. I think that's inappropriate."

The truth was that John took some pride in being Ground Zero in the coming Patriot wars, the personal front line of a citizens' army that stretched, as he put it, from Valley Highway all the way to New Hampshire. He swore that the New World Order wasn't going to take America as long as John Pitner was alive and fighting in Whatcom County. He wanted me to know that he had read the "signs" and that he was prepared. We had met exactly a week before his forty-fifth birthday, and I knew almost nothing about him then, other than that he ran a militia that some Bellingham liberals regarded as a menace and others as a bad joke. ("Those guys? You could take them out with a Girl Scout troop!" was what I'd heard.) But this much was clear: the fact that John Pitner had been born on April 19, 1951, in the state of Washington, was one of the few details in the story of his Patriot awakening that he hadn't had to change or fiddle to his advantage, because April 19th was the most important sign of all when it came to understanding the war for America, and what his role in the war would be, and even why it was going to start in Whatcom County. John did not believe in coincidence. He believed there was a reason why Janet Reno—"Janet Reno," he called her, "the illegal attorney general of the so-called United States"— had chosen April 19, 1993, to murder the people John thought of as "peaceful, religious folks, exercising their constitutional rights down in Waco, Texas," just as there was a reason why Clinton, the illegal president, had chosen April 19, 1995, to bomb the Alfred P. Murrah Federal Building in Oklahoma City, in order to blame Patriots like Terry Nichols and Timothy McVeigh, and reduce Americans to fear and panic. When John counted the dead—81 men, women, and children dead in Waco; 168 men, women, and children dead in Oklahoma City—it was obvious that all those American bodies had been signs to John Pitner, approaching his forty-fifth birthday. And those were merely the big signs. There were small ones too, directed entirely at him. "Yup, the messages" is the way he put it. The messages began to arrive one morning in the spring of 1995, when John woke up to an ear-splitting roar, rushed outside, and discovered an unmarked black helicopter hovering no more than a hundred feet above his flagpole. Then, no more than a year later, the FBI paid a visit to Valley Highway. A couple of suits came for John and drove him to an empty building at the Bellingham airport—sometimes, it was the

Seattle airport—and zapped his brain with lasers, and that was when he knew for certain that David Rockefeller had written "John Pitner" at the top of his list of targets.

It was John's belief that Rockefeller was the "true, secret power" behind the New World Order, and Rockefeller, to his credit, took John seriously—which was more than John could say for the liberals he knew in Bellingham. John hated Bellingham. It was the county seat, a pretty port town with a population of not much more than fifty thousand, but John viewed it with the kind of suspicion and alarm that most people reserve for the favelas of São Paulo or the bidonvilles of Cairo. Bellingham had sanctuary churches and human rights activists. It had a National Public Radio station and it had a university—Western Washington University—with a gay and lesbian hot line and it had a reputation on the funk-rock circuit and it had a bookstore called Village Books, whose owner boasted that he could spend a lifetime behind his cash register and never meet anyone who had voted for George Bush or Ronald Reagan. The people who lived in Bellingham were by and large serious citizens. They signed petitions and joined protests and sat through political debates and book club meetings and discussion panels with the Western Washington faculty. They complained a lot about the levels of fluoride dumped in Bellingham Bay by Georgia Pacific—whose chemical plant was the biggest industry in town—but, as one Bellingham professor put it, they did not believe that agents of the New World Order had dumped it there in order to make them sterile. Rockefeller, like John, knew better. John could picture Rockefeller, back east in his New York mansion, conspiring about things like fluoride with the generals and the bankers and the Wall Street Communists and the secretary-general of the

United Nations. He could almost hear the order go out to the troops that were already massing and operational, a few miles north of Valley Highway in Canada. "Take out Pitner!" Rockefeller always said. "Repeat. Take out Pitner!" As Debbie explained it when I knew her better, "John's this guy has a little touch of—what would you call it?—the hero complex."

For a while, by John's account, he held his own. He let it be known that Rockefeller was running scared. Then, in the winter of 1996, he read somewhere about Rockefeller cancelling a trip to Olympic National Park, just across Puget Sound from Seattle, and this, finally, was the proof he needed. It wasn't long before word went out on the Patriot Web sites that David Rockefeller had been so shaken at the prospect of having to face John Pitner and his militia at the park entrance, putting themselves between him and the land he was planning to seize from the American people and turn into an "ecosystem" (which, if you lived in Whatcom County, you knew was a code word for United Nations territory), that he not only cancelled his trip but actually postponed his invasion. Still, it wasn't until John was arrested and sent to jail that John could really begin to appreciate how, after such a big humiliation, Rockefeller had had no choice but to pull him in and order the judge to see to it that he was put away. "David Rockefeller pushed the button," John said to me once, during a lunch break at his trial. "David Rockefeller was really pissed off at me."

AT THE BEGINNING, not many people in Whatcom County, or even on John's particular stretch of Valley Highway, between Deming and Van Zandt, knew John. In fact, not many people had ever thought one way or another about John

Pitner before the fall of 1995—when he posted a notice inviting his neighbors to a gathering he would later refer to with historic solemnity as "the first public meeting of the Washington State Militia." About forty people came, among them the local Patriots, the sheriff, the Bellingham police chief, and a couple of informers for the FBI. They sat in the Rome Grange, in front of a big yellow banner with a black snake coiled on it—"Don't tread on me," the banner, and presumably the snake, said—and listened to John describe the terrible plot to enslave them. But even then, the most they could really have told you about John Pitner was that John was the stranger with the small spread down in the woods by the south fork of the Nooksack River, and that you got there by a dirt road, off the highway, which crossed some old Northern Pacific tracks and then dropped to a stretch of riverbank beach where the liberals in the South Fork Beach Association came to swim naked and, as one of the Whatcom preachers put it, "fornicate right in front of their own innocent babes." A few of John's neighbors claimed to have seen his house arrive, in sections, on the bed of a semi, six or seven years earlier. A few claimed to have seen Debbie—she was a big, blond, good-looking woman, over six feet tall, shy but hard to miss, even in a crowd—nursing a Bloody Mary, after work, at the Nooksack Indians' casino. And a few actually knew their daughter, Rachel, because Rachel was a friendly, high-spirited girl who had spent a couple of years at Mount Baker High, the local high school, and had earned her pocket money in Van Zandt, clerking at Everybody's Store, an old-fashioned general store which was called Everybody's so that everybody with an urge for a bagel or a bag of organic jellybeans or a stick of jerky would feel at home. But until the night of November 11, 1995, at the Rome Grange, all that most people really knew about John Pitner was that he flew his Stars and Stripes from the tallest flagpole on Valley Highway; they knew this because they could usually see the top of it poking through the trees. As John was fond of saying, the only thing that stood between the American flag and the flag of the United Nations were Patriots like him.

JOHN WAS KNOWN as a man who kept to himself. It was something his neighbors respected, maybe because so many of them had reason to keep to themselves, too. The woods of Whatcom County were full of men and women who wanted to be alone. People had been disappearing into those woods—disappearing into the wild ash groves and up the foothills rolling east to Mount Baker and the North Cascades—for as long as people had been coming to the state of Washington. You could say that this was the charm of Whatcom County, and the neighbors were not insensitive to it. They had respected the secretive, solitary ways of draft resisters and hippies and marijuana farmers and students who bicycled out to communes after class at Western Washington University. They had respected the ways of Second Amendment gun nuts and gyppo loggers and ecologists who came to preach against logging. They had respected the ways of homeschooling fundamentalists who came to protect their children from the influence of sex education and biology teachers, and of Vietnam veterans who came to grieve, and maybe even to chase their demons in backwoods cabins where nobody from what they called "the world" could find them. And now they respected the secretive, solitary ways of John Pitner. Leaving your neighbor alone, not asking your neighbor questions, understanding that a man had a right to his own thoughts and his own beliefs and his own insanity—people in Whatcom County said that not asking questions was what the American West was all about. It was a point of pride among them, and, of course, it was one of the reasons John Pitner came to Whatcom County. Nobody asked questions when his house went up, or was much surprised, over the years, by rumors that he had threatened a couple of nude bathers sunning on the South Fork beach or had filed suit against the beach association or had been seen trekking up Mount Baker with a group of odd-looking middle-aged men in combat clothes. It's probably safe to say that, out in the county, no one was even surprised to pick up the *Bellingham Herald* on the Monday morning after John's encounter with Special Agent Catherine Fahey and discover his picture on the front page, or even to read that he was locked in a jail, just south of Seattle, accused of conspiracy and waiting to be indicted.

In a way, getting arrested was a vindication for John, because he wasn't a very prepossessing man, not at all what you would have expected in the number one enemy of the New World Order. When people in the Patriot movement pictured a great leader, it was usually someone more in the line of John's mentor John Trochmann, the head of the Militia of Montana, or, as it was known affectionately in the movement, MOM. Trochmann was a hustler of such cunning and persuasive gravitas that he could sell you anything: the year John met him, or so John told me, he ran up a bill for $10,000 worth of MOM survival gear, conspiracy tapes, and loopy "documentary" videos. But Trochmann looked like a prophet. People who'd seen him said that, with his homespun clothes and his granite face and fine white beard and the fanatical fire in his eyes, he could have stepped right out of that famous portrait of John Brown—the one everyone knew, but couldn't name the painter—although they had to admit the resemblance ended there, since Brown's great passion was abolition, whereas Trochmann's was a credo called Christian Identity, and involved the conviction that God had made Negroes on the fifth day of His creation, along with the other beasts of the field, and not on the sixth day, when He made people.

John Pitner, on the other hand, was not the stuff of memorable paintings. His eyes held more petulance than passion. His hair was an ordinary brown, parted low and combed carefully across a slightly balding crown. He was short—about five feet seven—with big teeth and a rabbity smile and the bland babyish face of a man at some remove from the lessons of reality, not to mention from the doubts or reflections that eventually line the faces of the rest of us with what is usually called character or experience. Age had settled not so much on John's face as on top of it and around it, turning his mustache white and wiry and grizzling his sideburns with what he felt was the touch of maturity appropriate to a patriot leader. John wanted more than anything to be distinguished, but, in spite of the grizzled sideburns, distinction tended to elude him. What he had, at his most unguarded, was a kind of goofy charm. He blushed when he was proud of something, or delighted by something, or surprised. You would see his ears redden, and then his neck, and his face, and as soon as he was all red his cheeks would puff and he'd explode with a big heehaw. You would hear him laugh, and swear it was a donkey braying—or a child tasting ice cream for the first time.

John worked his meager charm. He was good on his feet;

he had hammy but effective timing. He would start a tirade about the New World Order and the coming war, and just before your eyes glazed over he would cut it short with a little joke at his own expense. He would pat his paunch, on a word like "patriot," and shrug, looking a little sheepish, and then the blush would start and he'd say, "Now if you're a Patriot, or a patriotic individual, you're a potgut, middle-aged, balding . . ." The sentence would trail off, with John braying in his aw-shucks way, because, after all, this was *the* John Pitner— John the Commander, his wife called him—taking a moment to step down from his pedestal and show you he was just as human as the next guy. It was not a sentence he was likely to have finished anyway; he was in fact quite vain. He steamed his face pink and shiny. He slicked his thin brown hair. He loved clothes and dressed with the rapt attention of a teenage boy, and what he lacked in taste he made up for in self-regard. I remember two or three times at home when he made his entrance in a new bathrobe, belted over a pair of immaculately creased pants. He was as proud of his bathrobes as he was of his $750 night-vision goggles. He had a purple velour bathrobe, blocked with the sort of pre-Columbian geometric pattern you sometimes saw on the floor models at a furniture warehouse sale. He had an apple-green terry cloth bathrobe so bright and starchy that it could have been trailing tissue paper and a price tag. He was very careful about entrances. When he had an appointment with someone he didn't know, he'd call a militiaman to come over and "run security" at the door—by which he meant open the door. He told me that Trochmann himself never saw anyone or went anywhere without security, but I suspect that John did it to give himself time to change out of the sweats he usually wore and choose the right clothes for the occasion. When I met him, security was a spectral recruit who lurked somewhere inside his own camouflage of black beard, baggy black overalls, dark glasses, and a black cap pulled so low on his forehead that all I could see of him besides his two pale hands was the tip of his nose. He circled the Pitners' living room, watching me closely in case I started opening drawers or filching papers, not saying a word until a door to the living room burst open and John emerged, in his terry cloth robe, with a clean white towel around his neck and a telephone at his ear. He dismissed the recruit, with a wave of his free hand, and for the next ten minutes he paced the room, barking into the cell phone. Eventually, he acknowledged me with a helpless smile. There were so many urgent matters competing for his attention, so many enemies threatening his America, that John, I could see, was running late just thinking about them all.

John longed to be a celebrity like Trochmann—someone the media called when a bomb went off, or when a bunch of Freemen, holed up on a ranch they didn't own, threatened to shoot the sheriff who came to evict them—and never mind that the Jewish bankers owned the media, or that, more often than not, the media was one nervous reporter sitting in John's living room. I was certainly nervous, those first few times at the house that John called "headquarters" or the "command post" or the "intel" (for "intelligence") "center" or "my private office and things of that nature." I didn't know then, and still don't know, if being nervous had to do with some atavistic terror at finding myself alone, in the woods, with a person who was convinced that eight Jewish bankers were selling America to the United Nations, or if it was a perfectly reasonable way to feel, given that I so obviously represented the kind of person who John claimed was making *him* nervous. I was a woman. I came from the East. I was liberal and educated and, by John's lights, prosperous. I was even on the Council on Foreign Relations—de facto part of the conspiracy. The nearest house was a developer's log cabin that was never used. And the closest neighbors were a couple of aging hippies who either sold or collected (they wouldn't say) rusty car parts and old mattress springs and abandoned logging gear at a campsite on another dirt road, about a quarter of a mile east of John's turnoff, and, to the west, an old Nooksack woman who lived in a ramshackle, riverbank cabin with an angry dog chained outside it, neither of whom encouraged company. And, as I soon learned, once John made an entrance and began talking, he was unlikely to be interrupted by anything more pressing than the urge for a cigarette or for one of the cookies he liked—the kind with M&Ms melted into the warm dough. Whoever found him at home at headquarters was there for the duration of a performance which John was polishing for the day the war started and the correspondents at CNN and CBS and all of the other big networks woke up to the truth of the conspiracy, and flew to Whatcom County to consult him.

It was a strange performance, and not really for being scary or ludicrous or mad or—as it was the first time I heard it—delivered by a damp stranger in a bathrobe. The strangest thing about John's performance was how American he made it seem, sitting there with his mug of instant coffee and his plate of cookies in the plasterboard parlor of his double-width manufactured home, sharing a faded flowered couch with a couple of drowsy cats that clearly had no plans for the invasion. John spoke in the flat, friendly, utterly uninflected voice of the television heartland, and when you heard that voice you felt you could easily be in any of a million other plasterboard American parlors—that the crazy literature and the hate videos stacked in a metal bookcase on his living room wall were somehow of a piece with the old television console on the floor beside him, and the coffee table with its laminated panels, and the couch with the matching armchairs, and the potted tree, and the exercise bicycle gathering dust in the corner. There were so many homey and attentive touches in that small, slightly shabby, prefabricated room—there were family pictures, and a framed needlepoint of a cardinal perched on a branch, and a tangled shag rug, black and orange, hanging behind the couch like an heirloom—that at first they made John's lunatic library, his conspiracy charts and gun manuals, his stacks of magazines about free men mining the universe for fun and profit, look like nothing more alarming than the guy stuff in Archie Bunker's garage.

JOHN'S PERFORMANCE rarely varied. The people who sat through it most often—his wife, his family, the militiamen who wandered in and out of what he called his private "leadership meetings"—were sometimes astonished by how little it changed, when the rest of the world was changing. "John, number one, he's a big bullshitter, everybody knows that," Jack Schleimer told me. Jack was an anxious Christian creationist who had spent a year and a half in the militia, going to those meetings (and was otherwise self-employed as a "bridge and inlay man," making false teeth in his Deming garage), and his view of John, months after he had quit, hadn't changed. "He's one of them kind of people—a good salesman, I guess," Jack said. "He made things up, stretched the truth. That's what he would do: spread suspicions . . . I'll say this off the top of my head, that he was practicing Hegelian dialectics. This is not to say he was a Communist. This is not to say that the info we got through the Patriot movement wasn't true." Certain things in America were particularly worrisome to John, and the one he began with, the "first and foremost" worrisome thing, was indeed the Council on Foreign Relations. He kept a chart—most Patriots had one—of all the important politicians on the CFR, cross-referenced with the membership list of the Trilateral Commission. He was convinced that the CFR and the TC (he always referred to them, ominously, by initials) were secret societies, and because of this, the chart counted as one of his most valuable documents, along with his copy of the "true" American Constitution and his printout of a nearly incoherent text entitled "Presidential Directive 25," which he claimed was Clinton's secret schedule for handing the American military over to the United Nations. He kept the chart displayed on his coffee table, like an art book or the latest issue of some glossy weekly, and he would often pick it up at the beginning of his litany of worrisome things and read out the title, "Political Dominance Through Four Administrations," pointing to where it said "David Rockefeller, chairman emeritus, CFR," and demand of his audience what better proof was needed that the American people had already been betrayed. From there, it was an easy jump to the worrisome black helicopter that still hovered over the Pitner household, though not, apparently, when anyone but John was around to see it. And then to the Federal Reserve, which John knew for a fact was a private bank—a bank with a huge warehouse, stacked with dollars—that laundered cash for the International Monetary Fund, which in turn used that cash to buy more armies for the United Nations, which itself was responsible for the tens of thousands of Russian troops training at that very moment close to Valley Highway, which everyone knew was already studded with microchips that tracked the lives of Whatcom County's children, controlling their moods and their movements and targeting any recalcitrant young Patriot for "special surveillance." John believed in his documents and his info and his intel the way a fundamentalist like Jack Schleimer believed in the Bible—not as *his* word but as the Word, absolute, incontrovertible, not open to discussion. You didn't argue with John. People who did were either in the conspiracy or a dupe to the conspiracy (as he warned me I was); and in any event they were wrong. John had done his research. He had seen the videos and heard the tapes and talked to the "experts" on the Patriot Web sites and ordered the right books, the ones you wouldn't find at the Bellingham Public Library, and it didn't matter if those books were written by the Founding Fathers or by conspiracy salesmen like Trochmann or Jack McLamb, the renegade Arizona police sergeant whose own contribution to the literature sold under the title *Operation Vampire Killer 2000*. By then, of course, John was an expert, too. His specialties were the Federal Reserve, the War Powers Act, and education—"Yup, I can't be an expert on everything," he told his admirers—because the Fed was stealing your money, the War Powers Act was stealing your freedom to make more money, and a modest teaching experiment in the Washington public schools, known to the right as Outcome Based Education and to the left as Performance Based Education, was stealing your children's will to resist the first two. Every day, John logged on to the computer in the spare bedroom where he kept his files, and downloaded the latest news on the conspiracy—the classified pictures of the concentration camps the government was building to exterminate Patriots like him, the secret accounts of Clinton's Arkansas drug-running operation—and, as he liked to say, he never saw anything to change his mind.

People living in the woods of Whatcom County tend to believe in enemies, and the ones who joined John's militia believed in them long before he moved there. ("I look at these people, I haven't seen one, not one, I can relate to," an agent working out of the FBI's Seattle office said to me that October. "It's a losers' club. This is where the danger lies.") They thought of the America "out there," the America that eluded them, the America spinning and speeding into a future way beyond their competence and even their comprehension, less as complicated than as hostile, which may be why John's delusions did, in the end, thrive in their occasional company. In fact, when you met the neighbors it was easy to believe that those delusions had as much to do with John living in Whatcom County as they did with anything John brought to Whatcom County. If John had been living in Boston, which he had as a small child, he might have had neighbors who took his stories about enemies and invasions and saving America from David Rockefeller, and put them down to something as banal as the midlife crisis of a man who had never amounted to much of anything and who saw his last chance to be someone who mattered, someone important. If he had been living in New York City, where he'd squatted briefly as a runaway teenage boy, he might even have had neighbors who took those stories not as delusions at all but as pure rainmaker rhetoric, and dismissed John Pitner as a kind of Elmer Gantry of Patriot paranoia. It's even possible that if John had been a Christian, in the Whatcom County, good-news sense of "Christian"—if he had done his preaching at one of the little Pentecostal churches on Valley Highway instead of at the Rome Grange under a banner with a snake on it—he might have been born again and got his ticket to heaven, just like that, and never have had to fret about looking good at the Apocalypse. It was certainly possible that if he had called a psychiatrist, instead of a Bellingham doctor with a family practice, after the FBI zapped his brain with lasers, he would have been persuaded to start a conversation about the New World Order with someone besides the kind of person who believed in lasers. If he had even talked to the right relative— like the deputy police chief down in Mountlake Terrace who had married his stepsister—instead of to two doting older sisters who wanted badly to believe that John was a leader of men, that all the people (including themselves) who had ever lost patience with John Pitner or written off John Pitner were wrong, he might have been forced back into reality. As it was, he wouldn't even listen to his wife when she grew a little skeptical about the war for America starting in their backyard, or when she complained because he had stopped working in order to prepare for it. John told Debbie that there was no use working, no use killing yourself working—not, she said, that she had ever known him to kill himself working—when the UN was planning to take your home anyway, and everything else you had. After a while, Debbie stopped complaining, because John had to be right, he had to be deferred to, he had to have the secret. The secret was all he had.

Two

TRAINING MILITIAS for war against the New World Order is only one of the things people in the Patriot movement do. In fact, it's likely that most Patriots have never even been to a militia meeting, and would not particularly want to now. In the lexicon of the far right, "Patriot" refers not so much to any particular group as to a kind of catchment population, which, like the militia population, can vary drastically according to who's counting and how loosely he defines the word. I've heard the number of Patriots put as high as twenty million, an estimate that clearly includes the activists on the far fringe of the fundamentalist right. Most Patriot watchers put the number much lower, at the three to four million white American men and women who claim to be the victims, real or intended, of an international plot to destroy their freedom and pollute their blood, and—inasmuch as they consider the United States party to this plot—have exempted themselves from many, and in some cases all, of the inconveniences of citizenship, from paying taxes to carrying drivers' licenses to obeying the laws that make it a crime to murder the people they resent. The Seattle journalist David Neiwert—who covered John's trial with me, and a few years later produced the book *In God's Country,* an exceptionally fine history of the Patriot movement in the Pacific Northwest—was convinced that the Patriots he'd studied were not only "quite diverse in their beliefs" but ranged in what you could call fanaticism and focus from "the cross-burning Christian Identity followers of the Hayden Lake variety to the buttoned-down advocates of 'constitutionalism,' from the bomb-flinging robbers of the Phineas Priesthood to the seemingly mild-mannered 'sovereign citizens' who quietly form 'common law' courts."

Without militias, there would still be Patriots. There would still be lunatic groups like the Ku Klux Klan, now in its eighty-second year and going strong, with chapters active all over the country. Or like the Aryan Nations, which was forced to sell its famous Idaho compound in the winter of 2001 (thanks to a harassment suit and a judgment involving several million dollars in damages), but, in the wake of the Al Qaeda attacks last September 11, is now said to be collecting large contributions toward a new one, perhaps in Pennsylvania. There would still be Freemen threatening the men and women who write judgments like the one in Idaho and, in fact, passing their own sentences against the clerks who file those judgments and the sheriffs who try to enforce them. There would still be terrorists like the Phineas Priests who not so long ago blew up a Spokane bank and the offices of a Spokane newspaper as an April Fool's gesture; there would still be neo-Nazi skinheads murdering immigrants; there would still be the peripatetic psychopaths known both to the Patriots who incite them and to the agents who hunt them as "the loose cannons" or "the lone wolves." And, of course, there would still be erstwhile militiamen, because distinctions at the far edges of the far right tend to blur. The militias, as David Neiwert says, are simply there "to enforce and defend" the revolution that most Patriots are convinced will save them, and transform their country into a better sort of neighborhood.

John considered himself an exemplary Patriot. He had the right enemies, although by Patriot standards he was tolerant. He didn't object to homosexuals—at any rate, not enough to refuse a $35,000 bail bond, a landscaping job, a comfortable bed, and a couple of months of home-cooked meals from his sister Susan, a happily partnered lesbian, when she and her companion, Betsey, offered their house as collateral in order to rescue him from the "ordeal" of his pretrial detention in a Kent, Washington, jail. Nor was he demonstrably concerned about the presence of blacks or Jews or Indians or immigrants or, for that matter, women in his imagined America, though when a black man did show up at a militia meeting, he described it—if not at the time, then to me, later—as an "attempt to infiltrate by a black individual." In public, he always delivered a cheerful pitch about the Washington State Militia welcoming "all races, religions, sexes, and things of that nature." But it has to be said that very few Patriot groups offered you what John and his militia, and, indeed, most militias, offered, which was the chance to bring your own enemies to the table, or to invent your enemies as you went along, or to spread the word among people who might be marginally less deluded than you that the violence you did was really your enemies' violence, planned and executed to discredit *them*. That, of course, was why people in some of those Patriot groups joined militias, or organized out of militias, and why the groups themselves used militias like the Washington State Militia to proselytize and recruit. John's conspiracy was a stockpot simmering in his head and his propaganda; you could add anything or anybody, and it only got tastier and more nutritious.

In one sense, all Patriot groups believe not only in the same conspiracy and the same conspirators, but in the same revenge. They line the same pockets in the big business of keeping America's white heroes in arms and real estate and rackets. They read the same literature, they keep in touch, and when it's in their interests, they cooperate. They are part of the same networks and sometimes even the same families. Timothy McVeigh—executed in the summer of 2001 for delivering the bomb that went off in Oklahoma City on John Pitner's forty-fourth birthday—was not only a regular on the midwestern militia circuit but also, by his own admission, a devotee of the cult novel *The Turner Diaries,* about the war of the whites against the dark forces of the conspiracy. *The Turner Diaries,* which was written and published in the late seventies by a Patriot named William Pierce, could best be described as the *War and Peace* of the white supremacy terrorist crowd, and by the time McVeigh read it, it had already inspired a couple of generations of terrorists—the most notorious among them being Robert Mathews, a violently anti-Semitic Arizonan with a gang he had named The Order, after the Patriot warriors in the book. Mathews and his men began by robbing banks and trucks, went on to counterfeiting, and ended up murdering a well-known Jewish talk-radio host from Denver named Alan Berg. And when Mathews himself was killed in the early eighties—he died in an island hideout on Puget Sound, at the end of a shoot-out between the gang and a small army of federal agents—his widow made her way to Idaho and the Aryan Nations compound at Hayden Lake, where *she* met and married the Phineas Priest who fifteen years later opened fire on the children at a Jewish Community Center in Los Angeles. The newlyweds were themselves close to the Christian Identity "Reverend" Richard Butler, the man who invented the Aryan Nations. Butler, in turn, was said to be close to the Trochmanns—John Trochmann, his wife, his brother Dave, and his nephew Randy—whose own compound was just a short drive over the state line in Montana. And John Trochmann, of course, was close to John Pitner. At least, John Pitner said so. The militias may not have been marching out publicly to murder talk-radio hosts or shoot children or set fire to black churches, or dump fake anthrax into the mailboxes of abortion clinics (more than a hundred and thirty-five envelopes in the 1990s), or for that matter send real anthrax to Democratic senators and network news anchors. But they thought about it, and talked about it, and more to the point, they made a comfortable, legal network of contacts for the kind of people who did. You could meet everybody there.

What the militias offered, too, was the false legitimacy of a false claim to American history and tradition. They offered Paul Revere and the Minutemen and the Second Amendment to the Constitution of the United States—the one-sentence amendment that reads, in full: "A well regulated Militia, being necessary to the security of a free State, the right of the people to keep and bear Arms, shall not be infringed." Constitutional scholars have been arguing about the Second Amendment for two centuries, arguing about everything in it from the meaning of "well regulated" and "State" to the placing of its two commas. But not many of those scholars have ever suggested that the Second Amendment guaranteed the right of insurrection to some people in some states, arming on their own behalf, rather than the right of the State to arm its citizens for the purpose of fighting insurrectionists or invaders. Or that it guaranteed the right to raise an army from the ranks of men with guns, or to "regulate" that army, to anyone besides the "people's" democratically elected servants. It certainly didn't promise the country to John Trochmann or John Pitner, although a country where the number of guns and rifles now in private hands amounts to three times the population could be said to have inspired, if not colluded in, that illusion. There were militias in every American state by the time John Pitner posted the notice for the first public meeting of the Washington State Militia. Even New York had militias. One was called the Manhattan Militia, and while it might have given a Patriot purist some pause—it was led by a woman, who had staked her claim to God's white wilderness in Washington Heights, a neighborhood of black and Latino families, old immigrant Jews, and polyglot Columbia-Presbyterian Medical Center interns—it was said to have a small following in Staten Island and Queens. New York's militiamen didn't stalk the city in camouflage clothes. You saw them in Queens, bidding on door prizes at National Rifle Association benefits. You saw them in Staten Island, where the NRA was offering training grants to any public school teachers of a mind to follow the good example of the nuns at some of the local parochial schools and to work late, teaching riflery, in order to cure their small charges of (as it was known to the natives) "the Bambi thing." You even saw them occasionally in Manhattan, down near City Hall, peering into the window of the old and venerable gun store, John Jovino, which was stocked from the Jovino family's own arms factory, out in Brooklyn.

The militiamen of New York were, in the main, Italian, and perhaps their problems had less to do with David Rockefeller and the New World Order than with too little exercise, too much (the lady in charge in Manhattan notwithstanding) machismo, the lamentable violence of the city's streets, and their own violent nostalgia for what one described to me as "the old Sicilian security." But they thought they represented the majority, and that, finally, was the illusion all American militias offered. In a few cases—given the distress they tapped —the militias weren't wrong. The first militia I encountered, the Maine Militia, was based in a small town on the Maine coast, and it was led by a man named Mack who (despite his unsettling habit of referring to the world beyond northeast Maine as "Boogaland") had perfectly reasonable questions to put to the country he had served and the town where generations of his family had lived and worked. Mack was a middle-aged biker with a passion for Harley-Davidsons that was equaled only by his passion for the hummingbirds' nests he collected and kept, along with his survival stores and his ammunition, in the abandoned railroad car he used as Maine Militia headquarters. But he was also a Vietnam vet and a laid-off railway worker, and his war was lost, his railroad was long gone, and the fish canneries where he had scrabbled together a living afterwards had closed. There was no work in a town that was all Mack knew besides Vietnam, nothing for him to do but ride his Harley and drink his beer and get in trouble and wonder why rich summer people had begun to cross the street when they saw him—why the son and grandson of a family that had put its faith and energies into building that town should end up shunned, broke, and camping in a railroad car, with hummingbirds' nests for company and no confidence left to start a life somewhere else. Mack had a couple of "co-commanders." One was a Calvinist homeschooler who believed that asking public school children to stand up in class and talk about their new baby sister or their summer vacation constituted a plot against the family, and whose qualifications to teach his own children seemed to consist entirely in having read "the Communist Manifesto, the Humanist Manifesto, and the Christian Manifesto," and in being able to recite the names of the presidents of the United States, in order. The other was a young, wild-eyed gun nut who brought to the Patriot cause a wardrobe of battle gear, a fondness for machine-gun meets (known in the movement as "Spray and Pray"), and a record of court-ordered psychiatric counseling. His complaint with the government, as far as I could tell, had mainly to do with what he called "my right to defend myself"—a right he had been deprived of when the local police chief held up his concealed-weapons permit for a two-week check. But the militia had been Mack's idea. He told me that one day he had "just got mad" and called the headquarters of the Michigan Militia—which was much in the news then, what with McVeigh and Nichols getting arrested and Norm Olson bragging about twelve thousand members—and left his name and his phone number. Two weeks later, Mack had members in thirteen of Maine's sixteen counties; a year later, he was pitching his revolution to an auditorium of students at the University of Maine. He told them that all they needed to join the battle for America was one rifle, a hundred rounds of ammunition, a knapsack, and a mess kit—"exactly what you needed to fight in the Revolutionary War." To their credit, most of the students laughed.

Mack wasn't looking for the West in Maine. He was looking for Maine. But in one way he and John Pitner were quite similar: they both believed that the enemy was everywhere, and, at the same time, "everywhere" was how they saw themselves. John, like Mack, believed the world was against him and the world was with him, and this indeed was his small attraction. He had never heard of Max Weber, but he seems to have tapped some native Weberian permutation in his own mind, and in the minds of his alarmed, excitable recruits. Somehow, John understood that in millennial America the idea of making good had become so fatally confused with the idea of getting saved that the choice for the failed and the poor was either to believe that they were damned themselves or else, like John, to believe that they were victims of a great conspiracy of the damned against them. He may have been deluded—there wasn't a prayer for John Pitner in that complicated American marketplace where nerve, character, and competence were still supposedly in as much demand as Patriot pyramid schemes and militia handbooks—but his biggest delusion was the one that sold. He said that America would be his again, once the war was won and the conspiracy shattered, and he promised to share it with anyone willing to join him, and to risk dying in the fight.

THERE WERE 150,000 PEOPLE in Whatcom County, and if you listened to John, you knew that meant 150,000 people sitting on two and a half million acres that the New World Order was determined to steal. Whatcom made an extravagant, empty sweep from the Pacific Ocean all the way up into the North Cascades. "God's country," people in the county called it, though provenance was pretty much all they did agree on. There was an ongoing, angry debate in Whatcom as to how God wanted His property looked after. Jeff Margolis, who owned Everybody's Store and reigned unchallenged as Whatcom's resident radical philosopher—or, as he liked to say, as "the I. F. Stone of Van Zandt"—described it this way: "When we came out here, I was thinking Émile Durkheim, I dreamed we could all be one family. But the only family in Whatcom County is the county." People who joined the militia tended to believe that God had put them in Whatcom County to make a fortune out of the county, and that once they were through stripping the mountains and turning their farms into shopping malls, He would see to it that the trees grew back and the water ran clean and the eagles nested. People like Jeff tended to believe that God preferred a Whatcom County that was more pristine. So did the state government and, for the moment, the federal government. By the time John discovered the conspiracy of the New World Order, two-thirds of the county had already been placed under one or another category of political or environmental protection—as parkland or reservation land or national forest or national wilderness area—making the use of that land and its resources highly regulated if not entirely forbidden. It didn't take very much wit to see that the real conspirators in the land-use business weren't the local ecologists, installed in some Bellingham walk-up office with their warming charts and their lists of endangered species; they were the big real estate developers and the men who ran the logging and mining consortiums—global consortiums—and you never saw them in Whatcom County, Washington, if for no reason than that they made their deals in the other Washington, and that those deals had long since smothered the small, local competition. But wit wasn't always in evidence in Whatcom County, despite the fact that John himself had enough of it to suspect that the place was a breeding ground for the kinds of political paranoia he was nurturing in his own head. There were certain givens in the county. Jeff's wife, Amy, who played violin with the Whatcom Symphony Orchestra, told me that, to understand it, I had to accept two things. "One, you come to Whatcom and then you get too poor to leave. Two, you come to Whatcom and you either get drunk or you get religion or you get mad." She may have meant "mad" in both its senses, since it was almost a point of pride among Whatcom's liberals that, acre by acre, their practically empty county held as dense a concentration of crazies as you were likely to find anywhere in the United States. Insofar as they were accurate, John's future seemed guaranteed. There was also, of course, a real enemy on hand in Whatcom County—the state, in all its intrusive, regulatory power—and one of the great ironies of life with an enemy like that was that it gave you all the privacy and isolation you needed if you were of a mind to turn your fantasies of cash and country into propane bombs and assault rifles. Whatcom was the sort of place where a man could safely bury the pails of earmuffs, ammunition, long johns, Band-Aids, jerky, water, flashlights, grenades, explosives, vitamin pills, American flags, and snapshots of the baby, known to the people who peddled everything in them but the snapshots as "survival caches," and at the same time learn to loathe the government that had made it possible.

The government was the *liaison* in John's conspiracy stockpot. It collected everyone's enemies in one sinister common cause, and it certainly made life simpler when you knew that all those enemies were either slaves of the government, instruments of the government, or, like Rockefeller and his friends at the Council on Foreign Relations, were telling the government what to do. Denizens of Whatcom County in the mid-nineties were eager for something simple, for some way to take their vague and unsettled grudges against the sort of people they were unlikely ever to encounter there—the immigrant hordes and ghetto masses waiting to swarm into the county after the invasion and rape their women, murder their children, and even steal their guns—and to connect those grudges to the taxes and zoning codes and environmental regulations that mocked their heritage as free white American men and, as real Patriots put it, "womenfolk." They wanted enemies who were *responsible,* the way Russia had been responsible, because now that the Berlin Wall was down and the Communists were gone, they seemed to have lost their bearings. They didn't know why, if the Russians had been to blame for every problem they had had at home, for every humiliation, every failure, they still suffered from the same problems. They didn't know why life wasn't perfect, why *they* weren't perfect, now that the Soviet Union had disappeared. In this, they were just like John.

When John first came to the county in 1981, he and Debbie moved into a trailer park at the edge of Lake Samish, a big water-fill just south of Bellingham, and started looking for a piece of land in the woods. John was certain about woods. He wanted to take Debbie and Rachel and settle the three of them into a house and a world as far from other people as he could manage. He was thirty years old and by most reckoning a failure, living from hand to mouth as an off-the-books electrostatic-spray painter for the big shipbuilders of the south Washington coast, and as an occasional summer yard-foreman in Alaska, making good money for a couple of months and then spending a whole season out of work, harboring a bitterness about the world, about people, about the injustices of his own life, that was not entirely due to the vagaries of Seattle shipyard economics or Alaska weather. "I've got a hard-on for humanity," is the way he put it to me. "I don't like very many humans." He complained that he was sick of humans, sick of cities, and it didn't take long before he was sick of life in a trailer park on a local developer's artificial lake, a park where the women wore housecoats, and the streets, such as they were, had postcard names like Autumn Lane. He hated it all, he said—the street signs, the picket fences, the little rose trellises up the fake-wood sidings, the fat, gossipy women keeping track of everybody else's business.

Lake Samish fell just within the Bellingham city limits, and John's trailer park was full of people who would have lived in Bellingham if they had had the jobs or the money for Bellingham, whereas John wanted nothing to do with Bellingham. In the spring of 1989, with Debbie working the graveyard shift at a local plant, he bought his ten acres on the south fork of the Nooksack River, and by November, when the Berlin Wall fell, he was deep in the woods in his manufactured home, waiting for his luck and the world to change. He was still waiting on April 19, 1993, on the morning of his forty-second birthday—

the morning of his first message from David Rockefeller, and, as he usually claimed, the morning he decided to start a militia and save America. Debbie had left for work while he was still sleeping. Rachel had left for Mount Baker High School. And John, who had nothing to do that morning, or for that matter most mornings lately, had just poured himself a cup of coffee and switched on the television to see what kind of terrible things were happening outside Whatcom County. Waco of course, was what was happening. The government was ending its long siege of the Branch Davidians' compound, and as John described it, "I turned the TV on and watched eighty-one women and children incinerated. . . . I watched tanks bulldoze the crime!"

It may be that Waco was a convenient symbol for John's distress. It certainly made an easy one. There were so many dead, there was such a terrifying show of government panic and government power, and millions of Americans saw that show on television. (Paul de Armond, Bellingham's most avid rights activist and, when I met him in 1996, the custodian of its Goodwill drop-off truck, once told me that he'd pegged John as a babe among the men of the Patriot movement as soon as he heard John's birthday story, because, as he put it, "you can always tell the men from the boys" by the way they use "Waco.") It may also be that John felt a real kinship with the Branch Davidians who died in Waco—with their isolation and their crazed resistance. It may be that, to him, they were just an extended version of the sort of weird American family—John preferred "dysfunctional family"—you found all over Whatcom County. Or it may be that he identified with the Davidian doomsday prophet who went by the name David Koresh, because he often used the word "martyr" to describe both Koresh and himself. Koresh was a ninth-grade dropout who had heard, from God, that he was the Christ of the Second Coming—the "Koresh" of Isaiah's prophecies—and had accordingly changed his name, which was really Vernon Howell, in order to announce the news. At the time of the siege, he was wanted for tax evasion and for the stockpiling of illegal weapons. He was also suspected of drugging and imprisoning the women and children in his cult for his own sexual use, and while that suspicion was never proven (or disproven), those women and children were his hostages against the kind of attack John saw on what he called "the morning of my awakening." It didn't matter that Koresh's Branch Davidian family was incestuous and polygamous, as well as white and pure; John decided that the Branch Davidians had died defending the family values of the American right. He had woken up and watched the news and it was "just like being in Russia or some Third World country." He "took Waco personally," and it wasn't long before he saw the advantage to himself, the compensatory glimmer, even the makings of a calling, in taking Waco personally.

John's story changed, by increments, in the telling. Sometimes, his awakening happened not on the morning of April 19, 1993, but on the evening of the 19th, after a birthday dinner with a group of Patriot friends who happened to drop by to discuss the tragedy. In that version, he and his friends vow that "another Waco" will never happen, and the Washington State Militia is born. In one version I heard, he had his awakening nine days later and founded the militia then. In the event, no one in John's family remembered April 19, 1993, as anything except John's birthday, and if John was outraged by the carnage at Waco—where eighty-one people, many of them women and twenty-one of them children, did die—it was an outrage shared by most of the people in the country. Debbie told me that John wasn't at all political then, or even much interested in politics. He certainly wasn't interested in collecting local Patriots to the Waco cause. He was pretty much of a recluse by the time Waco happened, and while Debbie did say that "after Waco he got active" and started talking politics, she also said that his "inspiration" for the Washington State Militia had nothing to do with Waco. The first time Debbie heard John use the word "militia" was about a year later, when he drove to Idaho and came home with the back of the car piled with conspiracy charts and handouts. He told Debbie they were "Patriot intel."

EVERY IDEOLOGY HAS a founding moment, which is more often than not a founding myth, and in the new American militia movement, among the Patriots whom Paul de Armond called "the men," that moment came eight months before Waco—in August of 1992—and it occurred in Ruby Ridge, Idaho. Ruby Ridge is a Patriot trope, and maybe *the* Patriot trope, standing as it does for the government's year-long siege of the mountain cabin of a white supremacist scofflaw named Randy Weaver, and for the shoot-out between Patriots and federal agents that ended the siege. It began on August 21st, when a United States marshal shot the Weavers' dog, Striker, and by the next day it had taken the lives of three people—an FBI agent named William Degan; Randy Weaver's wife, Vicki; and the Weavers' fourteen-year-old son, Sam—and entered the mythology as the OK Corral of the Patriot movement, something for Patriot connoisseurs. Ruby Ridge wasn't necessarily a useful myth—not, at any rate, in the practical way that Waco was useful eight months later—but then the Patriots who found Waco useful in raising militias rarely had an appetite for, let alone an interest in, the images that made it useful. The images of Ruby Ridge were something very different: a lonely cabin in the mountains; gun-toting homeschooled children; and a menstrual and birthing shed where women like Vicki Weaver, women who were proper Christian Identity wives, secluded themselves when, in the language of the group, they became "unclean." Ruby Ridge meant family ties with the Aryan Nations, an honor guard of skinheads, and the famous surrender of Randy Weaver, brokered by an ex–Green Beret lieutenant colonel named James "Bo" Gritz, who went on to run for vice president on David Duke's racist ticket, enlivening Duke's campaign with his own speeches about "Zionist Jews" leaving "the sign, scent, stain and mark of the beast" on God's America. Most of all, Ruby Ridge meant the white-tribe enclaves of the Idaho Panhandle, jutting to Canada in the far west of the state, between Washington and Montana, cut off by mountains, temperature, and temperament from the rest of a state that was hardly liberal to begin with. It meant Coeur d'Alene and Hayden Lake— God's America in every supremacist sense, as remote from the beast as you could get in America without huskies and a sled. The Idaho Panhandle was where white men dropped out of a world in which Satan looked like Alan Greenspan and into a wilderness they claimed as a separate nation. It was the America that God intended, and it certainly had nothing in common with David Koresh's Waco compound on a plot of dusty flatland that could have been Mexico.

John made his Idaho pilgrimage with a man he always referred to as "Jeffrey." There was never a last name (or even a description more detailed than that Jeffrey was some sort of "private" fencing or landscaping contractor). According to John, he and Jeffrey had wanted to check on some property for sale up near Hayden Lake—"What's that lake?" he asked me, when he finally mentioned Idaho, about six months into the ongoing story of his awakening—and the realtor who showed them around turned out to be a Patriot. He belonged to an Idaho militia, and from the things John told me about him, he could easily have belonged to the Aryan Nations, too. But to John and Jeffrey, he qualified as a specialist in the New World Order; he told them exactly who their enemies were. He told them about Bill Clinton running South American dope through a private airport in Little Rock. He told them "the truth" about Clinton's friend Vincent Foster; the papers were saying that Vince Foster had killed himself because of the terrible stress of the job he had as White House counsel, but in the Idaho Panhandle people knew that Clinton had murdered his friend when he broke down and threatened to expose Clinton's plans for selling the army to the United Nations and giving the money to the Federal Reserve. He told them to put *their* money into gold and silver and to stash it because soon the good Americans—Americans who knew the truth about Clinton, Americans like the Patriots whom John and Jeffrey had seen in the woods that day, training for war with 60-caliber machine guns—would be going underground. He showed them the buildings that he knew for a fact were New World Order concentration camps, and the ones that were New World Order crematoria. He played them videos. The video that impressed John most was "America in Peril"; it was a "documentary," patched together by a Michigan Patriot named Mark Koernke, and there were a million copies in circulation, which wasn't surprising when you considered what eager learners all those good Americans who bought them were. John himself learned several alarming things in Idaho, most of them having to do with the thousands of foreigners already in place in *his* United States: the Mossad SWAT teams and the Russian troops and the rest of the strange-looking people he'd noticed riding around in United Nations armored vehicles, looking as if they already owned the country. As John put it, "What I was learning fit my paranoia."

John and Jeffrey never did buy any Idaho property. Jeffrey's own paranoia was already so keen that, for all practical purposes, he lived in hiding ("about five thousand feet underground," is how John described it), and Idaho apparently put a damper on any plans he might have had to surface. John told me that, in fact, Jeffrey had come home from Idaho, packed up his house, fled to a cabin on one of the San Juan Islands, and moved his bed into the basement (a move that may also have had a lot to do with the IRS, which, according to John, was after Jeffrey with a bill for $30,000 in back taxes). John, on the other hand, came home from Idaho inspired. He started doing what he always described to me solemnly as "my research." He contacted John Trochmann and ordered his first batch of Patriot tapes, $600 in tapes, from Trochmann's Militia of Montana catalog. He went to the Bellingham library, where "I learned—yup!—the Federal Reserve was a private corporation." He wrote to a Patriot publisher in Arizona for pamphlets about the traitors sabotaging the Constitution. And he reconsidered his thoughts about the helicopter he had first seen circling over Whatcom County after a Nooksack River flood. He had assumed, until Idaho, that it was a relief helicopter—one of the dark green Federal Emergency Management Association choppers dispatched by the government to disaster areas. Now he knew that green was black, and that black was a code for UN forces. He studied the sinister helicopters in his MOM videos, and they were just like *his* helicopter. He said to himself, "Jesus, what the hell is this?" He told the family, "I've seen the black bird."

SOME OF THE FAMILY were quite worried about John. His half-brother Joey, down in Seattle, heard about the helicopters and the concentration camps and apparently phoned their father, on Whidbey Island, saying, "What's happening to my brother? He's a psycho!" His sister Susan, who told me she hadn't heard a word from John in two years, was so upset that she got in her car and drove to Whatcom County to see him. Susan had once put in ten years as an emergency-room nurse, and she said later that she should have seen the trouble coming, because John had the textbook signs. Bitterness. Regret careening toward entitlement. A desperate bravado that even in childhood had clearly been on the edge of delusion. "A problem with the truth," Susan called it. Yet none of these things could really begin to explain why John suddenly identified with George Washington and the Founding Fathers, or believed in an international conspiracy, or tried to raise his own army, or took the Word as it appeared in a militia mail-order catalog the way his fundamentalist neighbor Sharon Pietila, who lived in the woods just across Valley Highway, took the Bible—as the word that stopped the discussion. By the time Susan paid her visit to Whatcom County, the first two cells of the Washington State Militia were already holding secret meetings, and John was if anything even more disturbed. Susan couldn't remember the date, but she thought it was in the spring or early summer of 1995, not long after the bombing in Oklahoma City, because John talked all the time about Oklahoma City. "I remember, he couldn't sit still," she told me the month John's trial started. "He was crying. I said, 'What's going on?' That's the day we did target practice." The next time anyone in the family saw John, he was on television, talking about a militia, and by then even Debbie was talking about militias. Debbie had enrolled in a night school sociology class at Whatcom Community College and had written her term paper on militia history. "It freaked out my professor," she said, the day she handed me a copy. "He was very opinionated. But at the same time, he gave me a real good grade."

For a while, the family tried to believe in John, and in any event it wasn't a family that spent its time exploring Coleridgean distinctions between imagination and fantasy. Debbie herself wasn't worried. Debbie knew nothing at all about the Federal Reserve or the War Powers Act, and she had never worried about Rachel getting brainwashed at Mount Baker High because of an educational experiment that had mainly to do with moving children through their school subjects at their own pace, until they mastered the material. But she was so relieved to see John enthusiastic about something, even if that something was a war on Valley Highway, that, as she described it to me, much later, "I welcomed the militia." Before the militia, John had been hopelessly withdrawn. He would quit a job or talk himself into a get-rich scheme that ate her salary and lost their savings, and then his bravado would crack and he'd withdraw a little further into a kind of furious isolation. By the time he went to Idaho, he was "lost in society," Debbie said. He didn't know how to step back in, or even want to step back in, and that was when Debbie, by her account, "kind of strayed out of the relationship" and into her own life. But suddenly, after Idaho, John had *his* life. He was "John the Militiaman." He and Debbie started getting out and meeting people—Debbie thought they were "real nice people, real family people"—and it didn't much matter to her if those people saw black helicopters or believed the Bellingham airport was a concentration camp. Whatever some Pitners thought about John's Patriot obsessions, John himself was a new man, busy and actually cheerful as he got ready to die fighting David Rockefeller. And to some of those nice family people, bewildered by all the laws about not cutting a tree near an ecosystem and not grazing a milk cow near a bald eagle and not subdividing a piece of farmland to finance a retirement—to those people John was *their* man. He was even something of a mentor because, as he pointed out at every chance, he had done his research. He had "friends and important support" and secret allies in high places who had seen the "documents" of the conspiracy and knew for a fact that those wildlife and wilderness rules were part of the plot to impoverish and disenfranchise them. He could talk with authority about the invasion at hand, and how to resist it. Now he even had an in-house scholar. He ran Debbie's term paper in the first issue of "Sighting In," the Washington State Militia newsletter.

John told the neighbors who called up after the meeting at the Rome Grange that if they joined him in his militia they would all be equals in the leaderless resistance. The only difference between them—at least, as he explained it to me—was the old cautionary, "need-to-know," which, put plainly, meant that *he* needed to know where the guns were stashed and the money hidden and the battle plans stored and they did not. He said that the beautiful part of leaderless resistance was being able to put your trust in a leader, a leader like him, who wouldn't crack under the terrible tortures of the New World Order. Ignorance, he told them, was their protection, because it was certain that *they'd* crack—he wouldn't blame them, they didn't know the New World Order, they hadn't had the training he had—and end up handing all that valuable intel to the enemy. His scheme was a little bit Trochmann, a little bit Irish Republican Army, and a little bit Lenin, though he'd never admit to Lenin. It's doubtful that he knew anything about Lenin beyond the fact that Lenin was a Leninist, definitely part of the conspiracy, but he was careful to call his militia units "squads," not "cells," because he knew that cells were what Leninists had. He wanted his squads to be small. He liked the idea of four-to-six-man squads. Six men from the same town were only a couple of calls away from action when the invasion started; that is, if the enemy didn't remember to cut the phone lines first. Each squad would choose a leader, who in turn would report to a district leader, who in turn would report to John, making John the only man in the Washington State Militia to have anything like a list of members, or a cash or weapons tally, or, indeed, access to the men he referred to gravely as "my superiors." When anyone asked John about his superiors, he would shake his head or put a finger to his lips and say, "Need to know?" or, if pressed, the code names "White Buffalo" or "Daiwee." (Dai Uy means captain in Vietnamese.) As he explained it to me, Daiwee was his own special superior, though of course he had many more: important colonels and generals, down at Fort Lewis, who had keys to the arsenals where the big guns and the missiles were stored; important sympathizers in the FBI, who had the intel straight from the boardroom at the Council on Foreign Relations. John himself had a unique source of intel; he promoted his stepsister's husband, Larry—the policeman in Mountlake Terrace—into a high-ranking FBI agent who had been awakened, too. There was often a grain of truth in John's confabulations. Larry had apparently once been invited to Quantico with some other policemen, for a two-week course.

JOHN'S FIRST RECRUITS were mainly local talent. They weren't promising, but they had the advantage of being there. Of course, it was hard to tell if those recruits were all that was there, or were really, as John assured them, an "inner circle," the point men in a network of squads that stretched across the state of Washington. It was never easy to pin John down on figures. He could talk about having two armed-and-on-the-alert militia squads in Whatcom County, and in a few minutes talk about having sixteen squads, and then about having "hundreds." He could put the Washington State Militia at five thousand men, and the next day at six thousand, and then at eight thousand, and once at eighteen thousand. Not even the left, which tended to exaggerate the figures, did that. Paul de Armond put John's followers in the hundreds, not thousands. He liked to say that John's membership lists for the Washington State Militia had less to do with the number of armed white men who had actually placed their hands on his copy of the Bill of Rights and sworn "to protect and uphold the Constitution of the U.S. of A." than they did with the number of "Don't tread on me" militia badges that John and his recruits had managed to unload at gun shows and grange meetings and right-wing coffee klatches.

At the time, there were nine other known militias and Patriot armies in Washington State—the Lake Chelan Citizens Militia, the Sons of Liberty, the Olympic Sportsman Alliance, the Skamania Citizens Militia, the Unorganized Militia of Stevens County, the Yakima County Militia, the Minutemen Militia, We The People, and something called the Liaison Group—and probably just as many underground militias. Most, by reputation, sounded a good deal more menacing than John's, and places like Chelan County, east of the Cascades, were fairly menacing to begin with. Chelan had elected a Patriot sheriff and Patriot county supervisers, and some people in the county were said to have harbored terrorists: old fugitives from The Order and the Posse Comitatus; young fugitives from the Phineas Priests, among them a couple of Spokane bombers who hadn't been captured when their friends were. And as for western Washington, Scott North, a journalist who, when I met him, in 1996, was investigating Patriot crime for the *Everett Herald,* told me that even in counties like his, the so-called civilized counties on the coast between Whatcom County and Seattle, most serious militiamen ran their cells with a wary eye on the Washington State Militia and especially on John Pitner. The militiamen Scott knew, in Snohomish County, stayed underground. They kept their own counsel and their own caches—the sheriff there had unearthed one large arms cache before John's militia even surfaced—and they were not apt to be much interested in an outfit like John's, where the maps to their heavy weapons, the weapons the sheriff hadn't found, were going to end up sitting in a drawer on Valley Highway. But, as John was eager to point out, his militia was the only Washington *State* Militia. He claimed the rest of them. He said that, in the end, they would all get their "instructions" to report to him, and never mind that when people talked about his militia now, it was always the same few names you heard. The truth was that most militiamen hid their affiliation. They worried about their jobs, or their neighbors, or the police. They didn't advertise themselves. John liked to say that he did it for them.

Three

J OHN RAN THE SQUAD called Alpha One. He loved
the military sound of "Alpha." "Yup, I'm Alpha One,
I'm the idiot with the headaches," he told me. Alpha
One was his leadership squad, the place where the men with
Washington State Militia squads of their own—the local com-
manders with a little more "need to know" than the foot soldiers they had drafted—would trade intel and plot strategy
and brief their leader on what was happening in the war zone.
But the truth was that anyone who showed up regularly for
John's weekly meetings on Valley Highway could consider
himself Alpha One, and usually did. In a way, anyone willing
to supply John with a last name and a working phone number
was "leadership."

Some of the men in Alpha One were already acquainted
with the conspiracy (and with each other) through a loopy dis-

cussion group that met monthly in a public meeting hall on Bellingham Harbor—the hall was part of a port commission complex called Harbor Center—under the aegis of a retired post office worker and conspiracy expert named Ben Hinkle. Ben was seventy-one, living on his government pension, and when John joined the discussion, not long after the siege in Waco, he was devoting himself entirely to the Patriot cause. He called his own group Citizens for Liberty, which set the right patriotic tone and pleased the other old Whatcom Patriots, most of whom he had gotten to know quite well in the course of his long history as an after-hours agitator, and whom he was now providing with a list of guest speakers that included their earnest and accessible Sheriff Brandland. Ben had been involved in a right-wing party called the Populist Party of America and in a demonstrably racist networking and propaganda outfit called the Liberty Lobby, and once he left the post office and became a full-time Patriot with the official title of "Washington distributer of *The Spotlight*"— the Liberty Lobby's monthly tabloid—he could be seen, most days, wandering around Bellingham like a postman, with old plastic shopping bags full of *Spotlight*s and conspiracy books and the papers he liked to call his "documents." He was persistent, and not unsuccessful in finding converts. ("These guys, their history of the United States is Oliver Stone," one of the lawyers at the militia trial told me. "You could sell them anything. You could sell them the Book of Moroni.") And Ben liked reporters. I had hardly arrived in Bellingham when he rang my doorbell—the sheriff, who was known to be more obliging than discreet, had thought to supply him with my address—and demanded an appointment, and the next thing I knew I was sitting in a conference room at the Bellingham

Public Library, listening to Ben's Patriot lecture. Ben wanted converts, but he took no chances. He announced, straight off, that he was taping our conversation, and then, as one of his friends informed me weeks later, "he shared the conversation with us."

For a while, Ben tried training with Alpha One, but his combat skills were more than a little creaky, and his taste for the wilderness was nil. His real interest was the history of the New World Order, and John considered him a treasure trove of information. Ben could trace the conspiracy from its birth in 1776, in Germany, as Jakob Weishaupt's Brotherhood of Illuminati, to last year's gathering of Bilderbergers—"the elites" of the Communist East (they hadn't changed when the Wall fell) and the capitalist West, who had first convened in Amsterdam, at the Bilderberg Hotel, after the Second World War, in order to plan depressions and wars, manipulate the price of oil, and decide which nations were to be "eliminated." He could whip out a book to prove that the Rothschilds had paid Marx and Engels to write the *Communist Manifesto;* that China's red flag was a code for the *Rot Schild,* the red shield that had hung outside Mayer Amschel Rothschild's house in the Frankfurt ghetto; that the Rothschilds' investment-banking friends at Kuhn, Loeb, in New York City, had financed both the revolution in Russia and the Nazi takeover in Germany; that those same rich Jewish conspirators had even bombed the "Blitzkrieg" (he meant the Reichstag) in order to start the crackdown on an unsuspecting German people. He knew why the conspirators had put Masonic signs all over America's money, and why their cousins the Rockefellers had killed Sam Weaver's dog. He could tell you when the League of Nations changed its name to the Council on

Foreign Relations and began to plan for the world government called the United Nations. He knew for a fact that the United Nations was run by Zionists, but he claimed to have nothing at all against Jews—"Most of the information I have comes from Jewish Patriots," he told me—or for that matter against blacks. He apparently claimed to have a black grandchild, but that was a claim he made to the sheriff and not to me, and no one I knew in Bellingham could remember seeing the child or, indeed, its father. In the event, you wouldn't have found many of Bellingham's black citizens—there weren't many to begin with—buying *The Spotlight* on the third Friday of every month at the Harbor Center, or on Valley Highway, swapping bomb recipes with the Alpha One leadership.

JOHN'S SECOND-IN-COMMAND at Alpha One (the man he called "my deputy director") was a lily-white, over-weight, Bellingham contractor by the name of Frederick Benjamin Fisher. Fred was just past sixty and, like Ben, a grandfather, and according to John, everyone in the leadership squad admired him. "Most people who come . . . share our views," John once told me, and by all accounts Fred Fisher certainly shared them. Fred disliked the government and everything about the government, though his dislike may have had less to do with Patriot principles than with the time the government locked him up, on charges of "incest in the first degree," and then convicted him of those charges, thanks to the testimony of the sixteen-year-old stepdaughter he had been molesting since she was seven, and had begun raping when she was nine. By avoiding a trial (he pleaded guilty) and then requesting probation (as "the sole support" of his wife, his stepdaughter, and another daughter, who was fourteen), Fred had managed to get out of jail on the ninetieth day of a ten-year suspended sentence, so it wasn't surprising that, so many years later, he thought of the whole affair as an incident too trivial to mention to John or, for that matter, to any of the militiamen who admired him. John gave him the important job of "storing common ordnance," figuring, I imagine, that a stack of, say, propane cylinders wouldn't look suspicious, or even a little strange, in the basement of the proprietor of Fred Fisher Masonry. I never knew, and in the end it didn't matter, since Fred swore that he had never heard of a job called "storing common ordnance." What Fred wanted was for the militia to make a statement. He liked the idea of bombing a government building; he said so at one of the leadership meetings, or, more accurately—since I was never invited to a leadership meeting—in the transcript I have of a tape of that meeting. (John suggested the Sea-Tac Detention Center, between Tacoma and Seattle, which turned out to be the place he eventually went to prison.) But Fred's real influence on the group was moral influence. He was a staunch defender of what he called "the rights of the child." He worried that America was going to lose its children to the United Nations. He spoke of sinister plans to take children "from the moral authority of their parents" and force them into "contraceptives and gender relationships." "Beware, parents!" he told the audience at the Rome Grange. "The UN wants your children for its world plantation." He gave such an eloquent speech about family values, the night of that first public meeting, that even John got teary. "That was great, Fred," John said. "Left me all speechless here."

Fred had a young disciple named Marlin Lane Mack, who

started coming with him to Ben's Citizens for Liberty meetings and eventually to Alpha One. Marlin Mack was a tall, pasty-faced, sandy-haired man of twenty-three—a boy, really, whose own parents had been divorced for years. His father lived in Yakima, some two hundred miles to the east in south-central Washington, but he wasn't "militia"; in fact, he owned a chain of karate parlors and was apparently prosperous enough to have flown to Bosnia, with a shipment of medical supplies, the month of his son's arrest. But Marlin's two sisters had married militia, and one of those sisters lived in Whatcom County, and, according to Marlin's lawyer, James Roe, her husband was Fred Fisher's stepson. When Marlin arrived in Bellingham a year or two after high school, Fred took him in and put him to work as a mason, and in the end Marlin stayed. He liked the connection to such a patriotic Christian family. The family had prayed together and forgiven Fred. And as Debbie Pitner herself said—it was the fall of 1996, and Debbie was talking about how she'd felt, that spring, opening the *Herald* to discover Fred Fisher's indisputably ugly record—the Fishers were "so together it was inspirational." Fred's daughter and stepdaughter distributed militia tracts. Fred's wife, Maryann, took time out from her housework for target practice. Maryann was so devoted to the man who had raped her daughter that she started vacuum-packing the food he was going to need to see him through the invasion, and even organized a Washington State Militia tag sale in her front yard. The sale brought in $600; it was the first money the militia had ever made.

It didn't take long, in Fred's company, for Marlin to discover the conspiracy against the Fishers, not to mention the conspiracy against himself. His lawyer once told me to remember that Marlin was "insecure," that he hadn't had friends, or even a single date, in high school—that he'd always been a little too nervous, a little too wired for his classmates. But in John Pitner's militia, the more wired Marlin got, the more everybody seemed to like him. "If the person is wired, or nuts, we keep him in—to keep an eye on the loose cannons and not let them go sniping on the highway," John had said, the second or third time we talked. "With people in my unit, it's given them cohesion, purpose. Some of them were going crazy, they were suicidal. Now they're a community." But it was hard to credit John with keeping an eye on Marlin. Most people would say that John and the others cheered him on. Marlin, of course, had a right to speak his mind. One of his fantasies had to do with killing Sheriff Brandland, whose idea of "wired" was a testy night at the PTA, and another involved Cathy Logg, at the *Herald,* who'd made a sworn enemy of Marlin the day she broke the news about Fred's conviction. (It had been there, all along, in the public files at the Whatcom County Courthouse.) Some of the men in Alpha One had a Good Samaritan pitch, like John's. They used it among themselves, on occasion, maybe because it did them good to sit around, sometimes, pretending to be a public service—just a few neighborly guys on the ready to put out forest fires, or haul sandbags in a flood, or shovel a neighbor's road in a snowstorm. But Marlin had no interest in his neighbors' driveways. "Fucking saving people, my ass!" was the way he once put it. "We're going to go on a killing spree!" Marlin preferred talking about John's intel. He liked the meeting where John had gone through "Presidential Directive 25"—the one that turned the American army over to the United Nations— and the meeting where he first heard about the "counterintelligence bill" that had just made Israel part of the United States. But he couldn't have cared less about John Pitner's image in the *Herald,* or for that matter about his own. "I don't want any fuckin' stickers—save the planet, love whales, eat a flower, all that shit," as he once said.

Marlin became a kind of militia mascot. He made the men feel younger, although that wasn't hard, given the ages of some of them. Donald Ellwanger—or, as everyone called him, Doc Ellwanger—a local veterinarian and, for a time, Alpha One regular, was at least as old as Ben Hinkle and if anything even more impressionable. At some point into the 1980s, Doc Ellwanger had stopped paying taxes. He described his decision to me as "sovereign citizen principle," but the sheriff put it more precisely: Doc Ellwanger had fallen in with a self-styled minister who went by the name Roger Allen Davis of the Lord Jesus Christ and gave his address as "Kingdom of God, Washington Republic." Davis had provided him with sovereign citizen's papers (papers declaring Donald Ellwanger to be a sovereign citizen of the true United States and absolving him of any responsibilities to the United States he happened to live in now), and helped him file those papers, which of course had no legal standing, at the county courthouse. According to Doc's wife, Judie, the reverend also "took everything he had"—a transaction that had involved a trip to Costa Rica to which Judy was pointedly not invited—leaving the Ellwangers with a $130,000 debt to the Internal Revenue Service and no way to begin to pay it, should Doc Ellwanger ever consider paying, which he didn't. When this became clear, the government held a tax auction and sold the Ellwangers' Animal Birth Control Clinic—an artificial-insemination franchise, just east of Bellingham—to the highest bidder. And the result was that early in January 1994, Dale Brandland and a group of his deputies arrived at the clinic with orders to re-possess, and discovered forty or so of the Ellwangers' Patriot neighbors, John Pitner among them, holding up pickets and blocking their way. It wasn't Waco or Ruby Ridge, but it was a siege—in a reluctant, Whatcom County sort of fashion. The sheriff, who had already put off the eviction once (not want-ing to disturb the Ellwangers over Christmas), would drive over in the morning, with his men and his paperwork, and try to talk the neighbors into leaving; the neighbors would de-cline; the sheriff would get in his car and leave instead. John often described this amiable *face à face* as "our first action against the illegal government of the United States," though it was difficult to say *whose* action, since the Washington State Militia, if it existed at all then, was nevertheless two years away from declaring itself in a public meeting, and since the sheriff himself seems to have settled the matter peacefully. On the fourth morning of the siege—with a small subterfuge that to Brandland's mind was so resourceful he was still beaming about it two and a half years later—he called a truce. Every-one went home for a rest and some hot food, and as soon as the coast was clear, he and the deputies sneaked back to Ani-mal Birth Control with a big van, served the papers, sealed the premises, and—because Brandland himself liked Doc Ell-wanger, who was veterinarian to half the dogs and cats in the county, including his own—spent the next several hours pack-ing the furniture and files and moving them to the Ellwangers' house, a few miles up Hannigan Road in Lynden.

Judie Ellwanger accepted her husband philosophically. "Who else is going to take on an old bag like me, with twenty cats?" is how she described their marriage when I stopped to see her, a week or so into John's trial. Judie was a small, thin woman with a sharp face, a halo of tightly permed red curls, a cupid's bow etched in pink over a narrow mouth, and the wardrobe of a perky teenage girl. Her age was a "need-to-know" secret (she told me fifty-five). But her politics were pure Patriot. The day we met, she told me a story about a friend called Wayne, whose two children were at a school infiltrated by the New World Order: "His kids came home from school with a DNA project," Judie said. "You know, genetics. You fill out the eye color, et cetera. Well, he didn't want them to reveal anything. His daughter said, 'I like school. Don't force me to do any of this Patriot stuff.' But the son is pretty right-wing, like his dad. I said, 'Wayne, just write this across the top of his paper: "This is an invasion of privacy."' I said, 'It doesn't matter if he fills it out or not. They have the file on all of us.'"

Judie was the only woman among the first militia regulars, as well as the only regular who could match Marlin for profanity. She mothered Marlin, who brought out her "tenderness," she said, whereas she referred to her husband, at her most benign, as "Dipshit" (she called John Pitner "Asshole"). "I have an overactive thyroid," she once told me. She liked people who were lively, and she made it clear that "lively" was not a word that applied to the aging crowd you encountered at most Citizens for Liberty meetings. She preferred militia meetings, where you shot at paper cutouts and went endurance hiking and talked about weapons. John had tried assigning Judie to Fred Fisher's Bellingham squad, thinking that she'd want to help Fred's wife start a women's auxiliary to freeze-dry survival food and knit socks. When Fred lost patience and sent her packing—he didn't really approve of women who wanted to hike with the boys instead of freeze-drying at home with Maryann—she and Doc Ellwanger tried out a new squad. But they really considered themselves members of Alpha One, and, in a way, so did everyone else. The Ellwangers weren't leadership, but they gave the militia a folksy cachet, and maybe even made it seem a little less menacing than John or Fred or, certainly, Marlin might have wanted. People in Bellingham, liberal people, still talked with affection about "poor old Doc Ellwanger" and his way with a sick puppy, and about how little Doc Ellwanger charged them—"even now, under the circumstances." They would say, "We don't agree with poor old Doc Ellwanger's crazy views, but he's always been good to us," and the only other militiaman they said anything that nice about, the only militiaman who didn't seem to frighten or alarm them, was a seemingly mild-mannered and reclusive bachelor named Gary Marvin Kuehnoel, whose squad happened to be the one the Ellwangers joined after leaving Fred's. Gary Kuehnoel had come home from Alaska to take care of a dying mother and an ailing father, and he would cheerfully fix anything of his neighbors' that needed fixing, from the transmissions on their cars to their lawn mowers or their grandmothers' toasters. Gary was in fact a gunsmith—he had once tuned pistols for the Anchorage police—who could also turn a semiautomatic rifle into a fully automatic machine gun. He lived alone in a trailer on what was left of the Kuehnoel family farm, surrounded by the used law books and military histories and encyclopedias and army manuals he had collected over the years (he was addicted to yard sales, his father, Marvin, told me) and nursing the painful back he'd injured in a fall, during a stint on the Alaska pipeline; it made him limp badly, leading the neighbors to assume he was much older than the forty-eight years he claimed. Gary's books were one of his few pleasures. According to Marv, who was himself pretty much confined to a wheelchair by the time we met, at his place, in October of 1996, Gary "did an awful lot of reading, sitting there in that trailer." In fact, Marv thought it was probably all those old law books that had persuaded Gary to join a militia and defend himself. But the truth was, Gary hadn't been able to afford to do much *besides* read books that nobody else wanted —not since a brief, bankrupting marriage, in the early eighties, which had lasted, his father said, exactly as long as it took the good-looking martial arts instructor he'd met in Alaska and married in Bellingham to convince him to sell some property he had saved to buy in Alaska. She put the proceeds in her Phoenix bank.

Gary, as his father put it, "was always looking to do good," and even their neighbors—the ones who knew that Gary, like Doc Ellwanger, had crazy views—rarely talked about those views. What interested them were his views on toasters that had stopped popping, and on the homemade muffins and casseroles they brought to the Kuehnoels' farm, by way of a thank you. Most of the men who showed up at John Pitner's leadership meetings were better known for the trouble they caused their neighbors.

Jack Schleimer, for one, was famous among the parents and teachers at Mount Baker High School for having "a little problem with his temper," as was his eldest son, who had once been arrested and fined for shooting up a trophy case in the school lobby and, a month later, for shooting into the side of a pickup that belonged to a boy dating his ex-girlfriend. Jack, being fanatically Christian, didn't like seeing his youngest son, who was still a student at Mount Baker, come under the corrupting influence of people who weren't fanatically Christian, too—in particular, the "Communist evolutionists" sent by the New World Order to teach biology. He hassled the biology teacher. He went after the social science teacher—it happened at night, after a school-board meeting, according to a board member who was there—in the school parking lot, shouting "Fight me!" He upset the principal so much, during one of his unannounced visits, that the principal was rumored to have called the police. Even John allowed that the enemy had made Jack Schleimer a little strange. He wasn't like Brian McDugal, who was John's oldest friend, not to mention his key squad leader down the coast in Anacortes. Brian was definitely strange, but, as John said, he wasn't angry or suspicious, and he was certainly friendlier than Jack. You could even say that Brian was laid back, the sort of guy who could make you uneasy with a smile and a couple of reassuring words.

Anacortes was fifty miles from Valley Highway—a different need-to-know zone, John admitted—but Brian was welcome at Alpha One, and he made a point of attending. He was not only John's oldest friend, he was close to being his only friend. When John talked to me about the men he could count on, once the invasion started, "to sound the alert and activate the contingencies," Brian's was always the name he mentioned first. Brian didn't get arrested when John did (though there was a drug conviction from 1987 on his record, along with a few foreclosures). Through the winter of John's trial, you could still find Brian at work in black jeans and a denim shirt at Nesbit's Engine Supply, a Bellingham machine shop that kept him on, if with some anxiety, because of his fine hand with a broken motorcycle. "We don't agree with his politics!" the woman who let me in said, straight off, the night I rang the bell at Nesbit's—it was after hours—and asked to see him. In the event, it would have been hard to miss Brian. He was a huge, wiry character with wild blue eyes and shaggy blond hair and a big mustache, and some people had described him to me as "like a warrior." The truth, at least as he told it, was that he had once had every intention of making a warrior's career. According to Brian, he'd joined the Marines the week he finished high school, and he wanted me to know that in all likelihood he'd be running the Corps by now if it hadn't been for "a pair of mismatched dress boots that gave me heel contusions" in every parade and "put me in whirlpool therapy." His story began at Fort Pendleton, with Brian in basic training, his feet blistering in his boots, and ended with Brian picking up an ashtray and hurling it at the sergeant who, even then, wouldn't give him a better pair. He was put on the first plane out of San Diego. It was an experience that inspired, in Brian, a certain sympathy for John and what he called John's "authority problems." "I'm a protester of the highest order" was the way he started our conversation, building to the moment when he leaned over and looked me right in the eye and said, "I got this little nuclear reactor . . . down in the basement." He had made the reactor himself—he swore to it—and that wasn't all. There was also the matter of the $40,000 worth of raw nuclear fuel he kept in a couple of coffee cups on his basement table. He was not planning to confront the New World Order unprepared; still, but he was a forthright sort of person, and he thought that by talking to me he might be putting the enemy on notice. "It's a little bigger than God," he said, describing his reactor, and he must have known, because he'd already been dead three times and had "seen" Jesus. His girlfriend, Linda, disagreed about the reactor. She said there was a hundred times more power in the Holy Spirit.

It was easy to see what Brian had to offer John. His reactor. His nuclear coffee cups. His military "experience." Brian claimed to be "inner-circle" militia, the man with the contacts John talked about so much: the Fort Lewis brass with "the real serious arsenals." The Fort Lewis brass had been in touch with Brian, "personally in touch," ever since the Gulf War, which in militia circles counted as the war that had forced American soldiers out of the legitimate caps and hats of the American armed forces and into the blue berets of the United Nations. (Every militiaman knew the story of the brave captain who'd been court-martialed for refusing to change hats.) After the ignominy—the treason, really—of the blue berets, the brass shared most of its secrets with Brian. Brian learned all about the government letting Mossad operate out of Fort Lewis—it was Mossad's reward, from Clinton, for the assassination of Vincent Foster—not to mention letting its own Phoenix Program agents rise again, from the ashes of Vietnam, to orchestrate the massacre at Waco. He knew, of course, that there were also Russian troops at Fort Lewis. He knew there were real Patriots, too—Patriots who were eager to join the Washington State Militia as soon as the orders came down, as he put it, "to lock and load." But most of all, Brian was loyal to John. They went back twenty-five years and shared the same hard-on for humanity, and the same fantasies, and for this, if for no other reason, he was determined to protect John. He had a nose for spies, agents, informers, infiltrators, saboteurs, for anyone who could hurt his friend—which arguably John did not—and he reported to John when any militiaman said a word against him. Once, he called up the man himself and left a message on his answering machine: "I want you to know that my feelings about you are not very good. You're just a low-life piece of shit." He was very proud of that.

There was, of course, a certain attrition in John's high executive ranks. Some of the members fought, and left to start their own squads. Some dropped out when their wives started complaining about the grocery money going for gear and rifles. Some got tired waiting for an invasion that never came— or nervous, or scared, or even a little more paranoid than they normally tended to be. Ben Hinkle stopped coming; John thought he was worried about getting arrested and losing his post office pension, though the reason Ben gave was that he could do more good for the cause as the Washington State Militia's "independent counsel." Jack Schleimer stopped coming in the spring of 1996, saying that he wanted to spend more "quality time" with his family. What he meant—at least, what he told me later—was that he had begun to suspect John of being "somebody else," a cop or a federal agent sent into the county as part of an elaborate plot to entrap *him*. John called this the weeding-out process. He wanted leaders who were "in for the long haul," leaders who loved their country enough to be able to make it through a cold winter in a cave in the North Cascades, with the bombs dropping and the enemy already installed in Bellingham, and this narrowed the field to the kind of people who actually looked forward to winters in caves, at twenty below, on a diet of MOM's reconstituted powdered protein. John had a strong pedagogic streak, and he prided himself on being able to teach those people. He never got impatient, not even when Marlin Mack tried to convince him to start the revolution right away or Judie Ellwanger interrupted him in the middle of his best lecture on ammunition, asking, "What do you mean, John, 'Boom!'?" When something like that happened, he would stop talking, and think for a minute, and try to provide an answer. He didn't want his troops to take the revolution lightly, or ignore the gravity of their mission. Once, he told them—speaking softly and slowly, the way a general does when he knows the human cost, when he's had the *experience*—"You're gonna have to pull the trigger on a man. It'll be with you the rest of your life. So you better be prepared."

EARLY IN THE SUMMER of 1995, a new recruit called Edwin Graves Mauerer started showing up at militia meetings, sometimes at Fred's place in Bellingham, sometimes out in the county at John's. Ed Mauerer was an auto mechanic, a quiet, ordinary sort of person, short and spreading a little as he edged toward forty. He ran a Mobil station and garage in a town called Ferndale, and claimed to be able to rebuild any piece of machinery in any car, from the brakes to the air conditioner. Customers who didn't know him well enough or long enough to know about his history of passing bad checks, or his three convictions, or the sixty days he had spent in Dale Brandland's county jail, would drive in and look at Ed, with his neat brown beard and his plain, thick glasses, and think how lucky they were to have found someone they could trust with a busted engine, or with an old transmission some other mechanic had unloaded on them during a yearly checkup. One of those happy customers was Doc Ellwanger, who liked Ed Mauerer and didn't want him to have to face the invasion alone or unprepared. Doc Ellwanger invited Ed to the next Citizens for Liberty meeting, and then, encouraged, to another. Ed was so interested in what he learned at Citizens for Liberty, so eager to do something for the Patriot cause, that Doc Ellwanger figured it was time to bring him into the militia. One of the men Ed met that summer—he thought it was Fred, but it could have been Marlin—told him that Ben Hinkle's monthly evenings at Harbor Center were "where you kind of weed out who the believers are."

The militia, of course, was still secret. John himself was ready for what he called "public life," or, more heroically, "painting that target on my back." But he also knew how glamorous secrecy could be for a recruit like Ed, going to his first militia meeting at Fred's house and learning about the plot to turn Whatcom County into a UN park, or even just watching the video that showed you which herbs to gather if you got sick and Whatcom's hospitals were already closed. By July, Ed was going to every militia meeting Fred called. He tried to be helpful, and not just somebody out to impress the group, like the guy called Cliff—the one who kept volunteering to plant the bomb or kill the cop because he was "youngest." Ed was the kind of guy who contributed his own propane bottles, so they could actually make that bomb when the time came. By August, Ed was attending training weekends at John's house. He got to know the group. He met a man called Dan, who was introduced to him as the militia's "supply sergeant" and, at the time, was trying to talk John into buying a cache of hand grenades and claymore land mines from a young Patriot in Pennsylvania whose father wanted them out of his house fast. He met most of the other regulars, like Gary and Jack and Brian, and a new recruit by the name of Mark, who appeared one weekend for obstacle course training and sniper-detection practice, and was soon a regular himself. And, of course, he got to know John, who was eager to share with him the special "counterinsurgency" skills which he claimed had earned him "super-high marks" in the army, though they actually bore a strong resemblance to the kinds of skills you could master with a couple of free days and a MOM manual. John knew how to construct a barricade of bamboo sticks. (You whittled them into points, upended them in the ground, and covered them with leaves. He had even taught Rachel to build one, when she was a small girl, digging herself into a play fort on a hill behind Lake Samish.) He knew how to transform a mousetrap into a bomb with a blasting cap. He knew how to use a battery on a trip-wire to ignite a fuse. He knew how to pack a five-gallon pail so that everything you needed to survive in the mountains would fit: your drinking water; your socks and Sterno cans and matches; your freeze-dried soups and your canned meat, even your winter blanket and your waterproof tarp. And he knew how to make you feel at home at Command Central, with Debbie there to open the door and say hello and John himself so responsible and reassuring. "To reinforce the strength of our community, that's our primary mission," he told his recruits. When those recruits turned into regulars, he would make the point in an earthier, more military sort of way; "We're going to fuck with these people . . . fuck 'em up big time," he said at one meeting. But that was much later. At the beginning, he told them to think of their training as "a learning experience," something he was doing for them and they were doing for Whatcom County. He wanted them to count on him for everything. And for a while they did. Ed claimed later that by the fall of 1995 the garage at Command Central held the beginnings of a good-sized arsenal—dynamite, rifles, detonators, grenades, fertilizer for pipe bombs—and that John was planning to add some state-of-the-art night-vision goggles which he claimed had been stolen from Fort Davis through the good offices of the men he called "Daiwee" and "my superiors." John considered night-vision goggles essential gear. He was offering them to his own men at anywhere from $1,000 to $1,500 a pair. (Ed's story, or perhaps it was John's price, varied.) Ed gave him $500 in cash, right off, as a down payment.

John liked Ed. He liked his enthusiasm and his money and the fact that, in the course of the next year, Ed offered his house for meetings, and once even his garage—his private garage—when Gary needed a safe place for a demonstration in converting weapons. Ed was practical. He wanted to see the war start. He wasn't nervous like Jack, who suspected so many people of Leninism or Darwinism (or of some unknown "ism" designed to plague him) that he couldn't always tell where the New World Order stopped and the Washington State Militia began. He wasn't laconic like Gary, who could make poetry out of the workings of a good rifle but was notably silent on any other subject except his ex-wife, or volatile like Marlin, who liked the idea of what he called the "bang bangs" but had no patience for the intricacies of Patriot politics. If Ed had any doubts about John's competence, he never voiced them. For instance, he never came out and asked John how, precisely, he was going to blow up a UN troop train—it was a project John often mentioned—entering the tunnel between Vancouver and Whatcom County when he'd already sealed the tunnel at both ends, or for that matter how he planned to seal it to begin with. But Ed had a small problem with authority, too. Once, when John talked about Daiwee and the "quick response team" out of Fort Lewis that was ready to go to war at a sign from him, Ed asked, right in front of the men, "How'd you get so much more prepared than we are?" When John talked about serving in Panama with the army, Ed said, "Well, I was back in Vietnam." John preferred recruits who were a little more respectful—more on the order of Theodore R. Carter, Jr., the Bellingham chimney sweep who came out to a meeting at John's in February of 1996. Ted Carter, who was demonstrably dim himself, considered John a thinker and deferred to his experience. When Ted offered the possibility of a "larger version" of his special Fourth of July sparkler bomb, a version that "if somebody stepped on this, their foot wouldn't be there," he made some suggestions— wrapping nails around the bomb was one, or shattered safety glass, or poison—and then said, modestly, "John's the leader. I'll let him pick one." John liked that. It set the right tone for a leaderless resistance. He had introduced Ted to the group that night as an "anti-personnel expert," and then presented him with a militia badge and even swore him into Marlin's squad. "Hold up your right hand. Repeat after me, 'I, Ted Carter, hearby swear to serve and defend the Constitution of the United States, so help me God.' Welcome to the unit." But a few hours of glory at Command Central were enough for a sweet, limited, overgrown boy whose field of battle had been confined to Bellingham's chimneys. Everybody was nice, "real friendly," Ted testified a year later, but he had worried all evening about his sparkler bombs waking up Mrs. Pitner, or perhaps it was just thinking about the enemy, sitting there so close at hand with *its* bombs, that scared him. He had "cried some" when he got home, and he cried later, when he told the story in court.

John thought he handled his men well. He thought he handled his public well, too. The forty people who had shown up at the Rome Grange for his first public meeting seemed more than enthusiastic, though it's hard to say how many of them he converted. Don Pierce, who at the time was Bellingham's police chief (he's the police chief in Boise, Idaho, now), once told me that if you started counting bodies at public militia meetings you had to allow for the possibility that every second body was a plain-clothes cop or an undercover agent. And in Whatcom County that first night, you might also have had to allow for people who didn't have anything else to do, and for Christians who came for John's neighbor Sharon Pietila's speech about "touchy-feely education," and for "constitutionalists" who were interested in what Keith Anderson, the sovereign citizen imported from Port Townsend for the occasion, had to say about the government (which a few of them still secretly acknowledged by paying their taxes on the fifteenth of every April). But John felt he had hit the right note, holding up the Bible in one hand and the Constitution in the other, and then presenting a minister to say a prayer. It wasn't the "Patriot's Prayer" ("God grant me the serenity to accept the things I cannot change, the courage to change the things I can, and the weaponry to make the difference"), though that was available at the door, along with a broadsheet called "The 10 Planks of the Communist Manifesto" and a special issue of John's newsletter that traced the history of the Washington State Militia back through the "minutemen" [*sic*] of World War II and "Phillip II" [*sic*] to the Briton chieftain Cassivelaunus, who in John's version drove Julius Caesar out of England. Prayer, in John's opinion, made the right impression. It set the stage for the unnamed and slightly delirious veteran who took the podium at the Grange sporting a beard so matted, and a cap dangling so many buttons and medals, that you couldn't have known who he was anyway. And for Sharon and the constitutionalist, both of whom went on too long. And for Rachel Pitner, who had taken the time to drive out to the Grange to tell everyone how proud of her dad she was for painting the target on his back so she and her generation could live "free." Rachel wanted the neighbors to know that, as far as she was concerned, when your dad painted a target on *his* back you painted one on yours because "you were family." "That's my daughter!" John said afterward, turning red and starting to grin as he brushed away a tear. The neighbors liked that.

John saw no reason to bore his audiences with the sort of technical, soldierly details he taught his men—things like how you could fill a condom with Drāno, attach it to a stick of dynamite, light the fuse, and then "send that sucker up and let it drift over the fucking area and let that concussion [*sic*] explode"—although condom-bombing was certainly something many of them could do from home. John's language, like his details, varied with the crowd. It was "civil defense" to a reporter like Cathy Logg, and to a militiaman, maybe one who needed some fire in his belly, it could be, "We're going to fuck with these people, we're going to go in so hot and heavy that they're not going to know what the fuck hit them."

By the time Ted Carter brought his sparklers to Valley Highway, the group was primed for the invasion. If there was some breakdown in what John called "the chain of command" —if the men in one squad kept dropping in on somebody else's squad meetings, or were starting to meet separately, in pairs, or were even getting suspicious of one another—they were held together by John's success at the Grange and by their own anticipation. People were listening to John now. On the thirteenth of January, a hundred people had shown up to hear him speak at a public meeting in Port Angeles, out on the Olympic Peninsula. A day later, he had driven down to Mount Vernon, near Seattle, for a meeting of nearly four hundred people. John Trochmann was the guest speaker, and clearly the main attraction at Mount Vernon, but Trochmann gave a speech that most of the audience already knew by heart— the "Enemies, Foreign and Domestic" speech that went with the videos he sold, at a very handsome profit, at militia rallies. (His enemies included Communists, socialists, American corporations, traitors in the government, "commies" in law enforcement, "greenies," Baha'is, the Southern Poverty Law Center, the Anti-Defamation League of B'nai B'rith, and the Simon Wiesenthal Center.) And he was known for taking a good percentage of the gate to cover his expenses, which did not always endear him to the local Patriots. John Pitner, by comparison, was entertaining. He warmed up the crowd with a little of his bashful-middle-aged-hero routine: "I'm losing my hair, so if that makes me a skinhead, well, I don't know," he said, early on, and got everybody laughing. He watched his language. "Basically, this country is in deep doo-doo" was about the strongest thing he said, although calling the government "a crock of baloney" brought the most applause. He invited the protesters who were standing outside, blocked by militiamen, to come in and listen. ("And you don't need to be Jewish," he told them, by way of a small joke not one of them appreciated.) He even remembered to end his talk with "God bless America"—showing that touch of solemnity and reverence that had played so well at the Grange. He was so encouraged that he went on the road with Trochmann again, in

March—the meeting was in Fife this time—and a month later they were together in Seattle, with Trochmann debating an environmentalist at one of the local ABC affiliate's weekly "town meetings" and John, planted in the audience, standing up to speak for the concerned citizen.

It seemed to John, during those first few months of attention, that he had discovered a vast constituency. He could sit in the woods, alone with his computer, and log on to the Patriot Web sites, and see his name. He could tap a key and learn everything he needed to know about the world from "experts" who were counting on him, as he often said, to "share the intel." The world, in fact, leapt out at him from his small screen. He was privy to David Rockefeller's dark strategies. He was an instant specialist on the Federal Reserve. He was on intimate terms with the Joint Chiefs and the Jewish bankers. He was a ranking member of the global village and never mind *whose* village it was, or whether he had the experience or the education or the context or even the capacity to evaluate the words he read and the pictures he saw. The illusion held. He lived in a kind of unsourced-data fugue. He began to talk about the terrible news on his Patriot sites as if it were *his* news, something he'd unearthed, personally, every time he left the house. He referred to the Rockefellers and the Rothschilds as if they were upscale neighbors, people on the order of the nude bathers on the south fork or the parents lobbying to get *Silent Spring* put back onto the required-reading list at Mount Baker High—only twice as sinister and a lot richer. The more connected to the world he felt, the more isolated from the world he became. By the time I knew him, he was for all purposes incapable of reflection. He could talk, but he couldn't hear. His certainty was as seamless and deep and secret as first love, and perhaps because of this he began to work his head the way he had learned to work his computer, deleting reality as if it were a jealous or malign suitor. There were the people who knew, and the people who didn't, and the conversation stopped there. (The only time I ever heard John express a doubt about the configuration of the New World Order was when he told me that, to his mind, North Korea wasn't the "major player" most people in the Patriot movement believed it to be.) In a way, he was as much a victim of the information age as a participant in it; his access to truth, as he saw it, was so simple and direct that he had no need for an interlocator, only for an audience—which is probably why his fantasies could sprout like flowers in a biosphere. In the end, the more "information" he had, the more he extrapolated or invented, and there was no one around, really, to contradict him when he said that if the New World Order was on the march, then it was marching directly to Whatcom County and John Pitner was the reason. It had to be true, because it was what the Washington State Militia wanted to hear.

It may be that the worst thing that happened to John those first few years was that life went on so peaceably in Whatcom County. None of the serious training he'd organized, none of the serious talks he'd given about income and output and the cost of ordnance—Judie Ellwanger called it "Jewing," but Doc Ellwanger liked Jewing, because it gave him something practical to think about now that his artificial-insemination clinic was gone—made up for the fact that the invasion never came. For a while, of course, John's militia recruits were too busy to be impatient. Matt Ramsey, a young sheet-metal worker from Snohomish known to the local public-access television audience as "Militia Jim," told me about a very busy weekend he'd spent, supposedly in the fall of 1995, at one of John's secret training "encampments." Matt wasn't exactly sure where the encampment was, only that it was a half-hour's drive from the Bellingham parking lot where he and a group of other recruits—he said that John Lloyd Kirk, one of the Freemen arrested when John Pitner was, had been with them —were marched into a van in blindfolds. He did say that it must have been a very strategic site, because it was up on a cliff and you'd be able to see the enemy coming from three directions, but he was not what anyone would have called an entirely reliable informant. When I met him, about a year after his Whatcom weekend, he wolfed down two lunches at a Snohomish pizza parlor, sold me a Militia Jim video for ten dollars, and then proceeded to describe his mother as a left-wing social worker, a born-again Christian, and a founding member of the Spokane Hillary Clinton fan club. At the end of the day I wasn't really sure if his ghoulish performances as "Militia Jim" had been obsession or satire. His story was that, having been sworn into one of John's Snohomish squads in a small ceremony in a Denny's parking lot off the Interstate 5, he had promptly replaced his earlier program, "Matt Ramsey's House of Pain," with a militia program and—this much was true, anyway—interviewed John for the first "Militia Jim" broadcast. "A sense of humor, but he needs lithium," was how Scott North, at the *Everett Herald,* described him when he gave me Matt's phone number. But after twenty-six of those broadcasts, Matt did know something about militias. He said that the camp where he'd spent the weekend—with forty recruits and John, Fred, Marlin, and Gary as their "drill instructors"—not only had trenches, rifle ranges, and firing pits, and a shack for "tactical entry," but that he would have happily gone back if the praying that began and ended the weekend hadn't offended his "atheist principles." As it happened, he was never invited back, which offended him even more, since he'd already given John the fifty dollars that, according to him, John charged every new recruit for the "bunch of goodies" he was going to need at the invasion. John had promised to buy the goodies himself and then to bury them in some safe, secret, need-to-know piece of the wilderness. He wouldn't say what, precisely, you could expect for your fifty dollars, and naturally he couldn't say where you'd find it; he didn't want that intel falling into enemy hands. If you believed Matt's calculations, John had made as much as $2,000 that weekend.

Scott North, who'd been covering northwest Washington's militias so relentlessly that by 1996 his picture appeared regularly on a local Patriot "Most Unwanted" poster, once said that some of the militia recruits he'd met reminded him of the kids who joined gangs in big cities. "It's like when a gang starts," he told me, "and there's an incredible power association with being a member." He described John's men as "gang members with a little more age." They had a lot of the same fetishes: insignia, special clothes, weapons, turf. And they had the same impatience. The older militiamen wanted to see action before arthritis, or worse, kicked in, and the younger militiamen were bored and, given that this was small-town Washington, dangerously restless. They wanted to prove they were tough—as tough, anyway, as the Patriots in Spokane, where (as Matt Ramsey had put it nicely) "in terms of the violence level, one guy . . . is [considered] worth ten here." After a year's commute between the gangland East and the militia West, I suspected that Scott was right. Marlin, for instance, would demand: "If something goes down, where's the first place to hit?" Then John would have to think fast, and say something like, "The first place that gets it, the first thing to do, the first option to do is get the fuck out of Dodge and regroup. . . . Then wait for your orders. Your orders will come. . . . I have two sealed documents that are—that are placed in various places." It didn't take many exchanges like that for the men to start complaining among themselves. Marlin complained that they hadn't come very far, as a fighting force, since the night he had driven out to Command Central as a new recruit and seen his first rigged mousetrap and Molotov cocktail on John's coffee table. Fred complained because the big "cluster fuck" that John had promised them all hadn't happened. Ed, who had moved up and was now "second in command" in Gary's squad, complained because none of them knew where their money had gone, or where their weapons were cached, or for that matter where to sound the alert if the enemy struck and John, as most of the men put it, "was taken out." By then, there were six squads with connections to Alpha One meeting weekly in Whatcom County, and Marlin was getting promoted and would be leaving Gary's squad to start his own. And, as Scott predicted, most of the people in those squads were getting bored with the routine: the Pledge of Allegiance; the opening minutes; the short discussion of enemy activity known as "current events"; and the hour or so of "training" or "instruction" or "weapons news" or debate on, say, the comparative explosive properties of Epsom salts and cayenne pepper. Not that it was much livelier at Alpha One. If anyone dropped in on an Alpha One meeting, asking questions—and at one time or another a lot of the militiamen in the county did—he would have to sit through one of John's monologues on the theme of how much harder the waiting was for *him,* as their leader, than it was for them. John swore to the group that the invasion was close at hand; he swore that he had the intel; he swore that, at a word from him, the big Patriot guns and tanks would join the battle. But he couldn't provide his militiamen with that battle. The closest he came, during that spring of 1996, was the famous standoff in Jordan County, Montana, between the government and a group of Montana Freemen (who, not surprisingly, counted among their leaders a New York con man with a source of bogus checks), squatting on a ranch they claimed as sovereign territory. Jordan County, or "Justus Township," as the Freemen called their ranch, was Doc Ellwanger's clinic writ large, with the whole country watching. It wasn't Whatcom, but it was definitely a Patriot sort of confrontation. John, with some relief, told me that the moment of truth was finally at hand, the moment for the Washington State Militia to stand and fight for the Freemen's God-given right to a piece of the state of Montana—though of course he had to accept that his men might never make it to Montana. His intel was that the feds would be using "high-frequency sound and low-frequency microwave" to "pacify" them at the Montana state line. The Washington State Militia went on high alert anyway, which from what I could gather meant mainly that the militiamen kept calling Montana to compare the room rates at Jordan County's motels, and for at least a month, none of them even thought to ask where their money had gone. When the Freemen surrendered in June, without a shot fired, John announced that the Jordan Patriots had been seized as "sacrificial lambs" to the New World Order. He considered that a stirring explanation, but it was the only explanation he had, and it wasn't likely to make Whatcom's Patriots much happier than they had been before. John's troops were disappointed. They were even *alive*, which didn't do much for their image on their own turf. They thought they had ordered a revolution the way you ordered a hamburger with fries at Denny's. When the service was slow, they began to blame the waiter.

Four

O NE DAY, when John was a boy, he decided to fly.
He slid a piece of plywood through the handlebars
on his bicycle, took off from the top of a hill, let go,
and for as long as the ride, and the bike, lasted, he waited to
be wind-borne and "free." Then he fell. John was still dream-
ing of flying at forty-five. The copies he saved of *Science News*
and *Discover,* stacked on his living room floor beside a couple
of years' worth of a magazine called *Reason* ("Free Minds and
Free Markets," the cover said), were devoted to the entrepre-
neurial possibilities of space travel. John referred to them as
a kind of archive—proof that the ultimate, top-secret, treacherous aim of the New World Order was to keep the mineral
matériel of profit, the fuels and the ores of its industries and
the precious stones which he knew were floating around in the
universe, terrestrial. He meant, by terrestrial, in the hands of

the men who controlled them now. John once told me that if I thought of Earth as "just a little green ball in space" I would understand that "there's a hundred zillion trillion billion other little balls in space that we could have, too." His physics was not much more sophisticated than it had been when his bicycle crashed. What he had in mind was to build himself a small jet that would pick up speed, collecting hydrogen as it went along, and manufacture the oxidizers to burn that hydrogen, until it passed Pluto at the speed of light. It was a metaphor for his longing and his frustration and, at times, for the rage he felt when he logged on to the Militia of Montana catalog and ordered books like *Weather Control* ($5) and *The Mark of the New World Order* ($30) with Debbie's Visa card.

There were people in John's family who believed that, with a little encouragement and a measure of self-discipline, he could have gone to college and become a scientist, instead of a contract worker at the Seattle shipyards, spraying electrostatic paint onto the hulls of battleships and container carriers and ferryboats for companies like Lockheed, Todd, and Marine Power and Equipment, which is what he had done, off and on, before he moved north to the county in 1981. There were other people in the family who said, no, he could have been an artist, because the part of painting he liked best, the part that absorbed him, was the decoration. "The more intricate the colors and the design, the more I liked it," John himself said. Once, he told me that his happiest times as a painter had been the times some private client let him design a thunderbird and spray it onto the side of a house, or a truck, or a piece of equipment. He thought of his thunderbird as a logo, signifying John Pitner, and by the time I met him it meant the John Pitner trapped and grounded in "Amerika" by all the people who were determined to keep him from building his spacecraft and flying off to wildcat some convenient asteroid and returning with enough diamonds and gold to put De Beers and Anaconda out of business. It may be that, in his odyssey from the workers' suburbs of Roxbury and Dorchester, Massachusetts, to Valley Highway 9, John had used up his American birthright for terrestrial self-invention, and in the end the choice, for him, of an American West was either a cold bath in the Pacific or the warm fantasy of a universe dripping Patriot gold.

No one had thought to see to his education, and he never did much to correct that. Once, when we were talking about the spacecraft he planned to build as soon as the war was over, he claimed to have spent a year studying physics at a Jesuit college in Seattle. But the only Jesuit college listed in Seattle had no record of a student named "John Irvin Pitner"—not even Lockheed, where he'd supposedly worked most, painting ships, had a record of anyone named John Pitner—and the truth is that he never finished high school. Sometimes, he admitted to having dropped out after the tenth grade; other times, it was after the eleventh. His high school couldn't tell me, and the army, which he joined for three disastrous years in the late sixties, couldn't either. (His army records listed his education as eleventh grade on one page and ninth grade a couple of pages later.) Debbie maintained that while John had always had trouble sticking to anything for very long, his problem was never the studying or the work so much as it was the people. John hated to have to answer to other people. It didn't matter if those people were schoolteachers or sergeants or shipyard foremen or officers of the law. The only thing that had changed in John's life, as he came to understand it, was that now he knew this wasn't a problem at all, but the true sign of an independent American spirit. The way John saw things, the Bill of Rights was a bill of his own entitlement; he was as stubborn about his "rights" as a cowboy with a long rope. The more reality betrayed him, the more desperately and tenaciously he believed.

The Pitners were by Washington standards old family: white, Christian, European peasant stock with an exotic, which is to say appropriately Wild West, touch of Blackfoot and Potawatomi mixed over the years into the Pitner bloodline. Long before the Pacific coast became the Pacific Rim—back in the days when Seattle was a town of eighty thousand people and not looking to expand—there was a road called Pitner Avenue, off Lake Martha, a few miles out of the city, and the family owned a good deal of the land around it. John's great-grandfather, Grandpa Pitner to the family, was the Pitner patriarch. He was the first Washington Pitner, and Pitner Avenue was the end of a journey that had begun in a village in Bohemia, in 1878, when he was a boy of fourteen and decided to make his life in America. "Fourteen years old and fourteen bucks, American, in his pocket," is how John's father, Richard Pitner, a man with a reverence for hard knocks and American self-reliance, described Grandpa Pitner to me. "He walked into the streets of New York that way, nobody waiting for him with the rent paid for six months, and [nobody with] a bunch of food stamps and a couple of checks, either." Back in Bohemia, Grandpa Pitner had been an apprentice butcher. He had been hacking at carcasses since the age of six, so it wasn't entirely surprising that, at fourteen, he was able to pass in New York as something of an old pro, or that, by fifteen, he had his own butcher shop in the city, or that, by twenty-one, he had found his way to the Chicago stockyards and was making money out of seven successful butcher shops, or, you could say, a Pitner chain. He might have stopped in Chicago, and prospered, and changed the family story, but the West lured Grandpa Pitner and in the end ruined him. He sold his butcher shops for the price of a 3,000-acre wheat farm, a little to the west of Spokane, and for a while he did so well in the commodities market that he began to believe the price of wheat would be going up forever. The crash of 1929 caught him with 500,000 bushels of wheat on the market. The family says that he went to bed on the night of October 29th as a rich man and woke on the morning of the 30th without a dime. He lost the farm and never recovered.

In a way, it was the family that never recovered. John's grandfather had to homestead. He took a horse and some chain and cleared a plot in Idaho. Every night, he made a huge pile of the brush he had cut that day and lit a bonfire so blazing that Dick Pitner, as an old man, could still remember going to bed at the age of two or three with flames shooting up and lighting the night sky. At the end of a month of bonfires, he dug a big square hole in the ground and covered it with a sod roof, and that was home. It was a hardscrabble life, which may be why it became a sore point with Dick Pitner that the squirrel gun his mother had used, sitting on a box by their homestead door and shooting the heads off sage hens at eighty feet, was later described in court as part of a weapons stash that made his son John a menace to society. Dick had inherited the rifle from his parents. He called it a fourth-generation Pitner rifle, because everyone in the family down to John's daughter, Rachel, had tried it, although no one had done as well with it as that young Pitner bride sitting on a wooden box, picking off sage hens at eighty feet.

I often thought that the real story of the Pitner family was the story of the squirrel gun, handed down through the generations of Pitners like a prized teacup, or like one of those immigrant ancestral portraits where grandma and grandpa sit all dressed up in front of a photographer's drop-sheet mural that turns their life on the farm or in the sweatshop into a prosperous, genteel, and altogether enviable illusion of America. The gun, like some of the Pitners I got to know, had lost its purpose in its travels from Grandpa Pitner's glory days in Chicago to John Pitner's arrest in a Whatcom County manufactured home—from immigrant hope to Patriot expectation. John's grandfather left Idaho not much richer than when he came; he put down apple orchards in a valley near Yakima and tried to ride out the Depression that way. John's father left home and joined the navy at seventeen. "Dick's war" is what the family called the Second World War. It set the family standard and became a family legend, like Grandpa Pitner's seven butcher shops: four years in China on a Yangtze cruiser, patrolling the riverbank that was Chiang Kai-shek's last line of defense against the Japanese occupation armies, moving south; four years in the Pacific on the gunboat *Luzon;* action in Bougainville and the Solomons; the glory, at twenty-two, of becoming Chief Petty Officer Richard Pitner, the youngest chief petty officer in the American navy, not to mention its lightweight boxing champion. John grew up on stories about the heroes of the Yangtze River Patrol—a handful of American boys who had held off the Japanese for six long months, alone and for all practical purposes abandoned, because Franklin Roosevelt had already spent America's money on socialist schemes like the WPA.

Dick Pitner put in fourteen years of active duty in the navy, and, much later, six years in the National Guard reserves to bring the number up to twenty and qualify for his pension. By then, he had managed to pursue "a fractured education" in engineering, a process he described to me variously as "pieces here, pieces there" and "racheting my way through a bunch of crap." He enrolled in extension courses. He worked days as a salesman for engineering companies, and went to night school to study thermodynamics and applied mechanical engineering. He studied at the University of Michigan when he had a job in Michigan. He studied at Tufts when he found a better job in Massachusetts. He pasted a Yangtze River Patrol decal on the rear window of his car and kept in touch with his war buddies on a ham radio, and even when the good days ended—it didn't take long, once he left the navy—he never let anyone in the family forget that he had earned his right to tell them what to do.

JOHN'S MOTHER, who died in the 1980s, lived most of her life in Boston. Her name was Dorothy. "Dorothy One," Debbie called her the first few times we got together, so I wouldn't confuse that Dorothy with the Dorothy Pitner who has been John's stepmother for more than thirty years. Dorothy One was crazy. This was one thing everyone in the family agreed on. John's sister Susan called her a classic case of paranoid schizophrenia, but she said that when their mother was a young woman, the diagnosis at the Pitner house was simply "crazy." Crazy, dangerous, and scary. Dick had wanted the sort of wife he later recommended to John as a "kitchen and bedroom" woman, a port of call in his man's world, somebody not too difficult as women go, somebody obedient. And when they met and married in Boston—Dick a stranger from Washington, Dorothy One a stranger from Maine—he believed he had found one. By all accounts, he was stunned when the simple, God-fearing, Catholic country girl he had thought was going to run his house and cheerfully raise his children began to show signs of a strong, unnerving imagination, and even more stunned when she became convinced that she was actually possessed by demons. No one seems to have disabused her of the idea of demons, or tried seriously to help her, not even the Virgin, to whom she prayed regularly to exorcise those demons and save her from damnation; her prayers, at any rate, were unanswered. She had four children in the course of eight or nine years—Richard Jr., Sheila, Susan, and finally John, the baby. And she spent most of those years raising them on her own, since Dick was as often as not at sea. John, who tried to believe in a happier family history than the one he'd had, was the only child who remembered much joy or even much attention. "We're all survivors," Sheila once told me, referring mainly to herself and to the demonstrably lonely life she led, sustained by disability checks and depression medication, in a mobile home at the same Bellingham trailer park that John had been so eager to leave. Susan, who worried about her sister all the time, felt that, in Sheila's case, "survivor" was an understatement. Sheila had been the eldest girl, and according to Susan their mother tormented her—beat her, stabbed her, dragged her to the stove when she cried too loudly, or misbehaved, and slapped her hands onto the hot coils. But the truth was that none of the children

Dorothy One had with Dick Pitner survived their childhoods undamaged. Richard Jr., who was amiable, a little slow, and not what you would call a terrifically useful person, had had trouble with work, trouble with wives, trouble with the whole stressful and bewildering world. (When I met him, in the fall of 1996, he was working part time at a refinery and living with his fourth or fifth wife in a trailer near Sheila's.) Even Susan, who was competent and smart and had worked hard to make a life for herself, had, by her own account, a history of depressions, breakdowns, and sleep apnea, a condition she described to me medically, and then, in layman's terms, as "falling asleep, and your body forgets to breathe."

Dick Pitner didn't believe in psychiatrists. He believed in navy discipline. He had thought of his family as a ship at last under his command, and for him the turmoil at home was a kind of mutiny, as if his violently deranged wife and his terrorized, troubled children were setting that ship adrift, giving it a bad name and, it could be said, giving America a bad name. John was a baby when his parents started quarreling about divorce. The family was living in Washington then, and the divorce would certainly have happened there if Dorothy One hadn't crushed her leg in a car crash—she was drunk and driving—and been left for all practical purposes helpless. Dick moved everyone back to Boston, first to the suburb of Roxbury and then to Dorchester. It was an experience he remembered, at the age of seventy-eight, as "eight or ten thousand dollars on bone surgery." I visited Dick on Whidbey Island—it was November of 1996, and he and his second Dorothy were living in the small retirement house they'd built there—and asked him to tell me what, finally, had happened. He said, "You don't even leave a hurt dog laying in the street, so I stuck with her and took her back East. . . . And when I got her all well, she promptly limped her way off over the horizon again. So that's when we split up."

John was five. He and his brother and sisters spent most of the next several years in foster homes—the boys always with one family, the girls with another—either because his father couldn't keep them, or because he wouldn't keep them, or because he thought simply that, as a man, raising children was beneath him. John's mother was clearly too ill by then to raise them herself. (In time, she married again and produced a third son; the boy, in despair, hanged himself at the age of thirteen.) John missed Susan, who was closer to him in age and spirit than the other children, and had always mothered him at home. In fact, he came to believe that missing Susan was what made him, at five, so intractable that in very short order he was known throughout their Boston diocese as "the bad boy of Catholic Charities." He said that he went through five or six foster families, first in Boston and then, when his father moved home, in Washington, and that "every one [was] a bad experience." The feeling was evidently mutual, since one of those families went so far as to land him in an institution—a gesture that may have had something to do with his setting fire to the family's house, though he swore to his own family that it wasn't the house, it was the chicken coop. (He told *me* that he'd never set fire to anything; he said it was the other children, who hadn't liked him and had wanted him sent away.) The important thing, at least to John, was that his father had come to retrieve him every time he was "returned" to Catholic Charities, or got in trouble, or ran away. He converted those moments into a kind of parenting—"Dad has a lot of regrets, [but] he did the best he could as a parent," he said, solemnly—which may be one reason he kept getting himself "returned." His best memory from all those years in and out of foster families was the memory of bunking with his father, just the two of them alone in a Washington motel, while he was waiting for a new family to take him in. That was when he decided to fly, and put the plywood through his handlebars.

When John was nine or ten, Dick Pitner bought a house in Bothell, in the Seattle suburbs, near the street that was once called Pitner Avenue (and not far from where Susan and her companion, Betsey, were living when I first met them). And then he brought John to live in Bothell with him. There was a small private airport a short walk from the new house, the Kenmore Air Harbor, and one of the very few things that never changed in John's stories about his childhood was how much he loved that airport. He told me he'd head for the hangar every day, after school, just to listen to the pilots talk. He'd wash down the planes when they let him. If he was lucky, one of them would take him flying. There was nothing to keep him home. Susan was long gone. Their father, with his strong views about women's place, had never been interested in keeping a headstrong daughter. He had sent Susan away at twelve to work in Florida as a "mother's helper"—she told me "child labor" would be a more accurate description—and that was when she decided somehow to find a way out of the Pitner family. She joined the Air Force as soon as she turned seventeen.

By then, the Pitners were a huge family. "A huge *dysfunctional* family" as Susan (and sometimes John and Sheila) called it, because Dick in the meantime remarried, and the new Dorothy had arrived at the Bothell house with four children of her own. When I met Dorothy Pitner, on Whidbey Island in 1996, she was a storybook grandmother, sweet and prim, who fussed over her husband and, indeed, over the whole family, and the family adored her. But the Dorothy who'd moved to Bothell nearly forty years earlier was—if you asked the family that adored her now—as mean as a rattlesnake, with a sharp tongue, a venomous bite, and very little patience. She was a different kind of survivor, a woman who had held her own in a rough male world. She had survived the war years as a riveter at Boeing Aircraft and the next ten years as a logging-camp cook in Alaska, and she was determined to survive the Pitner children, too. She told them that she was nobody's servant, nobody's patsy, and nobody's fool, and she set out to prove it. The children (including a few of her own) took her for a sworn enemy, and Dorothy, for her part, didn't much like them, either. She especially did not like John. She liked John later—like his father, she thought that John Pitner, commander of the Washington State Militia, was a cross between Jesus and Nathan Hale—but at the time she thought that John was trouble, and John *knew* that she was trouble. They fought with the weapons they had. John's weapon was his reputation as the bad seed of the Catholic foster home circuit. Dorothy's weapon was a wifely knowledge of the family secrets. The most damning secret, from the point of view of a lonely boy of thirteen trying to please an opinionated and arguably difficult father, was that Dick Pitner may not have been his father at all.

By all the accounts I heard, John's natural father was a mild-mannered man from Boston. His name was either John (if you asked Sheila) or Howard (if you asked Debbie or Susan), but the women agreed that he had met Dorothy One when Dick was on one of his tours at sea. Howard hadn't known that Dorothy One was married or even, at first, that she had children, and he certainly hadn't known that she was mad. According to the family, he was her lover for a little more than two years, during which time—this happened early in 1951—Dick came home on leave and found his wife pregnant and, whether from shame or spite or, as Debbie, who told me the story first, described it, an impulse to "do the right thing" and keep the children together as a family, he decided to claim the baby as his own. The children, on the other hand, seem to have preferred it when Howard was keeping them together, which is apparently what Howard did whenever Dick Pitner was out of town. Susan said it this way: "Howard was such a wonderful man. One day with him was better than a lifetime with our father." And Debbie, who had heard the story from John, told me, "He kind of stepped into the role of father." She said he was attached to John and at one point wanted to raise John himself, but when he came to the house to take him, Dick was waiting, the two men argued, and Dick won. According to Debbie, the children never saw Howard again. Dick liked the idea of sons. He put his hopes in John and never told him about the man his older children remembered and sometimes missed. He wanted John to carry on the Pitner "tradition" and to have sons who, in time, would do the same thing. Perhaps he saw himself as the new Grandpa Pitner, paterfamilias to an important American military family. My impression was that if Vietnam hadn't happened for him, Dick would have started a war so John could fight for the United States.

Debbie assured me that "there's been times John was curious" about the man she called Howard, but John never mentioned those times to me. He never mentioned Howard at all. He never talked about what it was like to be thirteen, fighting with his stepmother and hearing the name Howard for the first time, or how he felt afterwards, or what he said to Dick Pitner, or for that matter to his mother, back in Boston, or what either of them said to him, and whether he felt guilty or grateful or worthless or mad or miserable or betrayed. There was no reason why he should have talked to me about it. By the end of his trial, in February of 1997, I was fairly convinced that he'd never told anyone outside his family, not even the Patriots he trusted most, the ones who had promised to die with him, defending America. On the other hand, he liked the fact that I was going to write about him. He told everyone who asked that I had come to Washington because of him, which was for the most part true, and he always tried to be interesting and dramatic and, in a way, a victim—so the reason may simply have been that, by the time I met him, his Patriot persona was so convoluted and confused that, to him, the most interesting stories he told were (almost by definition) the ones he invented. It certainly wasn't peculiar to the Pitner family that the women in it tended to be forthcoming and the men did not, at least when the family honor, as they understood honor, was at stake. And in fact, most of the times that John talked about his father—he meant, of course, Dick Pitner, and so do I—he was critical and even judgmental. Once, he spent the better part of an hour complaining about how stubborn his father was, and what a mess he'd made of the family finances. He told me about a wonderful house that Dick had bought, years earlier— a house that was much bigger than the one in Bothell—with a modest windfall from a small hydraulic-engineering company he had started. John had liked everything about that house. It was close to the Kenmore Air Harbor, close to the first school he had ever enjoyed, close to a planetarium, even close to a country club, and the neighbors were rich, which at the time was exactly what John wanted his father to be. But suddenly— "Just like that," John said—Dick sold the house to invest in a couple of condominiums that in the end he couldn't unload and couldn't even rent at a profit. John never forgave him for selling the house, or, for that matter, for losing his engineering company not much later. He told me that Dick had sold Western Hydraulics (it was a name he intoned) "for a million dollars," and would have been rich himself if he hadn't got stubborn about his expertise with a contract and wound up cheated out of three-quarters of the payment. According to John, his father had "screwed up" everything that way. The property he persisted in buying was always in the wrong place at the wrong time, and the result was that Dick Pitner was now in the middle of an island, still waiting to make his killing—persuaded that he was "sitting on a piece of property" everybody else wanted. Once, John went so far as to say that disappointment had turned his father into a racist, a chauvinist, a bitter old man. But he never blamed Dick for the pain in the Pitner family. John was clear about that. He could talk for hours about the Pitners' "American family values." He wanted me to know that he and his militia were all about those values, that they were fighting to reclaim an idyllic American past that was in many ways *his* past.

The problem for John, of course, was that the real Pitners—the ones with a history of infidelity or neglect or suicide or breakdown—were not the kind of family you were supposed to find in the America of God and the Founding Fathers and whoever else had passed the sword of liberty to

John Pitner. The real Pitners were the kind of family you were supposed to discover on the other side, the kind of family that foreigners and communists and people who lived in the "other Washington" had. The Pitner women may have been proud of having survived that family, but what John wanted to have survived was the New World Order and the United Nations and the traitorous bankers at the Federal Reserve. The fact that he had had a nasty experience called a childhood and that it was nonetheless an American childhood—in his short historical memory, an almost prelapsarian American childhood—was one of the things he found almost impossible to acknowledge. It made him suspect, unworthy. It tainted his Patriot credentials, like having a Zionist or a Stalinist in the family. I sometimes wondered if the Washington State Militia wasn't, at least in part, a way for him to rewrite the history of the Pitner family, and his own experience in and of that family, because the militia was a passion he and his father shared. Dick was too old, ill with cancer and according to John too cranky, to come to meetings or train in the hills with young men like Militia Jim, and there was no reason to believe that John would have invited him anyway. But for Dick, the Washington State Militia was the Yangtze River Patrol reborn—a reminiscence, a triumph of Patriot paternity. "Painted a target on his back!" he told me, when I asked his opinion of John's brief Patriot career. He was unconditionally, uncontrollably proud of his son. He said that he'd worried about John all the time then, and that he gave him high marks for vigilance and courage now. "Like father, like son," was the way he put it. Once I was back in New York, I would find him on the Internet, pleading John's cause, right below an old snapshot of John in the Arizona desert, posing beside a mock-up of the

Apollo space capsule. He used a Web site called "Caged Patriots." He posted dozens of open letters—they were letters he'd already sent to the Seattle press, and to his congressmen, and to Louis Freeh, at the FBI. In his letters, he referred to John not as "my son" but as "my Son." Jesus couldn't have asked for more attention.

JOHN ENLISTED in the army at seventeen. It wasn't Dick's navy, but it was going to be John's Vietnam. In June of 1968, a few days after school let out for the summer at Englemore High, John presented himself at his local draft board, ready to fight the Communists in Southeast Asia. He was still, by his own account, a scrappy kid, and pretty much at war with the world already. His stepmother wanted him out of the house, his father wanted him to make a man of himself—if not in battle, then at least in the trappings of battle—and it has to be said that John's milieu was not one in which you burned your draft card, or your grandmother marched for peace, or your dad withheld the Defense Department's portion of his federal income tax. Listening to John talk about the army, I had to remind myself that 1968 in the Pitner family was "1968": the year of the Paris barricades and the Columbia sit-ins and the Berkeley protests; the year of sex, beads, and flowers; the year when the chocolate chip cookies came laced with hashish and New Yorkers romped naked in Central Park; the year that many young American men lived in considerable dread of their own draft boards and Allen Ginsberg assured them that with the right mantra they could make Robert McNamara disappear. In 1968, some of my friends were making plans to move to Sweden or Canada, but John Pitner wasn't thinking about Canada. In John's world, you didn't flee to Canada and you didn't call the family doctor for a letter swearing you were homosexual or schizophrenic and you didn't join the Society of Friends, hoping to pass for a conscientious objector. If you were Dick Pitner's son, or wanted to be Dick Pitner's son, you proved yourself as a man and a patriot. You thought it was a fine thing that America finally had a president who wasn't distracted from the cause of freedom by a lot of socialist boondoggles, the way Roosevelt had been distracted when Dick was holding the line on his Yangtze cruiser.

John did his basic training at Fort Lewis, the army base just south of Tacoma, and from there he was sent to Fort Bliss, in Texas, for ambush training and an orientation course for Vietnam. In October of 1968, with an "excellent" in conduct and efficiency in Platoon Combat Skills, he was posted to Panama, to Battery B of the Fourth Missile Battalion of the 517th Artillery of the United States Southern Command at Fort Clayton, in the Canal Zone. His records list him as a cannoneer in a light air defense artillery unit, which is pretty much the artillery equivalent of an infantry grunt. It was an assignment that, in the interests of reputation in Whatcom County, he preferred to describe as "training for psy ops"— psychological operations—"in Brazil and Guatemala and Costa Rica" or, better still, as "training for Vietnam jungle warfare in the Special Forces." Occasionally, if he was on a roll, if his audience was with him and he was really confident, he was the guy training second lieutenants for the Special Forces. "Five months of crack training, survival training, grooming super-troopers," is how he put it. Once or twice, he was even inspired to promote himself to the head of the psy ops program, working top secret out of a place he referred to mysteriously as "Building 519." The American writer Richard Koster, who lives in Panama, told me that "519" was the big Fort Clayton building that, in fact, housed the base hospital.

In January of 1969, John was court-martialed. It was three months after his arrival in Panama and also, as it happened, three months after General Omar Torrijos's coup d'état. Several thousand Panamanians had rioted to protest the coup, which had overthrown their new president, and while there is no official record of American soldiers being used against the protesters, they were used in John's version of the story, and he was one of those soldiers. John's story was that at some point during the rioting three young Panamanians broke into an empty building on the Canal Zone's Balboa base and barricaded themselves in a room there, armed with a couple of stolen American army 50-caliber machine guns; that John and a group of soldiers from his unit were sent to disarm them, presenting weapons (sent, that is, with fixed bayonets on their rifles but no live ammunition); and that within the next few minutes John watched two of his friends die under machine-gun fire. As for the rest of the soldiers, John told me, "We broke ranks and hid every which way" and "were punished for it." That was the beginning of his "understanding," the moment, he said, he began to suspect that "Big Daddy Warbucks"—nobody called it the New World Order then—was running the world and that life was cheap to Big Daddy, American life included. He knew he was right when, not much later, he "witnessed" an American raid on a Panamanian village. This time, he claimed to have watched American soldiers set fire to a house with a twelve-year-old girl and an eight-year-old boy hiding inside, too terrified to leave. The children, he said, were burned alive. (There is no record of a raid then, either, though it would be ingenuous to assume that every action involving American soldiers and Panamanian civilians during the years America controlled the Zone went into the public record, especially given the number of "unrecorded" records that surfaced in the 1980s, after the American invasion.) The next thing that happened in John's Panama story was his own protest. He decided to expose the truth about Big Daddy Warbucks and rallied the troops at Fort Davis, the Tenth Infantry base across the isthmus from Fort Clayton, with his passionate speeches. He led those troops in huge, mutinous demonstrations, "because of the deaths of my friends and the deaths of [the] two children." And on January 24, 1969, he was court-martialed at Fort Davis by a commander determined to silence him before every grunt in the Canal Zone threw down his arms and refused to serve. Describing his court martial to me, the third or fourth time around, he said, "Yeah, I got up in my lieutenant commander's face, in his office, slammed my fist down on his desk, and he had a glass top on his desk, a cover, and I cracked that . . . and he was not too happy about that. . . . So because I staged those protests they had thrown me into the slammer, in the stockade." When I asked who "they" were, he said "a couple of majors and a couple of colonels down there who thought that what I was doing was standing up—that I had enough chutzpah to speak out when nobody else, you know, not even the majors, was speaking out about what was going on."

By then, of course, John had been working on his story for twenty-five years, though it was still basically the same story he had told to Dick Pitner when he came home to Kenmore, and to Debbie when they met a few years later in Anacortes, and eventually to the men in Whatcom County who joined the

Washington State Militia. People in the militia took it on faith, as proof that John Pitner was a hero, not only a leader of men but a freedom fighter so prescient that he was alert to the rumblings of the New World Order before it even had a name. The army had a different story: John never rallied the troops at Fort Davis in a protest; in fact, there were no protests at Fort Davis, and even if there had been, John was presumably nowhere near Fort Davis in January of 1969. John was AWOL for nearly half of January. By the 24th, he was locked up in the stockade at his battalion headquarters at Fort Clayton—he was court-martialed *there*—and three weeks later he was tried. The charges against him were not sedition or insurrection or even insubordination. John was accused of violating two articles of the Uniform Code of Military Justice. The first charges involved his being "absent without authority" from his unit twice—for six days early in January, and later in the month for eight days. The second charges had to do with the things he took with him when he went absent. For his first trip, John had apparently availed himself of one lieutenant colonel's twelve-bottle case of Diet Rite Cola and his five-dollar machete, another lieutenant colonel's hammock, and, moving up the Fort Clayton command, a colonel's folding chair and his stash of canned food. It wasn't grand larceny, but it was just right for, say, a couple of days on a Panama beach, and it was certainly bound to inconvenience three officers in Big Daddy Warbucks' service. John's second trip was bolder. For that, he stole an intelligence major's green MG.

John pleaded guilty and was found guilty. His pay was docked by seventy-three dollars a month for the next six months, and he was sentenced to six months of prison at hard labor—five of those months suspended. He served his month, and then in March, for reasons I never discovered, the suspension was revoked and John was ordered to complete his sentence. After six months in the Fort Clayton stockade, he was demoted and reassigned as a rifleman in the Fourth Battalion of the Tenth Infantry at Fort Davis—his first appearance at Fort Davis—where he was instructed in the use of a Browning automatic rifle and graded "unsatisfactory" for "conduct" and "efficiency." He was at Davis for a little over a year, though he never managed to raise his rank or his grade, and by then it's unlikely that he even tried. By his own admission, he was "seriously fucked" by what he had seen and learned about Big Daddy Warbucks. In November of 1970, his stepbrother Ricky committed suicide—Ricky was John's age and, at the time, his one real ally among Dorothy's children—and John was sent home to Washington, on "compassionate reassignment" to Fort Lewis. Three months later, he left the army with a "general discharge." This was a special (though not uncommon) category of discharge, neither "honorable" nor "dishonorable" nor "bad conduct," and when I asked John to explain it, he said it was part of the deal he'd negotiated with the brass in Panama. There would be no "dishonorable" on John's record, and John, in return, would never talk about the terrible and shocking things he had seen. It occurred to me, much later, that it could have been Dick Pitner, with his fine war record and his retirement rank as a sergeant major of the Washington National Guard, who had done the negotiating.

John had a favorite story about his record. He liked to say that his only trouble with the law was the time he'd shinnied up a flagpole in Anacortes on his twenty-first birthday, stolen the flag, and got thirty days in the slammer. He never told the rest of the family the truth about his court martial, and

Susan, for one, didn't even know he'd *been* court-martialed. His father never told anyone either, though Dick, as a military man, must have at least suspected that John had not done hard labor in Panama because of patriotic zeal. He would certainly have known that the commander of the United States Southern Command in Panama—a major general named Chester L. Johnson—had not, as John insisted, lost his post because a seventeen-year-old soldier told everyone in the Panama Canal Zone about his sending unarmed American boys against Panamanian insurgents, and, in John's words, "the scuttlebutt moved back uphill." It may be that, even then, Dick knew every detail of his son's disastrous service. He never said. But the rest of the family didn't know. The family thought that John had loved the army until the army betrayed him. The family remembered John, en route to Panama, as quite transformed from the boy they had known a few months earlier—the boy, as his sister Sheila, echoing Susan, put it, with "a lying problem." Dick himself told me that after three months' basic training, John had left for Panama "an entirely different young man." "He was proud of that uniform, and he was spic-and-span, and I looked him over and, of course, I'm an old brown shoe from the military, and he looked perfect to me. His shoes were shined, his uniform was perfect, his hair was cut. You could see that pride sticking out all over him. He was a real patriot."

By 1996, there were several versions of John's Panama story—John's versions, Dick's version, Debbie's version. But I'd heard only John's at the time I got hold of his records from the army's personnel record center, in St. Louis (they had been checked out without a signature, presumably by the FBI, in February of 1996 and returned a month before he was arrested), and tried to piece together what had really happened. John's Panama changed with the moment, the mood, and the audience, and in this the story wasn't so different from his stories about "watching Waco" on television. When he got those stories right, they held his world together, but they were not his life. He didn't have a life in any sense I recognized. He had two lives, the one he had lived and the one he invented, and his real biography seemed to me to be hidden somewhere in the commute he made between them. John's family told me about how terrible it had been for him when his two friends died, under fire and virtually unarmed. In fact, there were no American army casualties in Panama during the two years he was there, though there was a kernel of truth in his story, because American soldiers were sometimes deployed in bayonet lines against civilian demonstrators; they formed cordons along the Canal Zone borders to keep the demonstrators out. John may have based the story about his two dead friends on an incident in the Zone in January of 1964, when four American soldiers and twenty-five Panamanian rebels were killed in the course of four days of skirmishes along the border, except that those soldiers weren't part of a cordon or presenting weapons; they were on a mission, and they were under attack, and they were presumably armed. Or he may have based his story on the death of another young man—a Washingtonian, like him—sometime in 1967, except that that man wasn't even in the army; he was a radically disillusioned Vietnam vet who had joined a group of Panamanian dissidents and gotten himself arrested, and he died, horribly, in a local prison. (According to Koster, the last time anyone saw him alive he was in a cell, fitted with a noose that was strung just high enough to give him the choice of choking to death right away or standing, awake and on tiptoe, day and night, and choking later.) Nobody knows when, exactly, he did die, but once the news of his death came out the American consul resigned in protest, and *that* was in the papers for every American soldier in Panama to see. John was likely to have heard it, just as he was likely to have heard of the four American soldiers killed in 1964. And he certainly knew all about bayonet lines, since bayonet training was part of the drill in boot camp and, for that matter, in Panama. There was so much anti-American feeling in Panama by the late sixties that if the army hadn't used bayonet lines along the Zone borders—if soldiers had been ordered to open fire on demonstrators—the casualties would have been enormous. Even Dick Pitner acknowledged that the problem of dealing with angry demonstrators in somebody else's country was delicate. "This is the idea," he told me. "They didn't want the American soldiers to be making mistakes and shooting somebody and then they would have a huge political problem, an international incident."

Of course, none of this had much to do with John's story of helpless soldiers pitted against their own machine guns. Dick himself was incredulous. He told me, "I can't believe that our military would go into things like that. Here's a whole company of American infantry with no way to defend [itself] . . . and here's two fifty-caliber machine guns looking at them." But to some extent Dick did believe that. Everyone in the family believed it. John's sister Susan believed it until the day she went to the federal courthouse in Seattle, in the fall of 1996, for a pretrial summary of the discovery documents—Gary Kuehnoel's lawyer had put the summary together—and heard for the first time that John had been sent home from Panama as psychologically unfit for service. According to Susan, one document said that John had actually tried to kill himself in Panama; another said that he'd tried again in Washington, during the three months he was marking time at Fort Lewis, waiting to be discharged. By the time Susan told me about her shock at the courthouse that fall day, four months had passed and, as she said, she was still "reeling." But even then, she didn't know anything about John's being court-martialed, or about his putting in six months of hard labor in a Panama Canal Zone stockade. I'm not sure that even his wife knew that.

I remember the day in late June of 1996 when the fax arrived from Saint Louis with John's military records and how eagerly I read those records, as if I were finally going to locate some "real" John Pitner in the fiction called John the Militiaman, to trace the sources of his self-invention, to fix them in time and place, to check John out, as it were, against reality. Maybe it was a way of hoping: *This* is when it started. *This* is the moment the fear began or the resentment took hold. Maybe, too, it was a way of connecting the fatherless boy with the harsh, military father to the grown man who decided to have an army of his own. Dick Pitner remained convinced that the country was falling into the hands of communists or socialists or tyrants, and certainly John's Panama stories had confirmed that feeling. For Dick, it didn't matter if you were an army grunt in Panama or on a navy river patrol in China— you were still cannon fodder for the politicians. Rage at the government, rage at the ruling classes, was one of the leitmotifs in Dick's conversation, and maybe I thought that Panama had made it a rage the two of them shared. John told me he had asked nothing of the army besides that "general discharge" on his service record. No money for an education. No

Veterans Administration mortgage. None of the entitlements he said were due him, given the "deal" he had made. All he wanted was a clean record of how he had left the army, and if it ever occurred to him that the rest of his record would not inspire anyone's high regard, he may have assumed that no one whose regard he sought was ever very likely to see it. Of course, I know now that Panama was too easy an explanation. Panama was no more the beginning of John the Militiaman than that fall from his bicycle had been, or the fire in the chicken coop, or the day Dorothy told him about a man named Howard—or John.

In the end, what made Panama important to me was what it taught me about my own assumptions and, in fact, about the assumptions of most of the people I met in Washington that year, because people who weren't in militias, or hadn't covered militias, tended to assume that the men who *were* in them were the last victims of Vietnam, the brooding veterans who had come home from a war they couldn't win to a country that refused to credit, or even admit, their sacrifice. The assumption was someone like Mack, in Maine, exiled to a railroad car, unable to find his place in a world that had urged him to war and then dismissed him as part of its mistake. The assumption was Rambo, shamed, armed, aging, and abandoned, the hero nobody wanted to have around. But as often as not, the truth was a Brian McDugal or a John Pitner, the hero who in some way had shamed himself, the wanna-be warrior, the one who didn't go, and perhaps saw to it that he couldn't go—the one, even, who was frightened. The rule in John's family was that women got frightened and men did not, all evidence of breakdowns and suicides to the contrary. It didn't take much reflection or even much intelligence for

John to know enough to cover his disgrace in glory when he came home. Men have been known to lie about their courage, and in this John wasn't exceptional—only, in his own way, more desperately or relentlessly creative than most. He spun his Panama story like a fairy tale, and it could be he began to understand that spinning tales was his one real talent. It was a talent he shared with the Idaho butcher who introduced him to the conspiracy, and with John Trochmann, who sold him the conspiracy, and with the folks like Ben who kept it alive in Whatcom County. His stories were revisions of failure, emboldened by the certainties of self-regard, and, for a while, they collected his grievances into a kind of discipline, and even into a kind of eloquence. Once, not long before his trial was over, Susan mentioned how proud she'd been the first time she heard her brother on the radio. She couldn't get over how good he was, and she was right. He was good. "All that waste," she told me. "He could have run for office. He could have been a politician."

Five

J OHN HAD A LITTLE RIFF about his wife. He would
tell you that Debbie Pitner was the only woman he knew
who could "earn the money, shoot the bird, chop the
wood, and cook the dinner," and he could easily have added
"build the kitchen," since Debbie was largely responsible for
the labor that had gone into putting their house together. She
had run the wiring, laid the pipes, dug the septic system, *and*
cooked the dinners. At the time, of course, she'd thought of
the house as home and not as Command Central, though
when she finally left John in April of 1996 (after the last black
helicopter but before the lasers), he considered it not merely
a betrayal of the Patriot cause but another terrible message
from the enemy side. That was when he stopped telling his
Debbie story. He said to his men, "My wife . . . she might just
as well have been working for the New World Order." He told

them, "She cleaned me out." At a meeting in July, a couple of weeks before he was arrested, he described his predicament this way: "Being in the militia is a thankless task. You're going to bust your ass, you're going to do everything, and you're not going to get any thanks for it. . . . But I'll tell you one thing, the gratification comes from knowing that you know what's going on, and you're doing the best to combat that that you can. And I'll tell anybody to their fucking face right now that if they know what's going on in America today, and they don't do anything about it, they're a traitor."

Debbie was thirty-six when she left John. She had been living with him since she was thirteen. "John was my big romance," she told me, the second or third time we talked. She said it with a small, wry smile. She had no regrets. The smile was genuine. The story was still "romantic." She was this "dumb little Anacortes schoolgirl" just settling into her first week of the eighth grade. John was this "wonderful older man" of twenty, just back from adventures in the Panama jungle. And neither of them could really say they planned it— only that John had pulled up to the curb at her junior high school in a friend's car, and Debbie had slipped out of her homeroom, and by evening they were in Tacoma and no one knew where they were except, of course, the stepbrother of John's who lived in Tacoma and had had to put them up in his apartment. "Close quarters . . . but kind of glamorous, like Romeo and Juliet," is how Debbie described it. She was fourteen, living with John in Seattle (he said he was "working security" at a local motel) and still wondering what, and even whether, to tell her mother, when Rachel was born. She was twenty-four and living with John in the trailer park on Lake Samish, when a family therapist they'd started seeing remarked that, whatever John might have to say about welfare-check economics, perhaps it was time they "made a commitment" and got married. It hadn't been much of a life, as things turned out. She and John had made their way up the Interstate 5, from Tacoma to Whatcom County and even—when John had work there—to Alaska, but the farthest they had ever actually lived from the Interstate was a town called Winthrop, in eastern Washington; they'd stayed ten months and left before the first snows. That was the world Debbie knew, and John was the man who had introduced it to her. "I neglected her, lost track of her, didn't think of her needs, didn't put in enough quality time with Debbie," John told me, about a month after she had moved out of Command Central and settled into a nice Bellingham apartment with a view of the bay from the front windows. "But how come at least Ben's wife lasted [as a Patriot wife] twenty-five years? Mine couldn't last five."

In her way, Debbie was devoted to John. When he got in trouble, and everyone counted on her to rise to the occasion, or at least to the appearance of the occasion, she did it without a murmur. After his arrest, she moved back home. She took their house off the market, refinanced, and put it up as collateral toward his bail. She showed the court what a decent American family man John was, someone who may have talked tough but would never seriously have considered blowing up the railroad tunnel from Vancouver or taking out the sheriff. She stood by him while his trial lasted, and even testified for him as a loyal wife. Then she filed for divorce. Once, she told me to remember that for twenty-five years John had been her whole life. "My best friend," she said. "My brother." She was really saying that John was the only life she had had since she was thirteen, and that for a long time she had persuaded herself that John knew best, John knew everything. And what John knew was that his life on the run from reality was normal, and even that their isolation was normal. By the time John discovered the New World Order, it hadn't been hard for Debbie to persuade herself that his black moods and his crazy theories and his incapacity were normal, too. But there was clearly a part of her that "knew" better, because she'd learned, early on, to look after herself. She studied at home, wherever that happened to be. At fifteen, in a home program for teenage mothers, she graduated from high school. At twenty-four, the year she and John got married, she enrolled in Whatcom Community College and started studying nights toward the first of what would soon be two junior-college business degrees. By the time I met her, she was the inventory-control manager at Geographics Printing, with four or five people working under her. She was driving a big used Thunderbird and lifting weights at a Bellingham gym, and it wasn't long into John's trial that she started leaving town on weekends. ("Business trips," she told me when I called from Seattle, thinking to drive up to say hello.)

For years, Debbie kept the family accounts and conducted all its business in her maiden name. Even the telephone—the few years it was listed at all—was listed under the name Deborah Reece, as proof, perhaps, that John was not legally in residence and that therefore Debbie was eligible for welfare, should she need welfare. It was an arrangement that kept John a step ahead of the IRS or the state government (eleven state labor department tax warrants were filed against Deborah Reece in the three years before John's arrest) or, for that matter, of anyone in the county looking to get a bill paid. The

first time I checked on John in the records room of the Whatcom County Courthouse, I found seven months of documents
involving a single claim, from 1985, against Deborah Reece
and "John Doe Reece." The claimant was a medical group
called Bellingham Family Practice and the original bill was
"$37.87 for an office visit." After seven months of court costs,
the bill had doubled; the last document of the claim file was a
court order to Debbie's employer to put a quarter of what was
then a very small salary in escrow. There were also, of course,
a couple of claims against John—one from a local vet but
not, as it happened, Doc Ellwanger, who would probably have
waived it—and Debbie, as the partner with the visible and
steady job, was cited in those claims as co-respondent. John
himself wasn't interested in steady jobs. When Debbie began
to get out into the world and in her own way prosper, he
pretty much stopped looking for work at all. He told the family that he'd gone into the landscaping business with his friend
Jeffrey—the Jeffrey of his Idaho awakening—and he did occasionally sign on for some local yard work or house painting.
But Debbie said that by then he was "more like the house parent," the one who stays home and looks after the kids and
does the cleaning, and there wasn't much work in that once
Rachel finished school and moved out and started living in
Bellingham with her boyfriend. What friends they did have—
a few couples they used to go camping or boating with, or
invite to the house for potluck suppers—disappeared when
John founded the militia, and were replaced by Patriot families whose only redeeming quality, if you asked Debbie now,
was that, for a while at least, they believed in John.

It wasn't long before John depended on his wife entirely.
He sold their boat; he told Debbie the money went to the mili-

tia. He sold some wilderness land they had managed to buy, a couple of hundred miles up into the North Cascades, near a beautiful mountain pass. He left so many debts on Debbie's Visa card that she worried about it being cancelled. There was nothing in the least "romantic" between them now besides the years they had spent together, and a few good memories from those years. Debbie told me they were more like friends than lovers by the time John was arrested and went to jail. There had been "some problems, affairs," she said, before they married, and when she finally left him, he complained to some of the men in Alpha One about a boyfriend. In fact, a couple of weeks before she moved out, he had packed up her clothes, driven to Blaine, and dumped the suitcase in the middle of Geographics Printing's parking lot, convinced she was seeing the owner's son. But if John was jealous of the men he imagined in Debbie's life, he seemed notably uninterested in taking a lover for himself, though there must have been women in Whatcom County who found John the Militiaman as glamorous as Debbie, at thirteen, had found John the Veteran. There were certainly women on the fringe of the militia who would have made time for the man who was going to save America. Judy Ellwanger had sounded almost dewy, talking to me about "Mr. Leadershit." (The militiamen, on the other hand, thought she had her eye on Gary, or even on Marlin, who called her a tiresome old bag.) The truth was that John couldn't bear it when Debbie left. He thought she belonged to him, that her life and her discipline and her credit line belonged to him. "John is a lot like his Dad in a lot of ways," Debbie announced one night when we having dinner. "I can remember the one and only time I told him that. I said, 'You sound just like your dad.' It didn't go over real well."

Debbie was not what I would have expected in a militia wife. She wasn't trashy or edgy or furtive or crude. She wasn't battered. She wasn't born-again into the Christian Patriot cause, or much concerned with fighting Satan for the souls of Whatcom County's schoolchildren. She was soft-spoken, decorous, and to all appearances deferential, a woman who would open the door just long enough to shake your hand and hand you a cup of coffee and a plate of cookies before she made her excuses and disappeared. At thirty-six, with a plastic barrette in her neat blond hair and a touch of lipstick for makeup, she could have passed for an outsized teenage girl. When John was around, she shuffled her feet, scrunched her shoulders—she had good, broad shoulders—and hung her head, almost as if she were trying to fold her extraordinary height into some appropriately wifely and admiring shape. Once, she told me how difficult it was, from over six feet, to give John "the looking up to" he required, and in fact she loomed over John. It didn't take long for anyone who knew them both to see that she was at least as strong as he was, and far more competent. This was something of a problem for Dick Pitner, who referred to women generically, as "the weaker sex," and whose tirades against feminists were said to be at least as violent as his tirades against communists. But even Dick took a grudging pride in Debbie's size and her strength and her capacity for serious labor. When I met Dick and he started in on what the family had warned me was his favorite subject—the way the military, if not the whole country, had gone to hell by letting "the weaker sex into the foxholes"—he immediately excepted Debbie. He told me that Debbie had "soldierly qualities." "Oh, she's a big gal," Dick said. "If all the women in the United States were Debbie's size, I'd have to

shut up." It was as close as he came to what I would call a reflection on his son's marriage or, for that matter, on his son's
own soldierly qualities. (I'd heard that he often referred to
John and Debbie as "Mutt and Jeff," though never, of course,
in John's hearing.) But he must have wondered, sometimes,
what life would have been like for the Pitner clan if Debbie
had gone to Panama, instead.

Debbie looked after her husband with a guileless, almost
exasperating calm. It drove John crazy—he volunteered this—
but she didn't mind. She may have called him her best friend,
but she also said, "I kind of outgrew John. I wasn't the little
girl he married." Being of a literal turn of mind, she measured
her own maturity by the inches she had added since the eighth
grade, when she and John were, as she liked to put it, "eye-to-
eye" at five foot seven. She told me that John hadn't really
wanted the Debbie with the good job and the credit line. He
wanted the eighth-grader from the boondocks who thought
he was the smartest man ever to have set foot in the state of
Washington. She sometimes talked about how impressive he
had seemed then, eye-to-eye and just out of the army and
marking time in Anacortes, sorting through all the serious
things that were on his mind. John, in Anacortes, was bunking with another one of his stepbrothers—a man with a wife
and a job on *his* mind—but he was hanging out with a crowd
of high school boys and dropouts that at the time included
"little Debbie Reece's" oldest brother. There were a lot of parties, and Debbie showed up at them all. No one was at home
to watch her. Her father was long gone, her mother was bartending nights, and by her own account Debbie was running
wild—drinking and smoking dope and shooting up whatever
was being passed around. The party where she met John, in

the summer of 1971, was what she called "a drinking party." She told him she was seventeen, then sixteen. It took a few parties, and more than a few drinks, for her to admit to thirteen, but she always maintained that it hadn't mattered. What mattered to John was that thirteen-year-old Debbie Reece admired *him*. She gave him "trust, comfort, and adulation." She believed everything he said. "John *liked* how naïve I was. I wasn't conniving. I wasn't out for myself. . . . Here's a person wasn't going to hurt him. Just this naïve little soul."

Sometimes, when Debbie was talking to me about her life, she would fold her hands and lower her eyes, like a child wrapping herself in a pretty thought, and begin to reminisce about a place called Blakeley Island. Blakeley was not much more than a dot on a map of the San Juan Islands, a dot that you sailed past, summers, on your way up Puget Sound, but Debbie had spent nine of her first eleven years on Blakeley, nine years when the island was so remote, and literally so empty, that Herb and Pat Reece and their children counted as a fifth of the population. There were not much more than thirty people on Blakeley then, and the only regular boat from the mainland was the one that Santa Claus used at Christmas, for the presents. Herb Reece had moved the family to the island from Bellingham when Debbie was two, thinking to make a killing building houses for summer people, and in the nine years it took to disabuse him of the idea, Debbie had what she always referred to as "my childhood." She prowled the beaches with her mother, gathering shells. She played in the woods with her brothers and sisters. She went exploring with her dog. When the weather held, which it mainly didn't, she boarded a small boat and headed for an old frame schoolhouse on Orcas Island, twenty minutes away. The biggest town she had ever seen was Bellingham, where her grandparents still lived.

As Debbie told the story, her father was a drunk and a dreamer whose own father dealt in moonshine out of a Bellingham still. "Real backwoods people," she called the Reece family. "Other-side-of-the-tracks people. A little controversial." Pat Reece, on the other hand, had started out "respectable." She was a local machinist's daughter, and she had studied music at one of the state colleges, hoping to teach piano. She never expected to start her married life with the Bureau of Alcohol, Tobacco, and Firearms banging at her door, with an arrest warrant for her father-in-law, or for that matter to end it working nights in an Anacortes bar, with five children to support and her husband off with a woman Debbie referred to—at least, to me—only as the "tramp." But that was what in fact happened. Debbie, eleven years old in the big city of Anacortes—"thirty thousand people, almost as big as Bellingham," as she described it—missed her mother, who was never home. She missed her brothers and sisters, who had never been more than a couple of classrooms away in their Orcas schoolhouse. She had landed in Anacortes at the end of a 1960s I had never really imagined before: the sixties of working-class children, kicking aside the rules in small, poor, punishing towns; the sixties that ate their future instead of opening their world. Debbie said that John had saved her, and it may be that in a way he had. He asked her to stop taking drugs. He *insisted* she stop, she told me. "He wasn't an Anacortes country bumpkin," she said once. "He talked about astronomy, oceans, science. And he dressed nice. He wore slacks and shirts. Pressed! He was clean-shaven, and he had manners. I thought he was real cool."

IN THE END, it may have been easier for Debbie to leave John than to keep agreeing with him, though this wasn't a reason John considered. John blamed his father. "I listened to my dad," he told me, about a month after she had moved. "He says a woman's got to be told what to do—got to stay. So I guess I kind of threatened her. I said, 'Either get right home or I'll divorce you.' So she left." But Debbie didn't have the imagination for a life of enemies. She was, if anything, doggedly practical about the life she already had. She had worked with it and she had worked around it, and when it began to threaten her other life, the life she had carved for herself apart from John and his problems, she let it go. She wasn't philosophical, but what she did have was a sense of humor. She could even laugh at the New World Order. She'd say, "Well, John has his opinions and now I have different opinions." People who knew her wondered how she had managed to survive as long as she did in John's fantastical world. They talked about her placidity, if not precisely about her detachment. The local housewives—women like Sharon Pietila, across the highway—remarked that she never went to church, she never went to school board meetings, she never signed up for a tough-love group, or a property-rights group, she never called with a box of cookies, she never pretended to be at all interested in them. Sharon, who did all those things, thought that Debbie was "kind of snobbish." She considered herself a much more typical Whatcom County housewife. She was involved in a plan for her neighbors to secede from Whatcom County and establish their own county, Independence County, which would presumably leave them free to log their forests unrestricted (her husband, Dan, was a logger) and develop their wilderness land with condos and invest in shopping centers for the people who bought those condos and, especially, drive Satan from their schools. Sharon was hard put to name a subject at Mount Baker High School that didn't suffer from Satanic influence. She was the scourge of the Mount Baker school board: she wanted Darwin thrown out of the science lab (as he had apparently been at the Sehome, Nooksack, and Lynden high schools) and Rachel Carson kept out of the "connections" class and "relativism" out of the history class and "multiculturalism" out of the English class; she even wanted to abolish sports, which she considered subversive, on a level with sex education if not actually a plot on the part of faculty pedophiliacs, and which she never called "sports" anyway, but always "the touchy-feelies." Sharon, like Debbie, spoke with the authority of a sixties dropout, but in Sharon's case it was the authority of a dropout who wasn't accountable for the life she'd led before she met Jesus, in Whatcom County, and discovered that sports were touchy-feelies, and that the Holy Spirit was a bigger and much better high than marijuana, and that the disreputable son she'd had, years earlier, with a black boyfriend was living proof of "the sin of miscegenation." Sharon believed in tough love. She went to a tough-love group at church, and while she never joined the Washington State Militia, she thought that what John Pitner had been practicing, with his militia, might have been tough love, too—a kind of tough-love patriotism that wasn't so different from the tough-love parenting she practiced on her son when she baby-sat for his baby but at the same time refused to put up his bail or let him anywhere near her house. Debbie, on the other hand, wasn't interesting in parenting anyone but

Rachel. She was gracious and certainly friendly to the men who arrived at her house for Alpha One meetings, but then she'd go to a movie or even to bed. (She claimed, in court, to have slept through the sparkler-bomb demonstration that Ted Carter had been so worried would disturb her.) The only militia wife she liked or approved of, in the end, was Maryann Fisher. Whatever socializing she'd done with the other wives was pretty much confined to an occasional potluck supper at somebody else's house—she'd make a lasagna or dessert, or simply pick up some drinks and chips at one of the Bellingham malls—and, in the event, there weren't many of those suppers. By the time I knew her, she could laugh describing them.

It was hard to resist Debbie and her stories. I'd write them down and read them over, and they sounded true, which made them a huge relief from the stories John told. On the other hand, while John was hard work for anyone trying to pin down or piece together the facts of a life that had actually happened, his sentiments were, if the word applies, transparent. Debbie's sentiments were opaque. There was a kind of affectlessness in Debbie and in the stories she told, at least as she told them to me. She described shooting up in Anacortes, at the age of twelve, in the same pleasant, direct, humorous, accommodating tone she used to describe shopping for a pretty dress for one of her sisters' weddings or, for that matter, the inconvenience of driving to Seattle for her fifteen minutes behind the glass partition in the visitor's booth at the Kent jail. It was as if, for Debbie, there was nothing alarming or even unusual—only, perhaps, a little awkward—about her role as the wife of a man accused of mounting a conspiracy against the government of the United States. "John has his opinions and now I have different opinions" wasn't really much of an explanation, when you came down to it. Not when you were discussing a man who believed that the Federal Reserve belonged to a cabal of Jewish bankers or that the government was planting microchips in Valley Highway in order to track his movements. There seemed to be no real anger, no confusion or despair, not even any denial, in Debbie Pitner's conversations. She thought that John was foolish and impressionable; she said he'd been "spoon-fed by John Trochmann, spoon-fed some pieces of paper that somehow validated it all," but she sounded more irritated than appalled, saying it. The few arguments they'd had about the New World Order seem to have been no more disquieting to her than the arguments they'd had about putting up wallpaper in the kitchen—John was right, the wallpaper buckled the first time she boiled water—and perhaps they weren't. She told me her life was "on hold" for as long as John's trial lasted. Her loyalty was a given. But it occurred to me, after one or two days with Debbie, that in some ways John and his war of the worlds were a matter of as much indifference to her as the preteen party girl she described as "little Debbie Reece." In a way, Debbie had been born again, even if it wasn't a way her neighbor Sharon would have recognized. She went through the motions of her new life, which was not unsuccessful by Whatcom standards, not for a woman who had gone from waitressing to six years on the graveyard shift of an outboard motorboat factory to a job with a desk and, as she said, "staff"—but it was as hard to locate the person living that life as it was to locate John. She parceled her memories. There was Blakeley Island, the tranquillity there. There was another island off Alaska, a deserted island where she and John and Rachel had gone once on a picnic. There was the shock of looking up to discover their boat had drifted, the adventure of waiting, alone with a small, shivering child, and worrying about bears when John waded out of sight to find it. There was a campsite near the land they had once bought in Okanogan County, with John bursting into his sister Susan's tent in the middle of the night, pretending to *be* a bear. There was the fun they'd had afterward, sitting around the fire and laughing till morning. Those were the memories that Debbie salvaged, the ones that seemed to hold her feelings.

Debbie told me that the smartest man she had ever met was an old professor at Western Washington University, who taught a course called "manufacturing science." The professor had brought some students to the outboard factory where she was working then, and later he'd invited her to Western to speak to a few of his classes. "An old fellow . . . really kind of a mad scientist type of guy," she said. "Brilliant man. Supernerd. He's got tape on his glasses, you know, and pens in his pockets, but he's brilliant." She still ran into the professor sometimes, when he was taking his evening walk through the Bellingham mall they both used, and he was always courtly and polite, even after John was arrested and his picture was in the papers and everyone at Western saw that headline on the front page of the *New York Times,* the one with the word "terrorist." Debbie didn't seem to connect the word "terrorist" with anything that had happened on Valley Highway. Not with the explosions she said she'd slept through, not with the Patriot videos spilling out of her living room bookcase, not even with the weapons the FBI was claiming had disappeared from her garage. When John went to jail, she had cleared out the garage. "I can park my car in the garage again! You don't have to kick your way through it. I mean, I threw away twenty years of junk." Then she cleared out the extra bedroom—the room with the computer and the militia files and the blurry photographs of UN concentration camps that John had always referred to as "the intel center at Command Central"— saying, "John liked dark, dark furniture, dark pictures." She changed those pictures. "I brightened up the place," she told me. She threw out the orange-and-black shag hanging rug. She thought that shag rugs were "too seventies" and that they always looked dirty anyway. She bought a big new white rug for the living room floor. She hung valances, lacy white valances, over the windows. She refinished the dinner table. "I still respect John's opinion," she told me, a month after the redecoration. "But he thinks that I'm off base and I don't understand and I'm just immature and I don't see the big picture. And he's pretty much come out and said that in so many words." She sounded surprised, even a little aggrieved, but she allowed that this was the way men were. She remembered how once, just before Christmas in 1995, they were driving home from a holiday party at the house of the new militiaman Ed Mauerer and she mentioned being surprised by the Mauerer child's toys. "They had this child, a toddler—he was probably two or three years old—and this child had every imaginable play gun on the market," she told me. "And he was showing us all of them. Boxes of them. And he'd run around the house: 'Bang, bang, bang!' And that really took me back. I thought, God, what a violent child . . . It was weird, weird. And I remember saying something to John—that this was weird. And he just laughed it off, you know, like, 'Yeah, that is kind of strange.' But, you know, that wasn't important to him. I'm thinking back now: Why do you have to have so many play guns? Why is every toy a play gun?" She could have asked the same question of John, but according to her, she didn't.

Six

NOT LONG into my first trip to Whatcom County, I began to look for people who might not want a militia in their neighborhood and, more to the point, people who might be trying to do something about it. Bellingham itself was full of activists. Whenever there was an ugly incident—the beating of a black boy out walking with a white girl near the Western campus, the burning of a cross at the local immigrant farmworkers' hostel—people got out their "Not in Our Town" T-shirts, lit candles, and kept a vigil. In the main, those people were liberal in their politics and tolerant in their views, the kind of people who had come to Bellingham to study or teach, or to live near the kind of people who study and teach, or simply for the funky Victorian houses terracing the hills over Bellingham Bay, for the pleasure of having the Pacific at their front door and the North Cascades at their back door, for the clean air and the mild climate and the Chinook salmon and the oysters, out of the Lummi Indian beds, which were so enormous you could roast them in a barbecue, slice them, and eat them with a knife and fork, like a piece of prime filet. They came for the climbing and hiking and sailing and kayaking and mountain biking, all of it so close to the center of town that the take-out latte they stopped to buy on Sunday mornings at the Colophon Café—right beside Village Books, in the old seaport neighborhood called Fairhaven—would still be hot when they locked the car and started walking up a mountain or racing across the bay. Those people gave Bellingham a mood and a culture that despite the manifestly western wilderness around them was as much New England as Pacific Rim, though, to an easterner, they were perhaps a little ingenuous about their city and about what made it so appealing. The fact was that beyond the campus of their university, Bellingham was a lily-white town, a town where a black boy walking with a white girl got noticed. And most of its liberal citizens had little more experience living with minorities or immigrants or any of the other people whose rights they championed in their Whatcom Human Rights Task Force or their discussion groups at Beth Israel Synagogue and Christ the Servant, the Lutheran sanctuary church, than John Pitner did, holed up in the county in a house that was nearly impossible to find. Tolerance, in Bellingham, was rarely strained, and it seemed to me, arriving that first time from New York, that Bellinghamers pursued good causes the way my neighbors at home pursued opera tickets or restaurant reservations. That, in fact, it might be the absence of those selfish, satisfying, big-city distractions that left Bellinghamers with time to kill, evenings, and persuaded them to take up good citizenship as an entertainment.

But on the subject of John's militia, Bellingham was oddly quiet. No one called a "not in our town" demonstration after the first public militia meeting at the Rome Grange. No one marched in protest to Command Central. Not even the police seemed alarmed. The sheriff told me, "If push comes to shove, and we do have an incident in this county, I don't want them to say, 'He never listened to us.' . . . My feeling is, it would add validity to the things these people preach." It wasn't that Sheriff Brandland liked having militiamen in his county (although two of the fifty-six sheriff's deputies then on call were rumored to be either militia members or sympathizers). Brandland didn't even like guns. He told me that ten years on the Bellingham police department's SWAT team had cured him of any interest in weapons, regardless of what to me was his fairly baffling conviction that the right to carry a concealed weapon was "the foundation of the Constitution, and I feel it's a fundamental right and I guess I believe it." But the sheriff wasn't worried about the Washington State Militia. Not even Police Chief Pierce—a fairly sophisticated cop and member in good standing of the International Association of Chiefs of Police antiterrorism task force—seemed worried. Don Pierce liked saying that his job wasn't about groups, it was about crimes; it wasn't about attitude, it was about *behavior.* That was the law, he said, and that was also what his constituents must have wanted, because when it came to the militia most of them turned the other cheek and waited, as if by ignoring the militia they could make the militia go away, like a ketchup stain or a bad dream, or even convince themselves that the militia hadn't happened. Of course, the militia hadn't happened to *them*—not the way a beating had "happened" to a black student. Strictly speaking, the militia wasn't doing anything to Bellingham or its county, not unless you weighed the uneasiness people felt, or the potential for intimidation of an unseen "army" whose numbers they didn't know and whose weapons they couldn't count claiming to represent them, whether or not they wanted to be represented. As far as the militia went, most people practiced what the minister at Christ the Servant called "civility [as] a certain kind of confrontation." Perhaps they were in denial. Perhaps they took a long view, assuming that John's moment would eventually pass, the way troubling moments always passed in Whatcom County.

Bellinghamers took a slightly embarrassed pride in how resilient their county was—how, in the end, its decency always surfaced. They told stories about their wilder, woollier days as an army fort and a fish cannery port and a timber mill depot. Bellingham was never Dodge City, but it was lawless enough once—Western Washington University had a library annex full of archives to prove it—and the town had kept enough untamed county in its bourgeois heart to accommodate, if not encourage, a fanatical vigilante strain. It had survived the scab armies of the old canneries and logging companies, not to mention its own home-grown enthusiasts of the Klan and the John Birch Society and the Populist Party, and, as late as the 1980s, of Patriot outlaw bands like Posse Comitatus and The Order. And given a past like that, it wasn't unreasonable for Bellinghamers to assume that it would survive the militia, too. But to a stranger prowling the militia fringe, it sometimes seemed that the hardiest survivor was the fringe itself, that the biggest change from the days of those earlier groups was in the names that described them. Bellingham had never really shaken out its fanatics. For somebody, say, Marlin's age, the conspiracy was a discovery. But if you were Ben Hinkle's age and joined the militia, the chances were you had cut your Patriot teeth on John Birch and Joe McCarthy and had run for some local office on the Populist ticket and had ordered your bedside reading from the Posse and the Klan and maybe even sheltered one or two of the fugitives, en route to a hide-out in Chelan County or Hayden Lake. What the militia did mainly was to stir a new generation into John Pitner's conspiracy stockpot—adding fresh ingredients as the flavor of the old ones faded, proving the French maxim that, with a little attention, a good stock will simmer forever on the stove.

Bellingham's reticence about confronting its militia may have been a matter of etiquette—part cowboy code, part Emily Post—because the rule was that you didn't poke around in your neighbor's kitchen and you certainly didn't lift the lid of the pot on his back burner to test the strength or quantity of the stock base, or to sniff the smell. And John's part of the county was definitely back burner, a Potemkin Village of the wilderness. There were stretches off Mount Baker Highway, the road that ran east from Bellingham to the foothills of the North Cascades, that looked to be endless forest, until you started walking and a couple of hundred feet later discovered that the forest was scalped. The scrub bore witness to a hundred years of wanton logging, and perhaps to too many regrets for Bellingham's liberals not to feel a twinge of sympathy, or even of conscience, for the loggers who felt so betrayed by the rules that stopped them from cutting now, the ones who had arrived too late to do much except wonder where all the fabled prosperity had gone. Back in its glory days, the south county was at the center of a rush for timber and gold that had turned its tiny settlements into boom towns. The village of Deming, where Rachel had gone to high school and Debbie still stopped occasionally after work, had a population of ten thousand people at the turn of the twentieth century. By the turn of this century, there were fewer than a thousand, and pretty much all that was left of old Deming was a tavern featuring tough steaks and faded logging tintypes, and an annual loggers' show with barrel-jumping and chainsawing and booths where the gyppo wives, Sharon among them, passed out warnings about tree-spiking ecoterrorists from Earth First! It was difficult for the doctors and lawyers tucked into the good life in Bellingham's bayside Victorian houses—houses with pastel gingerbread trim and witty little rounded towers—to think of those people as very threatening as long as they weren't doing something threatening. Those people were in another world.

THE HISTORY OF TOWNS like Deming and the people in them in some ways mirrored the history of Henry Roeder, the man who could be said to have founded Whatcom County —a Great Lakes steamboat captain and adventurer who had gone from boom to bust to boom to bust in the course of his own particular Westward Ho. Henry Roeder was a man who had wanted one thing very badly in his life and that was to get rich quick, even (as he supposedly said once) if getting rich quick took years. He had tried, and failed at, gold mining in northern California, shopkeeping in Sacramento, and fish packing on the Columbia River, but his luck changed, with one of the first big San Francisco fires. It was a fire that devastated the city, destroying its wooden houses—which at the time meant pretty much all its houses—and persuading Roeder that there was a fortune to be made in timber for houses to replace them, with the lion's share of that fortune going to the first man with enough water power for a mill to cut the planks. Roeder headed north, looking for a waterfall. The closest falls were taken, but the captain went on, undaunted and avid. There were rumors circulating of a very big waterfall hundreds of miles north of San Francisco, in Olympia, Washington, and he aimed for that, certain that no one else would even attempt to reach it. By the time he got to Olympia —only to discover that, sadly, someone already had—he was so obsessed with his mission that he kept on moving north. Fifty miles short of the Canadian border, he stopped for the night at a Port Townsend tavern, where he shared a bottle with a local Indian who claimed to be an expert at finding waterfalls. His price was a dollar a day, and Roeder hired him. The story goes that at sunrise the next morning the two men climbed into the Indian's canoe and paddled across Bellingham Bay and into a cove with two small settlements and, at the mouth of the small river known now as Whatcom Creek, a fine waterfall that no one in either settlement had thought to claim. The day they landed was December 15, 1852, and it's famous in Whatcom County as the day Henry Roeder stood up in his guide's canoe and shouted something on the order of "Wow! Stop! Here's my mill!" Roeder looked east from the creek and saw nothing but trees and more trees, fifty miles of virgin forest stretching from the bay to the mountains. It was a lumberman's paradise.

I first heard the saga of Henry Roeder from a Washington writer named Mike Vouri, a decorated Vietnam veteran turned playwright, monologist, journalist, novelist, and peace activist, who had worked at the Whatcom County Historical Museum and the *Bellingham Herald,* and when I met him was commuting to Bellingham weekends from a new job as the park ranger and historian of San Juan Island National Historical Park. Mike was said to know more Whatcom County history than anyone else in the county, including the professors who taught Whatcom County history at Western Washington University. A generation of Bellingham children had been raised on his "history of the county" performances, one-man shows in which he took the parts of his favorite county characters, the most notable being General George Edward Pickett, famous in the Northwest not for being the commander who had led the Confederate charge at Gettysburg but for being the man who ten years earlier had secured the Washington Territory for America and made it safe for pioneering entrepreneurs like Henry Roeder. It was Mike's theory that the peculiarly "American" passion of those pioneers, and the legacy of that passion, had a great deal to do with the distress in Whatcom County at the turn of the twenty-first century. He said that, for a stranger like me, the important thing was to understand that their passion wasn't the same mercantile passion of the British pioneer-traders, a few miles north of Whatcom in British Columbia—that while the Americans had wanted to strike it rich at least as much as the British, they had also wanted to *stay* where they struck it rich. They had a passion for settlement. Mike called it "a passion for real estate, for getting in on the ground floor with your six hundred and forty acres free and clear." And it was certainly American, when you considered that in the space of less than two years in the middle of the nineteenth century, the white population of the entire Pacific Northwest went, as Mike put it, "from three hundred Englishmen to eight thousand Americans."

His point, I think, was that a passion having originally and essentially to do with a settler's right to his own square mile of America, free and clear, could easily, in a complicated new economy of skills and specialties and services and regulations, turn into a cult of guns and property among people who had been left behind by the change. The rhetoric of entitlement was really the propaganda of expansion. It was scrip only for as long as it took the continent to be cleared, though this was clearly one detail no one had bothered to share with John Pitner or his neighbors. In a way, John and his neighbors still thought of themselves as settlers, and, as Mike liked to remind his audiences, in Washington's history a settler's home wasn't just his castle but everything he saw from his castle, and thought to claim. It all depended on what you meant by castle, and to John, for one, it meant a great deal. When John talked about wildcatting in the solar system, it was almost as if he was staking a claim to a slice of the universe as his homestead acreage. He thought that that slice of the universe was his, by right, as an American, the way the weapons he supposedly started caching "after Waco" were his by right. He didn't believe the government had any business regulating his claim to his share of what he called the "ground floor" of outer space, and in this he wasn't so different from Bill Gates, ninety-five miles south in Redmond, who didn't believe the government had any business regulating *his* claim to cyberspace. You could find this same odd synergy of American pathology and American mythology, this entitlement to whatever "space" you chose to inhabit—from the space in your head to the space of the range to the space of the market—all over the state of Washington, maybe because so much of the real space *was* empty. Poor people in Whatcom County, people living what they sometimes referred to as "the potato chip life," were no more mystified by the land-use laws than the Microsoft billionaires, down in Redmond, were mystified by the antitrust laws. They were all like Henry Roeder, looking across the bay from a canoe and saying, "Here's my mill!"

It was hard to elicit a sense of what you would call community in a place where everyone was Henry Roeder. Most people didn't move to Whatcom County to find community, not even to find a community of fanatics. The rich vein of fanaticism that ran so close to the surface of that stubborn discretion which in the county passed for manners could lie untapped for years before anyone thought to mine it. Whatcom may have had an unusually dense concentration of crazies, but John's militia by no means held the monopoly—not when you considered how odd most people in the county were. There were the Dutch dairy farmers who lived in a small, anomalous patch of the northwest county, a place of tulip gardens and gentle pastures and sheltering oaks and rosy, billowing clouds that seemed to have been painted onto the landscape to make them feel at home. Those farmers practiced a Calvinism so pious and bizarre that it was forbidden by local statute to drink and dance in the same room or, for that matter, to have sex standing, in any room, the theory being that sex might *lead* to dancing, which was worse. (In the event, both were discouraged.) There were the Evangelicals who got themselves born again every Sunday and were otherwise so amenable to ecstatic trance that the Holy Spirit felt free to interrupt them in the middle of a quilting bee—quilting was considered a Christian virtue in Whatcom County—or a check-out line at the supermarket. There were the Bellingham lawyers tapping on their laptops at the nude beach on warm weekends, and the ex-Marines hiding from the Cong in trip-wired tents and cabins, and the old hippies painting Haight-Ashbury murals on the walls of the same houses they had squatted thirty years earlier, and the New Age families, anxious and organic, who wore their crystals to the Whatcom Symphony in order to trap the vibrato of the strings. And, of course, there were the people John Pitner called "just good American folks," the people against the New World Order, living in trailers next to old family homes they couldn't afford to maintain, on land they couldn't afford to farm—surviving, mainly, because Whatcom's county council operated on the principle that you could do your neighbor an occasional good turn if you did it in a cause that made the liberals mad. Left to themselves, a lot of those American folks would probably have stayed piecemeal activists, nursing their grudges in the abstract company of radio agitators and Internet racists sounding the alarm for God, family, and the white fetus. You'd know them by the stickers on their pickups—"America, Love It or Leave It"— and by the rifles *in* the pickups, by the T-shirts and kitchen posters that said "White Man: Endangered Species," and by the silence and click on the other end of the line when you answered the phone after a difficult meeting of the PTA. But Whatcom County had been discovered, and by the mid-nineties it was hard to find anyone with a flag on his porch, even his trailer porch, who hadn't been courted by the money interests of the radical right and by the property-rights lobbyists and the gun lobbyists and the lobbyists of Christian values, all of them hoping to raise a constituency among the county's most disgruntled citizens. Whatcom was susceptible.

It didn't take much to convince those citizens that a vote for, say, a high school gym levy was a vote for what Jack Schleimer called "Darwinism-Leninism" in the classroom, or for that matter for immigrants, AIDS, dope dealers, welfare mothers, and the Brady Bill. It didn't even take much to convince them that a vote to keep the local loggers away from a tree with a nesting owl meant the same thing. They were not a community until the propagandists of the radical right and the salesmen of the armed right and the crusaders of the Christian right turned some of them into a constituency that thought a militia was a perfectly reasonable "American" addition to the neighborhood.

In the fall of 1993, a year before the radical right took over the American Congress and Washington's own congressional delegation went from a liberal majority of eight-to-one to a radically conservative majority of seven-to-two, there were local elections for the Whatcom County Council. People remarked that the good old boys they had always counted on as fixers were beginning to look different. They looked, suddenly, like politicians with a plan. They began to talk about Bellingham as if it were a suburb of the other Washington. A couple of them even talked about seceding from Bellingham. That was when John's neighbor Sharon began collecting signatures for the referendum she was hoping would turn some thirty thousand east county people into the new citizens of Independence County, with their own sheriff and a government of three commissioners—"directly responsible to the people," as Sharon said—who would share a proper "rural perspective" when it came to zoning. ("Rural perspective" was a code for development easements and a way of circumventing the state's growth management laws.) At the same time, some like-minded northwest county people also began collecting secession signatures, with a mind to slicing off another chunk of Whatcom County and calling it Pioneer County. These county secessionists went door-to-door, talking about the Bellingham bureaucracy as if Bellingham were twenty-five hundred miles away and (the sheriff's words) as "terrifying in its inaccessibility" as the federal government. They looked at the county the way John looked at the solar system. They wanted to "take back the land," they said, from the New World Order and its local "enforcers." They didn't know why Bellinghamers got to build shopping malls and they did not, although they were hard put to explain where they were going to find the customers for their malls. An itinerant developer and pentecostal preacher who had appeared in John's part of the county a few years earlier had already rented part of a bleak little strip mall on Mount Baker Highway, not far from the Valley Highway turnoff, and that mall was notable mainly for its vacancies. It was a problem the preacher had tried to obscure by installing two of his children in one of the empty storefronts, where they stood behind a counter selling weak instant coffee to the occasional customer who dropped in from the "headquarters" of Independence County, in the storefront next door.

The storefront was usually closed, but the window was full of flyers promoting the causes and obsessions of the people who made up the Independence County "leadership"—causes that pretty much described the world in which John's militia flourished. Sharon herself was promoting a group called BEST (Basic Education Support Team), which intended to steer Independence County's schools into what she called "a return to the basics" of reading, writing, and the Creation.

Shirley Hardy, the wife of a dairy farmer north of Deming, served potluck suppers on behalf of a property rights group called CLUE (Coalition for Land Use Education), which was itself the project of an energetic though, at the time, largely unsuccessful Bellingham wetlands developer named Skip Richards, who had an interest in encouraging county people (it didn't matter if they said Whatcom or Independence or Pioneer) to defy the growth-management statutes that he claimed had been ruining *him*. Richards, in turn, had been encouraged by the visits of a Battle Ground grass-roots property rights agitator named Chuck Cushman, whose own small group in southern Washington had done so well in the course of the last few years that he was now the director of a national group called American Land Rights, and able to pay the salary of a full-time lobbyist in the capital. Cushman was himself connected to a Wise Use propagandist and organizer by the name of Ron Arnold, who in an earlier life and enthusiasm had helped to found the Sierra Club and now shared offices in Liberty Park—a conservative office complex in the Seattle suburbs that had once housed the American headquarters of the Reverend Sun Myung Moon's Unification Church—with a convicted tax felon from Queens named Alan Gottlieb, an ardent convert to the Second Amendment and the Catholic church, and Gottlieb's wife, Julie, who published gun magazines. In the mid-nineties, Liberty Park was the place where you could begin to trace a path from the crazies of Whatcom County to the power brokers of the radical right. The names on Alan Gottlieb's various doors included: Citizens Committee for the Right to Keep and Bear Arms; Second Amendment Foundation ("dedicated to promoting a better understanding about our constitutional heritage to privately own and possess firearms," according to its journal); Center for the Defense of Free Enterprise; and, what was presumably the cash cow in the middle of the foundation barn, a supplier of mailing lists (and mailings) that went by the name Creative Advertising and Marketing: Direct Response Specialists. Gottlieb had gotten his start as a specialist in direct mailings when he was on the board of the Young Americans for Freedom.

There were liberals in Bellingham who saw a conspiracy in this. They believed that powerful reactionaries in politics and the military were using the "slicks" like Alan Gottlieb and Ron Arnold to recruit the "hicks" who joined John's militia and went to Shirley Hardy's potluck suppers and gave their money to Independence County. They believed this as much as John believed that the New World Order was something more sinister than a coincidence of common causes and common economic interests discussed at a couple of clubs on the East Coast. The difference was, of course, guns. The armed right had very little interest in community, if by community you meant anything besides *its* community; or in consensus, if by consensus you meant anything besides a consensus about strategy within its own groups; or in elections or, for that matter, in democracy. "We're a republic, not a democracy," John told me, more than once. The armed right considered itself at war with the government, and to the extent you accepted that the United States had a legal claim on your tax income, and the law some claim on your attention, the armed right considered itself at war with you, too. It was the idea of war that brought together a hyperactive mason's assistant not much past twenty and the middle-aged wife of a bankrupt veterinarian to discuss new formulas for making pipe bombs and to shoot at paper silhouettes. So, in one sense, the Bel-

lingham liberals were right when they said that strange en-
thusiasms had their moment in Whatcom County and faded,
and sometimes, somewhere along the way, a few people actually objected—or at any rate roused themselves from restful
apathy to an exhilarating panic. It could be said that, in this,
the militia served a useful civic purpose.

Vigilantes, good ones and bad ones, are obviously part of
the landscape of the American West, and have been since the
first sheriff raised the first posse to rout a cattle rustler or, indeed, a United States marshal. And certainly guns are part
of that landscape. You took more of a risk driving an Avis in
rural Washington than you did packing a weapon without a
permit. (The first cop who spotted my rental plates wanted
cash, the second was a trooper waiting for strangers, or perhaps for me, on the road to Dick Pitner's house on Whidbey
Island.) Unless you were known as a criminal, or were under
surveillance, or had a swastika shaved onto your scalp, or the
wild stare of a crack addict, the assumption was that you were
exercising your God-given right to bear arms, but had practiced the western courtesy of letting the police know. Guns
were as plentiful in Whatcom County as Chinook salmon, and
were considered just as sweet. There were gun shows and gun
stores and gun-trade classifieds posted in shop windows. It
wasn't a matter of left or right. Jeff Margolis, at Everybody's
Store, owned rifles. Even Paul de Armond had a collection of
vintage rifles; he sold them, not long after I got to Bellingham,
in order to pay the bills from his Internet server. In some
places, it might seem odd, even in hunting season, to walk
into your neighbor's house and see rifles stacked by the um-
brella stand or flung casually on the coffee table, like designer
accents (and it would certainly seem odd to see a rifle poking

out from behind the hot-water heater in the bathroom, the way, according to the FBI, you did at John's). But not in Whatcom County. Don Pierce, in his office at Bellingham's police headquarters, tried to take a long view of the county's gun practices. Pierce wasn't provincial; he knew that the police chiefs he met in cities like Rotterdam, at his task force meetings, were a little baffled by the evidence that Whatcom's citizens seemed to care as much about their right to handguns and semiautomatic weapons as they did about, say, their right to health care or good public education. But when I asked him if he worried about militia violence, he said that, to his mind, the problem of violence in America wouldn't be solved by more "feel-good legislation"; it would be solved when lawmen like him got the money and the personnel to implement the laws they already had. Pierce allowed that, as a police chief in a town with a militia next door, he had no way of controlling attitudes about guns. The most he could do was dispatch some volunteers from the force to the local schools and maybe provide the kids there with a little preventative education. (In Whatcom County, this could amount to "gross government interference.") He trusted his men—I met some admirable Bellingham cops—but he couldn't swear that all of them were as skeptical as he was about the Good Samaritan face of the Washington State Militia. He knew that the police chief in Puyallup, a small town between Seattle and Tacoma, had had some trouble about militiamen on *his* force, but he said that there was no way of really screening a police department, not as long as militias were legal.

Out in the county, of course, Don Pierce was considered just another Bellingham liberal. No one expected him to be sympathetic to John's small army. People figured that if any lawman was going to be open to the militia cause it would be the sheriff—maybe because of the Westerns they watched, or maybe because of Patriot doctrine, or maybe because Dale Brandland, while lamenting the incredible volume of weapons trading that went (the law allowed this) unrecorded, did take the Constitution to mean that a citizen of Whatcom County not only had the right to bear arms but also the right to conceal whatever arms he bore without the inconvenience of having to show cause why concealment was necessary or even useful to the security of a free state. The Washington State Militia was, in this sense, right in the Whatcom character. It may have been no more than a handful of local characters or it may have been the thousands of men-at-arms John claimed; after John went public at the Rome Grange, it didn't really matter. What gave him the small power he had in Whatcom County wasn't guns. It was the sense of occasion signaled by his smiling concern, and the threat behind it, which is why it didn't take long for people to start worrying about John and his men, however philosophical they were about the prerogatives of angry or reluctant citizens. They worried about some parent arriving at the PTA one night with reinforcements. They worried about some householder presenting his weapons the next time Sheriff Brandland arrived with a foreclosure order and a moving van. They even worried about someone assassinating the sheriff, now that John had stood up at a Citizens for Liberty meeting and accused him of "treason against the Constitution." (Brandland had lost John's vote by refusing to take an oath to fire on any federal agent who attempted to "violate" the home of a Whatcom County citizen.) They wondered if there was muscle behind John's posturing, and some sort of murderous longing behind all his Second Amend-

ment speeches. John's view of the Constitution was idiosyn-
cratic to begin with, and once he had proof that the "true"
Constitution ended at the Twelfth Amendment, with the re-
form of the Electoral College—sometimes it was the Thirteenth or the Fourteenth, and the betrayal was different—and
consequently that every American government since 1804 had
been illegal, he also knew why Doc Ellwanger didn't have to
pay his taxes. This was not a point he deigned to discuss with
most people, including with me. He said it was incontrovertible. You couldn't argue with the intel, and sooner or later the
people who tried—the sheriff, for one, doing the friendly thing
and stating his case for the Citizens for Liberty—began asking
themselves how long and how much they could disagree with
John before they ended up on some Patriot enemies list. The
question was this, really: When did an enemy became a target?

The fear showed in different ways. Some people stopped
talking. Some people decided that perhaps it wasn't the time
to show up at a school board meeting or host a coffee hour for
the North Cascades Eco-System Alliance. "We stay neutral,"
those people would say when I asked what they thought of
the militia—the ones, that is, who admitted there was a militia. "We stay neutral." I heard it first from a woman who had
gone into business selling chipped fifties crockery and black-
powder rifles at the roadside café she called A Dab of the
Primitive Café and Gift Shop. And as the months went by, and
the tension in the county grew, I heard it more and more. No
one denied that the radical, Christian right had an agenda in
Whatcom County, or even that, for its own immediate purposes, the militia was useful. The radical right had been fielding candidates in local Republican primary elections all over
the state of Washington, and winning enough to start slipping

its people into place in the Republican leadership; by 1996, it had virtually taken over the state party. But I hadn't really grasped how silencing that grassroots strategy had been until I got to Whatcom County, expecting to witness some exemplary unfolding of America's ongoing Manichaean drama, even if it was only a small showdown, and not *High Noon* on Valley Highway. I know now that only an easterner would have expected a Western in the turn-of-the-twenty-first-century American West. Even in Bellingham—a town whose synagogue had been advised to drop its listing in the phone book and remove the sign on its door—most people still believed that by refusing to acknowledge the militia they could make the militia go away.

OBVIOUSLY, A FEW PEOPLE did make the militia a cause, people who weren't undone by the apathy, or by the knowledge that they got more encouragement from watchdog groups outside the county than from their own neighbors, or that at home in Bellingham—most of them lived in Bellingham—they were considered a little embarrassing, a little strident, even a little obsessional, as if by calling John Pitner publicly to task they were breaching the etiquette of that "all-American city" (as the sign at the town line said) where everyone was happy and where, with faith and patience, the system worked. Often, they weren't the natives. Vernon—his friends called him "Damani"—Johnson, a black political scientist who taught at Western, came from Ohio. Damani had helped found the Whatcom Human Rights Task Force, and while he allowed that it could feel "strange, being African-American in this lily-white society and active against the militia," it was clear that a black man who'd honeymooned with a white wife in Coeur d'Alene, Idaho, a few miles from what was then the Aryan Nations compound, was not someone likely to be cowed by John Pitner. Then there was Cathy Logg, from Florida, at the *Bellingham Herald,* which was part of the Gannett chain and, to Cathy, almost offensively delicate on the subject of John Pitner. (A few weeks into the Montana Freemen standoff, the paper commended John for his peaceful restraint in "working within the system.") Cathy certainly wasn't cowed. Being an ex-Marine—and by her own account a law-and-order person, demonstrably more at home with a cop or an FBI agent than she would be with an American Civil Liberties Union lawyer pleading John's First Amendment rights—she enjoyed her pursuit of John Pitner and his men nearly as much as she enjoyed Sunday picnics with her grandson. She wanted to see the leadership of the Washington State Militia locked up in some high-security federal prison. In the sixteen months she followed the militia, her house had been broken into, her computer trashed, her message machine clogged with threats, and her car tailed, late at night, and it wasn't surprising that she suspected militiamen, or militia sympathizers, were involved, especially after learning at the trial that one militiaman, at least, had talked about killing her. (Now she works at the *Everett Herald,* which is one of the New York Times Company papers.) Finally, there was Paul de Armond, who came from Seattle. Paul had been living in Bellingham since his student days at Fairhaven—Western's experimental college—and, after twenty-five years of persistent if not obsessive research, he was the man you saw when it came to documenting the facts and unraveling the fictions of Whatcom County's Patriots. This was partly a matter of temperament and partly a matter of family mission, or, you could say, an homage to his father, who'd been a well-known Washington documentary film-maker until his career was all but shattered by a John Birch Society witch-hunt. When Paul wasn't minding the truck for Goodwill Industries, a seven-dollar-an-hour job, he was tracking activity on the far right, including the activity of John's militia. He would sit up nights at his computer, chain smoking and surrounded by empty bags of chips and tacos, while he traded news and argued interpretation with hundreds of other obsessives across the country. His state of mind, at three in the morning, was by his own account "friendly paranoia." He was looking for patterns ("for conspiracies," some people said). He could take a militiaman like John and trace his connections to a whole network of Patriot groups and ideologues and criminals in no more time than it had taken to enter the name. He could read, in that militiaman, a whole history of fanatics creating fictions about Antinomians and Illuminati and Elders of Zion.

Paul was a believer. He believed that the country belonged to anyone lucky enough to be here, and smart enough to like being here, and that those people were the patriots, not the people like John Pitner. On the other hand, he thought that with enough affectionate attention you could rescue the John Pitners from the brink of their own delusions. He stalked the Patriots of Whatcom County, dressed like a logger-priest in baggy overalls and red suspenders, appearing at every right-wing meeting he could get himself into, taking notes, making tapes, politely offering his opinions. He was hassled, harangued, and threatened, but he always refused to leave unless somebody actually picked him up and threw him out the door. He knew more terrible things about more people in

Whatcom County than anyone else I met there—he spent his life looking for terrible things—but he refused to give up on any of those people. He thought that I took a narrow, punishing, eastern view of John, whereas *he* took a generous western view, and believed in "the people," whoever they were. (When we got to be friends, I preferred to think of it as a kind of Rousseauian conviction that "the people" were born smart and grew not so much stupid as stupefied by the system, and that a good argument, patiently pursued, could save them.) So he believed that he could even redeem John, who was demonstrably one of "the people," sitting there in the woods of Whatcom County with a mortgage due and a rifle behind the water heater, getting paunchy from too much beer and too many cookies, addled by laser zappings and by all the dangerous waves that David Rockefeller was beaming on Valley Highway from his big radio tower in Alaska. John, however, didn't think he needed redeeming. He maintained (depending on when he told the story) that the waves were designed either to muddle the minds of Whatcom's Patriots so that they'd start to love the New World Order, or to ruin the weather and demoralize them so that they'd lose the will to resist the New World Order when it came. He thought that this was why it always rained in the state of Washington. He said that no one would ever be able to convince him otherwise. Paul bet me that someone could.

Seven

KEVIN "ROCK" JACKSON WENT TO his first militia meeting in April of 1996, a month or two after he appeared in Bellingham, looking for people who might be interested in doing business. Rock was a dealer in stolen weapons. He let it be known that he worked through a friend in the army in southern California—the friend supplied, Rock sold—and that they both were eager to expand their operations into northern Washington, which was known for its lively gun and drug traffic back and forth across the Canadian border. Ed Mauerer, who had known Rock's family in California, vouched for him with the local underworld. He introduced Rock to a group of Bellingham gangsters, led by a patriarch named Ike Lantis, and while Lantis was also more interested in selling than in buying—his offer to Rock involved a cache of shotguns, bullet-proof vests, SWAT batons, pepper spray, combat boots, and gas masks from a heist at an army surplus store—Rock obliged him, sealing his reputation as a player when he talked Ike Lantis into accepting a thousand dollars for what was said to amount to $27,000 worth of stolen hardware.

It wasn't long before Rock began showing up for meetings with Marlin's squad. (John, who'd heard vaguely about a good new member, didn't actually meet Rock until the end of May, at a meeting at Ed's.) Marlin worshiped Rock. Rock had money in his pocket and action in his head. He was Marlin's idea of a real leader, tough talking and direct, not nervous and evasive like John, and what's more he looked like a leader, blond and trim, with a strong square jaw. His looks were American (or, you could say, Aryan). There was nothing dark or dumpy or foreign about him. He even claimed to have been a skinhead, back when he was still living in California, but everyone knew that the skins weren't smart, and Rock was smart. Very smart—Marlin could see that—and the kind of person who fit in fast once he'd decided that the Whatcom life pleased him. Rock dressed "Whatcom," in jeans, T-shirt, and a lumberjack's flannel shirt, and he even looked Whatcom, now that his hair had grown and he'd acquired a beard to match it. He gave the men a sense of purpose. In no time, he was virtually running Marlin's squad, though Marlin himself never suspected it. Marlin was so proud of his new prominence as Rock's best friend, the guy Rock chose to show him Bellingham's "strategic points" and join him for target practice, that he started calling *their* squad Alpha One.

In a way, Rock opened up Marlin's world, because Marlin began to see that when the war came it would be *everyone* against the New World Order—the militias, the Aryan Nations, even the black separatist groups that wanted *their* own nation—that it would be, in Marlin's words, "like biblical!" Nothing that Rock told Marlin and the others was really so different from what John had told them: "If you're in the militia, you got to carry yourself above the norm," John had said. "You got to help old ladies across the street. There's no 'nigger this' or 'nigger that.' . . . We need their help." The difference was that Rock put his time and his money where his mouth was. He set up bomb drops and financed gun transfers. He took delivery of explosives and saw to it that his friends got good emergency IDs from a couple of Seattle Freemen (homemade-bomb specialists whom John himself had met for a "secret strategy session" at the Snohomish Howard Johnson's, a few days into the Jordan, Montana, siege). That June, Rock even supplied some of the leadership with proper headquarters, a place that was safe. Safer, at any rate, than Ed Mauerer's garage had been on the day one of those Freemen showed up for a demonstration involving pipe bombs, and Ed's small daughter, a few feet away in the backyard, was having her birthday party. The new headquarters was on the second floor of an office building in a Bellingham mall called Haskell Business Park. Rock envisioned it as part warehouse, part classroom, and every inch of it was a secret, so secret that not even John knew it was there. In fact, for a long time the only other militiamen who did know were Ed, Marlin, and Gary—the "tri-lateral" council, Rock called them, though the reference may have been lost on anyone but Rock himself—and a couple of men from a squad in the town of Mount Vernon.

Rock had a talent for bringing out the best in people. He was willing to leave the spotlight to John and concentrate on his new friends. He saw potential where John saw mainly his own reflection. Gary, for instance, was famously taciturn. "Gary's a little dour," people who liked him would say, shaking their heads and laughing. Gary talked so little about himself at meetings that John had trouble remembering his last name, let alone spelling it, at least when I asked him. ("K-A-N-A-O," he said, finally.) But Rock believed that with a little prodding Gary would make an eloquent teacher, and Gary proved it one afternoon in the warehouse by taking Rock, step-by-step, through a couple of hours of filing and fitting that turned at least one semiautomatic into very marketable machine gun. Rock encouraged the men to "contribute" their ideas. Gary came up with one; he thought the militia might consider planting some explosives in an empty house, alerting the FBI with an anonymous phone call, and blowing up the agents who arrived to check it out. Fred Fisher had an idea, too; he thought you should take out the agents with hand grenades. Even Marlin had something to contribute; Marlin was interested in chemical warfare, and his idea was to kill the agents slowly, with "festive mortar balls" carrying hepatitis, or even blowguns and poison darts. Rock took all their ideas to heart, but in the end the best idea was his own. It wasn't exactly war, but it held the prospect of being profitable. What Rock wanted was to put his new friends in the pipe-bomb business—he offered to broker the sales—with part of the profits going to the Washington State Militia. He knew how hard it must be for boys like Marlin, waiting and waiting for something interesting to happen. "With these younger guys, there's none of this 'Wait for the right time,' " he said later, at the trial. "Give them what they need, they'll create mayhem." And he must have felt for the older militiamen, like Fred, whom John had hurt, taking away his title as deputy director of the Washington State Militia just because of one story about Fred and his stepdaughter in the *Herald*—telling Fred that it was a matter of image, not trust or friendship, but not even having the Christian courtesy to consult Fred first.

John, admittedly, wasn't thinking clearly. He had a lot on his mind beside Rock Jackson's ambitions or Fred Fisher's sensitivities. ("A little problem," was how he described Fred's incest conviction to me.) For one thing, there was the matter of Debbie's leaving. It wasn't the first time she had left, but it was the first time she had actually stayed away. Then there was the matter of living with a zapped brain. John told me the story this way: A few days after Debbie left him, he was out on his deck, at the picnic table, nursing a cup of coffee and fretting about his marriage, fretting about the Montana Freemen, fretting about the war he had promised to start if any of the Freemen were harmed. He felt a jolt and collapsed onto the table from "all that voltage" passing through his head. When he woke, trembling in a pool of sweat, he couldn't remember anything that had happened in the past five days. Scott Tarleton, the family practitioner he went to see in Bellingham, disagreed with his diagnosis; Dr. Tarleton didn't think that the FBI was responsible. At first, he thought that John had possibly had a mild stroke—a "reversible stroke," he testified at the trial—or even a short epileptic seizure, and so he ordered tests in Seattle. When the tests came back "entirely normal," he changed his mind and decided that John had almost certainly had "some type of stress conversion reaction . . . [which indicates] that the person is experiencing things that are more than they really feel they're able to cope with."

And he may have been right about that, because John was running out of stories. He had told his men about big guns and weapons stashes, but none of them knew where to find those stashes. He had told them about "contributions"—$5,000 for guns from one Seattle admirer—but none of them knew where those contributions had gone or even where the $600 from Maryann Fisher's yard sale had gone. He had told them about secret lists—the whole hierarchy of the Patriot revolution—but none of them knew where he kept those lists. None of them even had a name and number to call for help when the war started in their own county and John was dead, the first martyr to the Patriot cause, and they were cut off and under fire and hiding in a couple of freezing caves without a clue as to where John had buried the buckets with their long johns and their matches, let alone their ammunition. John's advice, on reflection, seemed a little perfunctory: "At night, you hunker down, cover yourself with leaves, go to sleep," he told them. (He was still repeating it a month later.) It wasn't exactly Clausewitz as a battle plan, but, as he said, the rest was need-to-know, and the men were getting a little impatient with need-to-know.

John didn't want the men to worry. He told them if he got taken out in that first battle, one of them—the militiaman knew who he was—would get his instructions. Sometimes he said the militiaman already had his instructions, or at least a phone number that would "activate" the instructions. Occasionally, he even said who that militiaman was. Most often, it was Fred Fisher. (To me, though, it was "Gary Kanao.") John claimed that, when the time came, he would see to it that Fred knew what to do, but the men, Fred included, were beginning to ask themselves how John would be able to see to anything, dead or zapped into another amnesiac stupor or under torture in one of David Rockefeller's grisly camps. What John called his "fall-back" plan—the plan he later described to Special Agent Fahey, with the warning that militias all over the country would go on "tac-4 alert" if he was out of contact for more than twenty-four hours—didn't solve the problem of how Whatcom County's own patriots were supposed to survive those twenty-four hours. John, in fact, was becoming so evasive on the subject of their survival that some of the men began to wonder whether he was some sort of federal agent, under cover for the FBI, or for the Bureau of Alcohol, Tobacco, and Firearms, which was precisely what John was beginning to wonder about them. Rumors about spies went around the group, and it was not a group given to dismissing rumors. John himself wanted to hold a "court martial" for one militiaman who he claimed had been spreading militia secrets. He fought with another militiaman who'd referred to what John called a "covert" member by his last name. He started asking questions about Marlin, and even about his crown-and-bridge friend Jack Schleimer, who'd been one of his first recruits. Jack, when I talked to him, put it down to "the enemy using false information and rumors . . . to spread dissension," and in the event he had stopped going to meetings early that spring. No one in the militia was apparently much distressed by Jack's departure. Jack had so many enemies in his own head by then that he couldn't sit still in church, during the Sunday morning sermon, without twisting around and peering into the crowd, as if he were expecting to catch Lenin among the worshipers.

The week I met John Pitner was the week Rock Jackson went to his first militia meeting in Whatcom County. John, by his own account, was on top of the world then, maybe because he was still able to field the grumblings in his ranks with evidence that other people in the movement held him in some regard, and that those people were counting on him to lead the fight in Washington. Even his new friends from the Seattle suburbs—there were eight Seattle Freemen at John's Howard Johnson summit—counted on him to "act as one [with them] against the feds." They worried that John Trochmann, who should have been putting his own men between the Montana Freemen and the agents waiting outside their ranch, was selling out to the government, but they didn't worry about John. John knew that the feds didn't belong in Justus Township. He couldn't understand why the Jordan sheriff had refused to accept it as his duty to stop agents who came into the county armed and expecting to march on Freemen property, or for that matter why the Freemen should be forced to pay taxes in a country that wasn't "playing by the rules"—though he wanted me to know that, of course, *he* paid taxes. Twelve hundred dollars a year in property taxes, he said. Sixty percent of his income, all told. (I didn't ask, What income?) On the other hand, talking about Debbie a few weeks later, he told me, "I haven't used my Social Security number for five years." He thought that the least he could do for the cause was not "contribute" to the system—not to the Social Security system (which sent your money straight to the enemy through the International Monetary Fund) and certainly not to the "counterfeiters" at the Federal Reserve.

It wasn't surprising that the militiamen were confused. One of the John Pitners I was getting (in a manner of speaking) to know had a shrewd sense of what he was offering the losers and loonies of Whatcom County. He understood that the reason some of his men weren't out on the highway, shooting, was that "they've got a place to call now, to talk out, to come to meetings. We give them a job. A militia job. It's a hell of a brass ring to give someone, [and] it means nothing." (A psychiatrist in New York, who wrote about group paranoia, told me the same thing.) John Pitner could talk about Panama and make some sense out of what he called "my disillusion." "We cut a sixty-mile swath in the middle of the country, and we told them how they'd live, what kind of money they could use, what rules and regulations they had to live under," he told me. "And we constantly lied to them about events down in, about our involvement in, Bolivia, Costa Rica. . . . No wonder the people down in South America hate our guts." He could talk about his summers working the shipyards in Ketchikan, Alaska, making $2,000 for a seven-day, sixty-hour week, and say, "The few jobs I got, working under the table, I figured I was owed it," and I had to admit a lot of perfectly decent people would have felt the same way. He could talk about all the petty government codes and licenses and regulations that kept a bureaucracy leisurely employed and forced the hardworking little guy out of business, and I could sympathize with that, too. But when he blamed the interstate commerce laws for the fact that "I can't deliver my cabbage to New York," I had to remind myself that John had never had occasion to try delivering anything to New York, let alone cabbage. When he said that his men were being demonized by the *Herald* for "learning cardiopulmonary resuscitation," I had to remind *him* that they were also learning how to make war on the United States. He would tell me that he was broke, wiped out by a selfish wife, and in the next breath talk about how he'd taken every cent he and Debbie had and blown it on his ungrateful army. "I used to have a nice boat, five or six Mustangs, a bunch of motorcycles," he told me. Once, complaining about the ingratitude of his men, he said, "All my nest egg, all my income . . . I have a hundred thousand dollars invested in the movement." (On the same day, he also claimed to have spent $40,000 suing the South Fork Beach Association.) He told his men that Debbie was unfaithful and that he was paying two men to follow her round-the-clock to prove it. He told *me* that Debbie had come undone, worrying about him. "The militia scared the holy bejeebers out of her," he said. But, whatever story he told, it was clear that Debbie's defection confirmed his place—at least, to him—in the pantheon of Patriot martyrs. "This happened to our forefathers too: a lot of men losing wives," he said, sighing. "I won't be the last."

Sometime in May—I was in New York the week it happened—John told a few of his men that he was taking a leave from his responsibilities as director of the Washington State Militia. He wasn't leaving the militia, and he certainly wasn't breaking its ties, or his own, with the Seattle Freemen. In fact, there were days that spring and summer when he seemed to have forgotten that he had stepped down. He still introduced himself as the head of the Washington State Militia, and not many militiamen were aware that anything had changed. But he stopped holding his weekly Alpha One meetings. He told me he needed to recover from the zapping, he needed to recover from Debbie, he needed to recover from Fred Fisher— who, as he remembered it now, *had* mentioned something once about a felony conviction—and, most of all, he needed to let the militiamen who were starting to bellyache about John Pitner at squad meetings see just how long they could "float" without him. It wasn't only his men in Whatcom County. The men in Snohomish County were complaining, too, calling him naïve, or worse, for talking to the press, going on television, having interviews. He thought he'd give them a taste of life alone. "I've got my ass in a sling . . . ," he said at one point. "They won't speak out, but if I decide to they're all over me." Later, he said, "I read them the riot act. I said, next time you jump on my butt for talking to the media, you speak out." He knew, of course, that a militia had to have two kinds of people. "The overts and the coverts," he called them. He had figured, at most, twenty overts to a county, and as for the rest—well, the coverts couldn't be blamed for keeping their asses out of slings, not when they risked getting fired, or hassled by the IRS or the FBI, or even by their own sheriff. Without those coverts, John would never have got away with claiming eight thousand Washington State Militia members. There were thousands of members, he told me, whose names he didn't even know, but there was also the fact that not even Gary was willing to make a public statement about the terrible siege that was taking place in Montana. John was tired. Being a leader of men was tiring. He knew that John Trochmann had saved *his* ass by calling himself "the founder" of MOM, never "the director." Nobody challenged Trochmann about need-to-know, or demanded accountings of where the big guns were hidden or the money had gone.

John had liked being called "responsible" in a *Bellingham Herald* editorial. He didn't understand why the paper had changed its mind and been so nasty after he announced that any move on Justus Township would amount to "a declaration of war," and more to the point, he didn't understand why his own men had also got nasty. It seemed to John that the only militiaman he could talk to lately was his friend Brian, who suspected everyone *except* John of telling lies or making trouble or simply being trouble, though the truth was that some of the men were sympathetic, if not precisely compassionate. Marlin maintained that you couldn't expect John to be up to form after a 44,000-volt zapping. Ed said that you had to understand how distracted John was, riding around all day trying to discover his wife's boyfriend. The militiamen wished John well. They hoped he got better. All they wanted from him were a couple of telephone numbers and a map of their ordnance stashes on Mount Baker. And, in their own way, they let him know. The phone would ring at Command Central, and when John picked up there'd be a husky threat or a long silence. He walked outside one morning to find the tires on his pickup slashed. He might just as well have been Cathy Logg, or Don Shepherd, the biology teacher at Mount Baker, or one of those women who kept knocking on doors for a new school levy. John was frightened. In early July, he called his sister Susan, asking if he could sign on with her gardening service for a couple of weeks while he did some "thinking and things of that nature." He felt beleaguered, like the fighting men who had got the treacherous memo called Presidential Directive 25—the one from Clinton, ordering them to swear to serve and defend the United Nations. The order was out now, and in a manner of speaking, John was, too.

John's troubles put him in a reminiscing mood. By July, I knew all about the good citizen he had tried to be in Whatcom County, the kind of citizen who, if his neighbor had problems, went out and helped him. He told me about the time he and a couple of friends had risked their lives trying to run some drug dealers out of town and make the neighborhood "safe for the children." "Some of the things I did was [*sic*] questionable, and I was bending the law to say the least, but I was effective and that's what counted," he said. "I didn't want them bastards getting *my* kid hooked on drugs." He told me about the time he'd persuaded a friend of Rachel's—a friend whose father had raped her, holding a hammer over her head—to report him to the Bellingham Child Protection Services. That, of course, was before John knew about the local cops doing big business with the dealers, and the people at Child Protection getting a "$5,000 bounty" for every child they could hound into signing a statement. That was before he had seen "America in Peril," or had read Orwell and discovered Big Brother, who was just as dangerous as Daddy Warbucks but a lot harder to pin down. He hadn't a clue then, compared to what he knew now. He hadn't seen that it was all part of the conspiracy. "I've always been very skeptical," he told me. "I have to really chew on things and see them and get to verify the proof, and it takes quite a while." But now he knew. The conspiracy was everywhere. It was behind the gun laws, and the drug laws, and the seatbelt laws, and the motorcycle-helmet laws, and for all he knew, they were going to make it a crime if your cholesterol count went over two hundred. There wasn't much time to stop them. They had already arrested John Trochmann—the charges, according to John, involved "criminal syndicalism," although he couldn't tell me what the term meant and, in the event, those charges were dropped a few days later—and while it was clear from the start that they'd have to release Trochmann, the message was "out there." John figured that he'd be next; his cholesterol was up. So he was "going underground" in Bothell. His sister was gay. She had voted for Clinton. She ran a business and paid her taxes and didn't believe in the concentration camp near Sea-Tac Airport. But you couldn't have everything. The Patriot wars would have to wait until John Pitner had his R and R.

Eight

THE MAN IN CHARGE of the Bellingham office of the FBI was a special agent by the name of Ramon Garcia. It wasn't a big office, just Garcia and Cathy Fahey, but everyone knew that it was there and that Ramon ran it. You could say "Ramon" anywhere in Whatcom County and people would understand exactly *which* Ramon you meant—not that there were many Ramons or, for that matter, Garcias in the county to begin with. Ramon had been with the FBI for thirteen years. He had started out as a special agent in Las Vegas, attached to the Bureau's organized-crime division, and had arrived in Bellingham in 1990, from postings in Cincinnati and Puerto Rico, with an assignment to investigate mob gambling operations on the Lummi Indian reservation. It was a nice job, but six years later Ramon Garcia was still in Bellingham, and Bellingham was a backwater—despite the

Mafia's interest in developing Whatcom's Native American casinos, and despite the border traffic in AK-47s, and despite what you could call a post-Prohibition revival of night boating that involved some of the old smuggler coves, up and down the coast, and the drug runners who had thought to try them, and even despite the presence of a group of peculiar characters preparing for war against the United States. Ramon wasn't, by reputation, brilliant or imposing. He was a small, squat, anxious-looking person, not someone you'd really noticed unless he was staring at you. But it's safe to assume that he would have preferred a more glamorous posting, like Seattle, and perhaps a little more renown. A hundred Washington agents reported to Seattle. Undercover operatives assigned to the Pacific Northwest were processed *through* Seattle. The Bureau's Seattle office was a big modern building, with the kind of high technology that people who worked there swore they were not allowed to use against you. Special Agent Ramon Garcia made do with Cathy Fahey and a message machine he never seemed to answer—not, at any rate, when I called, hoping to go over and introduce myself and make an appointment for a background briefing, the way you would in most places.

In the spring of 1996, Garcia was said to be working with the local police on the problem of one Ike Lantis, whose "crime ring" (as the *Herald* called it) seemed to consist of Lantis, his son Donald, and the various punks who wandered in and out of their operation. Not much else was happening in Whatcom County. There wasn't a lot of traffic at the Washington-Canada border, nothing the ATF couldn't handle. Four years later, an Algerian with ties to Osama bin Laden and his North American network was arrested at a border crossing, carrying explosives and heading into Washington, but in the spring and early summer of 1996 the border was quiet. Bellingham was quiet. Even the county was quiet. John hadn't led his men to war in Montana, and the men were too busy arguing about *him* to go themselves, even assuming they discovered the weapons caches they'd be needing. Rock was easing his trilateral council into the bomb trade, starting to arrange meetings and exchanges with John's Seattle Freemen. John himself was mostly alone at Command Central, brooding over his life, his wife, and the intel on his Patriot Web sites. Once, when he seemed especially upset and I asked why, he said that he'd just confirmed the fact that there were German troops training in New Mexico—at Hollerman Air Force Base, he told me—and that those troops already had "forty warships down there, and they plan on having another hundred come in." (I assumed he was talking about planes.) What was clear, to John, was that the New World Order had sent the warships *and* the Germans, and that it was only a matter of time before Germany had access to all the secret technology America was keeping from its own citizens. The two-hundred-year light bulb. The toaster that lasted a lifetime. The two-hundred-mile-a-gallon carburetor. (David Rockefeller and his friends had paid off the man who invented it.) The supersonic water engine. (They'd killed the man who invented that.) The giant magnets for launching cheap space payloads. (They'd be looking for John now, since he was the one working on his own "grav-lift.") According to John, he would make this alarming intel public as soon as "the FBI in New Hampshire" had checked it out for him. He didn't control the New Hampshire FBI. He wanted to be clear on that. But there were Patriots in every FBI office, and he also wanted to be clear on the fact that those Patriots "know what I represent." "So I have a lot more power than even I know about," is how he explained it then. Another time, he said it came down to trust. If there were feds who trusted John completely, they had every reason: "I'm about as uncorruptible as uncorruptible can get," he told me. "I don't have an inflated ego. I don't have this need or desire to be liked by bunches of people. . . . It's the way I was raised. It's the way I evolved as an individual." There was, of course, the other FBI. There was Ramon, who had interviewed Militia Jim but had never shown the slightest patriotic interest in John; there were the three suits who had tried to work John over in the secret interrogation center at Sea-Tac Airport; there were the 44,000 bolts of laser. But as John once said, the real Patriots in the Bureau—his "brother-in-law" in Mountlake Terrace was a good example—were on his side. Real Patriots never got co-opted. They were a breed apart from the federal marshals who leapt out of their helicopters dressed like Ninjas, or, for that matter, from the suits at the airport. One of those suits had been so angry and uptight that he'd reminded John of the kind of wife who, "when you go into the kitchen, all the cans of beans have got to be labeled out, stacked just right, in the right spot."

Actually, there wasn't much besides beans in the kitchen at Command Central once Debbie left (though Debbie said she'd made a point of driving out three or four times a week with groceries). John himself didn't shop; most days, he didn't even know where he would be by lunch time. He would wake up, ready to move to Susan's the way he'd planned, and then he'd say to himself, No, much better to try to borrow some money and take "a couple of months off," somewhere like Australia. Or he'd decide, suddenly, to step back into "the leadership," since it was clear that none of the men had come forward, or even had the capacity to come forward, to take his place as director. "It's too much pressure for them," he told me. "They aren't suited to do this kind of battle. I am." It wasn't everyone who could lead men and "make a . . . difference." The important thing was, "God, that word is escaping me. What is it? Wisdom."

There were good days and bad days. "I've got to get the point across and I just can't falter," he said on one of the good ones, when he wasn't looking gray or scared or complaining about losing Debbie. That was the day he talked about how "selfless" and "neighborly" he'd always been—how selfless and neighborly most Americans had been, before the Federal Reserve stole their money and the War Powers Act started eating away their liberty. He wasn't sure when this had actually happened. Sometimes, in our conversations, he dated the War Powers Act at 1794, sometimes at 1933, but never at 1973, which was when it, in fact, was drafted. And in the event he got the terms backwards. (It was an article of Patriot faith that the War Powers Act gave American presidents the right to seize public moneys to finance armies and wage undeclared wars, whereas the act was written, in response to an escalating Vietnam War, in order to prevent that from happening again.) Talking law with somebody like John, somebody who believed that the War Powers Act was responsible for drivers' licenses and the Rothschild family for capital gains taxes, was an exercise in patience, since he could always claim, and usually did claim, that my copies of the *Britannica* and the *Congressional Record* and even the Constitution were forgeries, straight from the printing press of the conspiracy. He maintained that the Founders' America had been a rosy place where "the townspeople got together [and] if they wanted a new road, they all contributed money and they built a new road, if they wanted a new library, they all contributed money and built a new library." And it was brave of him to say so, because he also believed that men like him, who told the truth, got murdered. The feds used poison, he said, although he did add, on reflection, that you couldn't be sure the hit men themselves were agents. The example he gave was "William Tuttle," the agent who had lured him to Sea-Tac for interrogation. John had checked with his sources and there was no one named William Tuttle in the Bureau; and now he figured that Tuttle must have been Interpol, a hired hand from "as high as you can get up in the food chain" of the New World Order's international police. You couldn't escape Interpol unless you ran to ground in the wilderness in Australia, which was one reason he had thought about going there. He wasn't scared to travel—"I've always liked to travel, that's why I've grown so much as a person," he told me—but he knew in his heart that it would be wrong to go. "For me to know what I know and not do anything about it is treason" was how he put it. He didn't want to be responsible when his men fell into "the worker-bee mentality" that was destroying Americans "as a race, as a people." He had let them know this, and even now, as we spoke, they were busy looking for the right place to hold a meeting, a meeting where the people of Washington would welcome John Pitner back to office. He told me about a Cotton Tree Inn in Skagit County that sounded promising (at any rate, much better than the Rome Grange, which had closed its doors to the militia after that first public meeting). It had to be soon, or his men would miss the action that was about to start because of Montana—and because of Georgia and Texas and California and Arizona and just about everywhere else you looked. Patriots all over the country were being deprived of their God-given constitutional rights, and as Norm Olson, from the Michigan Militia, said once, "When you take justice out of the equation, the people have nothing left but retribution." Olson, it was true, may have been a little too eager for retribution, and in the event his publicity was so bad after he went on television playing war games that his own militia had thrown him out. John knew, of course, that the media, being in enemy hands, was under orders to give the Patriot movement bad publicity. "You don't have to be a rocket scientist or a really talented chopper and whopper in the news room to put together footage to make somebody look dangerous," he told me, and that much, at least, was true. He didn't think *I* was in enemy hands, not precisely. He thought of me more as his own personal proof that the New World Order was so pervasive, and so effective, that you could be part of it and not even suspect you were. Despite his promises, he never let me watch the Washington State Militia train. By then, it was doubtful that he could have.

SOME OF THE MEN wanted to take out John. His absence, if anything, made them more suspicious, because at meetings he had always been able to second-guess them, to take their arguments about need-to-know and convince them that they all knew *something*, even if they had no idea what that something was. He could convince them that the ordnance was there, the arsenal was stacked, the big Patriot money was behind him, and never mind if he had just been griping about how broke he was, living without a cent to his name, having to sell his house just to keep himself in cigarettes and coffee. But he couldn't convince them of anything, sitting on his deck with a reporter for an audience.

He wasn't entirely out of touch. He still talked on the phone to Ed and Gary; he still consulted his Seattle Freemen; and he certainly saw Brian, who went to squad meetings and continued to report back on what was happening, and especially on what the men were saying about him. The problem for John was that they met at all. Gary, for one, was still counting on conflagration in Montana. "Any way you look at it, it'll be gunfire before it's all over with, anyhow," he said (I couldn't tell from the transcript if he said it sadly or hopefully) at a meeting that was mainly devoted to discussing the cheapest, easiest way to put together a homemade claymore mine. Waiting for war had not only loosened Gary's tongue but had stirred his imagination. He began to talk about taking revenge on the FBI and on anyone else who was closing in on the Montana Patriots. He thought of the siege of Justus Township as something happening to him. "What we're gonna have to decide, okay, when do we say, 'Fuck this shit, enough's enough'?" he said at another meeting, a few weeks later. His idea of justice was to "meet that guy in the middle of the night when he's coming home and just pulverize the shit out of him. Explain to him what's gonna happen to him and his family and then do it. . . . God damn right, the whole works." It was not a sentiment that his neighbors—the ones who called him sweet and shy, and admired his way with a broken toaster— would have recognized.

Brian wasn't discouraged, either. It would have been out of character if he had been. "Hi, everybody, I'm here, let's make bombs," he announced, walking into one meeting and promptly rattling off a small-bomb shopping list that ran from lead arsenate and silver fulminate and sulfuric acid to the granulated chlorine mix that went so well with brake fluid. Nothing was impossible to come by, not for a man with a hydrogen bomb in his basement, and Brian was nothing if not creative. He knew how you juiced up an old Egyptian Mac-90 "squirt gun"; he offered to wear his Clinton mask for a demonstration, if Marlin would promise to videotape it with his camcorder. He even knew how to solve the problem of buying suspiciously large quantities of chlorine. You did that by walking into your local Ace Hardware, all by yourself, and saying, "Hey, my hot tub is starting to stink like somebody's armpit. You know, what do I need?" It was clear that, whatever affection he felt for John, Brian was managing to survive without him. Certainly Ed was managing. Marlin was managing. (Marlin was even cheerful, telling the men about his new inventions: the little cardboard bomb you could make with bits of leftover fuse; the barrel for shooting crossbow arrows out of a 10-22 rifle, with only the whispery "pop" of a cap gun.) And as for Rock, who hardly knew John, Rock didn't have the time or the interest to start worrying about him now. Rock was always busy doing something—driving to Oregon to pick up chemicals, driving to Tukwila to pick up a pipe bomb from the Freeman John Kirk, helping Gary locate the right machine-gun parts, or Marlin an untraceable source of cannon fuse. And now that he had practically replaced John, he had serious responsibilities, such as deciding which militiamen were "hard core" and "operational"—trustworthy enough to be invited to the Washington State Militia's new headquarters. John was definitely not operational. Nor, for that matter, was the militiaman he had once accused of using last names in what he called an "insecure setting." (The problem was solved with a short death threat, whispered into the telephone; the man never came to another meeting.) And then there was the question of what to do about the Ellwangers, who in Rock's opinion should be kept away from headquarters; and in Ed's opinion should be escorted in and out of headquarters blindfolded; and in Marlin's more respectful opinion should be confined, unsuspecting, to a kind of headquarters sitting room—he offered to fix one up—with a flag, a couple of nice couches, and a secret door to the room where the weapons would presumably soon be stored.

Of course, the group that was left wasn't a group most people would have described as trustworthy. Marlin, for one, got so excited about their new headquarters that he started bragging about it to the kind of people who wouldn't even consider *themselves* trustworthy, let alone quiet, let alone friends. It was hard to think of Gary, with his bad back, as operational. He was in obvious, wincing pain, and some days he needed a cane to be able to walk at all. The Freemen, who had started coming to headquarters every week for training and were by anyone's standards hard core, were a little too casual with ordnance to be considered trustworthy *or* operational. (Once, when Rock drove down to Tukwila with Ed to collect some pipe bombs at John Kirk's house, he discovered that Kirk had left the bombs in a bag in the barbecue in his backyard, where his grandchildren were playing, and had gone out. His only message—his wife repeated it, handing the bag to Rock—was "Don't drop it.") None of the men really liked the Freemen. Fred thought that John Kirk was a terrible anti-Semite, and so did his wife, Maryann, who said that she wouldn't have John Kirk in her house. And Fred himself wasn't much interested in being operational. He was still smarting over his disgrace. People recognized him now. Strangers looked at him in the street—a portly, balding man with eyes that twinkled behind his glasses, the kind of man you would expect to see pitching lawn mowers on an infomercial or sporting a red suit and a long white Dacron beard at your church Christmas party—and saw a man who had gone to jail for abusing his wife's daughter. When Fred wasn't plotting his revenge on Cathy, at the *Herald,* he was plotting his revenge on John, who had not only taken away his title but had told everyone who asked that it probably wasn't the moment for Fred to be up there, in public, giving his speech about family values. Fred got so mad thinking about John that he stopped passing out his Washington State Militia calling cards, the ones with John's number on them. In fact, he hadn't even seen John since the time they ran into each other on a Bellingham street corner, right near the spot where Fred usually parked his truck. As Fred described it at the next militia meeting, John had been sitting there on his motorcycle. Just sitting. He seemed to be waiting for something, and when Fred asked him what he was waiting for, he said he was doing "motorcycle recon" on a guy in Fred's neighborhood—a mechanic, he thought—who was rumored to be Debbie's new boyfriend. That was the end of their conversation, but Fred said it had got him thinking about how John was able to afford the two men he was supposedly paying to watch Debbie's new apartment, which of course got him thinking about money, and about where the militia's money had gone, and why John was telling everyone that it had gone for arms caches and that Fred Fisher knew where the caches were, when Fred didn't know a goddamn thing about caches, not even the caches of freeze-dried chile, let alone caches of weapons buried under some bridge no one could remember seeing. Fred knew nothing at all about caches. He certainly knew nothing about the famous envelope with the lists and the maps and the phone numbers and the battle plans that was supposed to be someplace in his house, "in case the shit hits the fan, [and] 'course, if I ever find it." And when he thought about that, he was ready to kill John, or so he said. Not just to call him up, the way Marlin wanted to, and whisper "I'm going to fucking kill you," but to get him alone in the woods and wrap some wire around his neck and make him suffer, the way the men knew Fred was suffering because of all those people who would now think twice about calling Fred Fisher Masonry. Even Gary, who had bought a computer and was counting on John to teach him how to surf the Internet, referred to John now as that "fucking son of a bitch." Gary didn't see any point in killing John. He thought it was better to use John, the way he'd used *them*. "Play the game out, let him be the face out there that everybody gets to see, but he's never going to know what we're doing," he said one night, early in July. The men liked the part about John not knowing. They'd say "Need-to-know!" and start laughing—because if John wanted their intel, he'd have to come up with some intel of his own. The problem was that by now, no one really believed he would. Rock put it neatly: they'd been screwed.

Nine

EVERY COMMUNITY has its own confessional form. Catholics go into a small booth, Evangelicals "witness." Some people confess and are born again into fresh, new, blameless souls. Some people get forgiven. Among the Inuit, in Alaska, men recount their sins or their crimes or their failings to a circle of neighbors, who chant something on the order of "We like you anyway, whatever it was you did." Some people get punished. The Mafia calls, or the judge hands down a sentence. In the militia movement, where everyone is suspect or, you could say, no one is entirely free from secrets, the form of choice has been a kind of collective inquisitorial raid on the man suspected of lying, cheating, stealing, talking, spying, informing, or displaying an inadequate rejection of reality. The militiamen I met compared it to a group of relatives bursting into the house of a troublesome cousin with a stash of empty gin bottles underneath the couch, and administering enough hot shame to convert him to a life of remorseful sobriety and imported water. In Alcoholics Anonymous, it is called an "intervention," but in the Washington State Militia, it was usually called "the hot seat." John, who approved of the practice but thought "court martial" was the better term, had already put one militiaman in the hot seat (the man who'd made the mistake of using last names) and by all reports had handled himself like a real commander, shouting and shaking his fist and even, at one point, throwing a pillow in the defendant's face. Now it was John's turn.

The meeting took place in Ed Mauerer's garage, on the evening of July 9, 1996. It began about an hour before John was due to arrive, and according to the transcript, Rock, Ed, Marlin, Gary, Fred, and Brian were there, along with three other militiamen whose names I recognized and at least one man who wasn't identified at all. John may have expected trouble, but from what he told me, at his real trial, it was his first leadership meeting in at least two months and he had expected a hero's welcome. (In fact, there'd been an earlier meeting at the end of May, and John took part.) Most of the militiamen who came were more or less Alpha One, though there were a couple of men from Skagit who called themselves Alpha Two, and, of course, there was also Brian. They had made a point of inviting Brian, because he'd known John for twenty-five years, much longer than the rest of them put together, and they thought maybe he'd have something important to tell them, some insight that would make sense of John's behavior. Somewhere in the house, a couple of children were playing with their toy guns, punctuating the drone of a

country and western tape—"If you don't love me no more . . .
I've got no reason to live"—with whoops and bangs. Ed's wife
was in the kitchen, baking something that smelled like cookies to some of the men, and to others like steak-and-cheese
sandwiches—and, at any rate, made all of them hungry. It
was a good-natured gathering, at least at first. Rock informed
Brian that they had some questions, because John had "kind
of told everybody a different story," and Fred added politely
that this was making them all "you know, a little uncomfort-
able," and then Gary mentioned that "there's been some subjects come up that don't jibe," such as the arms caches none of
them knew where to find. Brian tried to clear up some of the
misunderstandings. For one thing, he could definitely state—
both as a scientist with "three years up here at Bellingham
Tech" and as a medical expert who had coached his own wife
through medical school "twice"—that what other people
might see as odd or confused or even dishonest behavior on
John's part was really "laser shock." "Indicative to laser . . . he
has the phenomenon," is how Brian put it. He couldn't really
explain why John had boasted that he and Ed and even Marlin
were Special Forces, especially when Marlin was only a few
years out of high school, any more than he could explain why
John had told them there were twenty-six thousand militia
members, or had started spreading suspicion among the men
who *were* members, talking about spies and moles and informers and, as Marlin said, getting "everybody like looking
at everybody else." What Brian could tell them was that John
was thick with some pretty serious military people and that
those people would never have bothered with John if he hadn't
been pretty serious himself. "He's been a fucking bomb-head
all his life," Brian said, perhaps by way of a reassurance. "He

blew up his dad's garage. I mean, he really did that. And lots of times. He blows things up . . . I think that's why he went into Special Forces or whatever he went into. Because he's got that little bit of a touch."

There were times when Brian would listen to something the men said, and acknowledge, "That's scary." But it's likely that the scariest thing any of them heard that night, in Ed's garage, was something Brian himself said when they asked him about Daiwee and he replied that Daiwee wasn't the code name for a group of forty important army officers from Special Forces—was the last description of Daiwee that John had given—but a "psycho" living near Seattle in a cabin stuffed with dynamite and grenades and M-16 and AK-47 rifles, a psycho who had once been arrested and thrown out of the army for his part in a village massacre in Vietnam. Brian knew Daiwee, and so did his buddy "Dave," a veteran who trained the militiamen in Mount Vernon and who, according to Brian, was definitely Special Forces, with "the Israeli assault, the Seven [sic] Day War, all of this shit" on his résumé. But Brian didn't encourage paying Daiwee a friendly visit on the subject of need-to-know. As one of guests from Skagit put it, "He's too scary to go to visit unless he gave you a personal invitation personally."

There wasn't much for the men to do then, besides run through their old litany of complaints. Fred was still worried about the Alpha One "escape route." He thought that the route John favored—up into the mountains, through Hannegan's Pass, and across Ross Lake toward eastern Washington—was "one of the poorest escape routes" you could ever imagine, inasmuch as it took a good half hour to paddle across Ross Lake, and that meant half an hour as a sitting target for the air force jets that could reach the lake from the nearest base in five minutes. Gary, on the other hand, was worried about himself. He said that someone—was it John?—had been spreading rumors about him being a Satan worshiper, and while there were always rumors about gunsmiths, who were known in the trade as alchemists, his point was that people hearing those rumors now were freaking out, and he wanted to make it clear that "I believe in Jesus Christ, and I pray to him." As for Marlin, he just wanted to know where the twenty-four combat rifles and the forty thousand rounds of ammunition, the ordnance John claimed to have bought with the $5,000 from his mysterious, big-brass, "fairy godmother" down in Seattle or Fort Lewis, were buried. Marlin was beginning to wonder if there was a fairy godmother, and, assuming there was, if John had spent the money on himself. Everyone agreed that John's directions to the rifles—you followed that beaver stream on Mount Baker, crossed that little bridge, you couldn't miss it, and turned left and looked for those three white rocks that were "pointed kind of like in a 'Y,'" and then you started digging—didn't exactly add up to a working map, not when you didn't know which stream, or which bridge, or which rocks, not when you'd be waist-deep in briars anyway, with no way to see three white rocks unless you tripped on them.

If John was shaken, walking into the crowd in Ed's garage, he didn't show it. He took the offensive. The first thing he said (at what could be called the second court martial of his career) was, "Are we reduced to meeting in garages now?" and the second thing was, "I don't see a flag in here, I'm leaving. . . . Bad. No flag." He would have expected the men to remember that you couldn't have a meeting of Patriots without a flag, and he wasn't talking about the kind of flag the feds flew, which was an admiralty flag, with gold fringes, and amounted to a sign that the country was under martial law. He was talking about the only American flag a real Patriot recognized and revered. ("Take the fringe off, and you've got Old Glory" was the way he'd described it to me.) The men were so surprised, or possibly so ashamed, that no one could think of an answer. After a while, Fred tried passing around a Patriot reading list he had put together, but John found something to criticize in that, too. He looked over Fred's list and barked, "This isn't spell-checked!"

It has to be said that John, under pressure, gave one of his best performances. When Fred brought up the caches—"I wanted to clarify one thing . . . ," Fred said. "I heard from some of the guys that I'm supposed to know"—John answered calmly, "You do know." When Fred said no, he didn't know, John told him, "There's some information that you're in possession of that you don't even know that you have. It's going to stay that way." And when Fred persisted, "See, that makes me really insecure," John explained why "not knowing" should be making Fred *more* secure, not less, because when Fred got captured and ended up in some New World Order torture chair, with the wires hooked up to his teeth and his brain full of sodium pentothal, he was going to talk. "No matter how big of a Patriot, no matter how big of a man, or whatever it is that you are, you're going to talk." It was clear to John that if none of the men could understand that, then they hadn't understood anything he'd ever told them about how terrible the war was going to be. The question they should have been asking themselves was, "How the hell are we going to get ahold of everybody anyways if the shit hits the fan?" because when that happened, when the fight for freedom really started, they would almost certainly be cut off and on their own. Daiwee would get to them if Daiwee could— "that's why Daiwee's in charge of it"—but John's advice to the men was that they'd better start thinking about how to get to Daiwee. "You don't know them and they don't know you, all right," he said. "Start to think about the shoe. On one foot or the other, it works both ways." When he put it like that, it was hard to argue. He was doing this for them. "If I get taken out, I'd like to know that everybody is going to be okay," he said. "I'd like to hold that knowledge close to me."

Marlin tried arguing. He understood need-to-know, and even so, he couldn't help wondering what would happen to the rest of them if John got hit in the head again with a laser. But it didn't matter how many times Marlin or anyone else in Ed's garage that night asked the question, or how differently each man phrased it, John always had an answer. "Fred is in possession of information he doesn't know he has" was one answer. "I'm the kind of guy who likes to let things happen very, very slowly . . . so as things progress, as we get to know one another, as we get to trust one another, things of that nature, then we'll, you know, you'll get to know more" was another answer. Once, John answered by saying that "loose as a goose" was *his* strategy. Loose as a goose was best because "if things were tight-knit, and really well thought out, and really well planned," there would naturally be more to lose when the bad guys infiltrated; and one thing the men could be sure of was that the bad guys were going to infiltrate, no matter what you did to keep them out. The bad guys were capable of anything. Look at the way they had "demonized" those Arizona Patriots, the ones with the Viper Militia, claiming that they had threatened to kill a congressman. (According to the congressman, the police, and the feds, they had.) They could break into your house and find fifty pounds of Tide in your washroom and haul you in for being "a fucking anarchist." That was the kind of thing the bad guys did, and they were doing it now, and as far as John was concerned, "I'll tell anybody to their fucking face right now that if they know what's going on in America today, and they don't do anything about it, they're a traitor and they should be treated as a traitor." Still, John took heart from knowing that this time, finally, the Patriots were ready. Brian had just been talking about some Patriots *he* knew, in Anacortes, who'd already bought two helicopters and a stockpile of guns and ammo that filled a room the size of Ed's garage. That meant two helicopters and a lot more guns for the Washington State Militia, because Anacortes's Patriots were going to sign on soon. Brian said so, and John not only seconded that but added, "There's *more* people that Brian doesn't even know about, less than a mile away from his house, and that's the way it's going to stay."

Every now and again, one of the men would make an attempt to catch John lying. The militiaman named Mark, the one who'd joined around the time Ed had, tried asking John why he had gone to the men in Mark's squad, behind his back, and accused him of spying for the sheriff. John said that he hadn't accused Mark, he'd accused Jack Schleimer. Marlin said no, it was Mark; Marlin had been there himself and heard it. The men waited for an answer, and a minute later John said "Okay," and the subject was closed. Nothing that night seemed to rattle John, though he was certainly rattled later. Perhaps he had figured that a need-to-know silence was his best defense, or perhaps he was so frightened in his hot seat that he'd simply stopped hearing. Not even Rock was able

to break through his unnerving calm. Rock tried asking for his
orders; he was the new guy and wanted to know what, specif-
ically, he had to do if the chain of command broke down—if,
say, the feds killed Daiwee before Daiwee had a chance to dig
up the 150 pounds of TNT that John had told them was ear-
marked for the Washington State Militia. "There's other people who know where everything is, and I'm not going to sit
here and tell you names," John said, and that was all he said.
Once, he suggested that the men stop focusing on Daiwee and
start thinking about buying shortwave radios and burying
their *own* weapons and learning the kinds of things Daiwee
already knew. He doubted that any of them knew how to use
their own sweat to detonate a stick of dynamite, but Daiwee
knew. He said to remember Vietnam, where soldiers cut off
from their companies had "had to rely on their shit, they had
to rely on their knowledge, their expertise to get their ass out
of that bind," and never mind Rock saying that the soldiers in
Nam had radios *and* call numbers, whereas the men in Alpha
One could go out and buy a hundred radios and still have no
one to call for reinforcements. "There's no finger pointing
here," John told him. And as for Fred, who said that if just a
few people in the leadership squad (it didn't have to be more
than two or three, and it didn't have to include him) knew
where the ordnance was "it would ease the tensions," John
thought Fred should concentrate on the things he could handle, like having another yard sale. Yard sales were important.
Anything that made money for the group was important.
John himself was planning to start a militia company that
specialized in selling "small, compact, emergency survival
equipment," the kind of equipment you could keep in your
car or your boat in case the war started when you were on the

road. He even had a name for the company: Northwest Survival. It may be that he was thinking about his own survival, because he knew for a fact that Janet Reno had offered a $100,000 bounty for information that led to the arrest of militia leaders like him. By then, of course—what with a bounty on John's head and a female attorney general as big as Debbie for him to worry about—it should have been clear to the men that the only serious complaints were John's. John's wife had defected. The man who manufactured his "Don't tread on me" badges had stopped accepting orders. (It was a misunderstanding, having to do with 250 badges and the fake credit card that John had used to pay for them.) John was not only broke, he was at the mercy of his "donators." He was sorry to disappoint young Marlin, who wanted to know why the tanks he'd promised them hadn't come rolling into Whatcom County, but "it just hasn't worked out." Northwest Survival was definitely the way to go if you wanted money for a tank. John Trochmann, he said, had made over $8,000 selling survival gear and manuals at the Washington State Militia's Fife meeting, while the militia itself, with nothing of its own to peddle, had made a grand total of $184. It was worth thinking about that.

THE MEETING LASTED for at least an hour after John drove home, and in the end the only thing the militiamen agreed on was that they hadn't learned anything from John at all. Some of the old-timers—not Ed or Rock, but the men who had known him for a few years—still blamed the lasers for his strange behavior. Some blamed the Seattle Freemen. Fred, for one, had come right out and told John he didn't want people like John Kirk at meetings in Whatcom County. "The guy is a fucking jerk. That's the God honest truth. . . . He's dangerous," Fred had said. "Worse than a skinhead." Fred didn't like the way Kirk kept talking about "kill a Jew this and kill a Jew that"; he didn't like Kirk, period. Even Marlin allowed that Kirk was "scary." He said that Kirk and his Freemen friends had once told him that Jews were children of the anti-Christ, and they had talked about killing blacks, too. "Let's kill them all," Kirk had said, and to Marlin that was a lot different from killing feds. The feds deserved it. They were already killing Patriots in six states, and they were planning to "do a biological"—John had said so—at the Olympic Games in Atlanta that summer. Thousands of people were going to die then; Clinton would have the excuse he wanted to cancel the next elections, and when that happened he and David Rockefeller would own the world. Marlin had agreed with John about the situation in Atlanta. Brian had brought up Atlanta, but it was John who'd had the strategy: once the elections were cancelled, John was going to take them "up to the hills like I told you, for fourteen days. We're going to get into gear and then we're going to come back down and then we're going to tear some ass." By "some ass," he meant the "world citizens" (he'd described them to me as "the five hundred families of the elite") who didn't think twice about wasting four or five million people "just to get their way." For a few minutes, John had taken over his own hot-seat meeting, and anyone listening to him then would have had to admit that he sounded almost like his old self. He had fired questions at them: What were those stories he'd heard about the men renting a Bellingham office? (One man told him it wasn't true; the office they'd wanted had been too expensive.) He had made suggestions:

There was a place in Deming that rented for half the price. He had given advice: Don't buy Chinese ammo; it was cheap but it got your gun dirty. He had even shared some intel: Did they know about the Belgian troops shipping into Fort Lewis and the Russian brass settling into condos near Mount Baker?

Still, that wasn't the intel they wanted, and John himself hadn't confessed to anything, though it has to be said no one seemed to expect he would. The most rueful thing John had said, leaving his hot seat for the drive out to his empty house, was this: "There's no guarantees. When you're in a miltia, your ass is whistling in the wind. . . . all we're doing is we're doing the best we can." And if some of the men felt sorry for him then, those men were in the minority. Rock thought John had been very clear. John had asked for their money, and they had nothing to show for it now. They were on their own. "Oh, Daiwee will call you! Yeah, I'm supposed to buy that," was what Rock said. "Yeah, fuck that, I don't trust the mother-fucker" was Marlin's view. There wasn't really anything left to discuss except whether or not you trusted John. A few militia-men made desultory plans to get together later in the week and buy a metal detector and comb the land near Hannegan's Pass for the cache of combat rifles, but those were the ones who believed there actually were rifles. Most of the men had pretty much given up on John by then. They hoped he was scared—"I bet he's fucking in his boots," Marlin said, and no one disputed that—and figured he'd probably leave the county that night, or the next morning at the latest. They as-sumed he'd be heading south, to his Freemen friends near Seattle, looking for suckers, looking for sympathy, telling the Freemen they were *all* moles up in Whatcom County. Some of them still wanted to take John out but there really was only one man smart enough to it without getting arrested, or killed himself, and Rock didn't volunteer. Rock wasn't interested in John. He was interested in John's weapons, and Ed must have agreed with him, because a few days later Ed called Command Central, discovered that John was still around, and tried to stroke him for information. He told John about the new Bellingham headquarters. He wanted to say how sorry he was to have lied before, how sorry he was not to have come right out and told John about the wonderful new place that was sitting there waiting for John to finish his R and R. He talked about trust and troublemakers and about the two of them being straight and sharing with each other from then on, but John wasn't sharing, maybe because Brian had driven out to Valley Highway, right after the meeting ended, and told him everything the men had said about him when he wasn't there. John was understanding. He allowed that Fred was feeling "a little bit jilted," and that he probably should have gone over and talked to Fred and made him feel wanted—or at least let Fred know "how lucky he was that I didn't punch . . . his fucking lights out." He even allowed that it was time to think about cutting short his R and R and stepping back into the leadership, especially now that Ed admitted that "me and Gary can't run this thing." "We've tried," Ed told him. "We don't have the ability to do it, neither one of us. We're not, I hate to say it—I'm not leadership material." Ed was so humble on the telephone that he even offered to show the headquarters to John that day. But John said no, he couldn't make it, he'd be gone in a few hours, he couldn't say where, just that he'd be "flitting around here and there, trying to pull this together, pull that together," and "meeting with a lot of people," and getting ready for his big debate with Bill Wassmuth, the head of the Northwest Coalition Against Malicious Harassment, and doing the various kinds of important things that leaders do. Ed tried calling again, about a week later, but by then John had already spent a week at his sister's house, where he'd had the time and the coddling to be able to think things over, and he had worked himself into such a rage against his treacherous friends that he was very nearly incoherent. He railed against Fred, and against Marlin, and against everyone else who was "gonna get us fucking killed," digging up ordnance. But he never forgot his need-to-know or produced the names and numbers and directions Ed wanted, not even when Ed talked him into paying a visit to the new office, and he was confronted with an unmarked map of Whatcom County on the wall. It was after that visit that the men began to discuss killing John in earnest. Marlin liked the idea of wiring John's teeth first, to make him talk, because wiring teeth was the example John himself often used, and then finishing him off with something quiet—maybe a cyanide dart. Fred, who didn't have anything to wire John's teeth *to*, offered his ax and his hunting knife for the interrogation. He thought that the best way to make John talk would be to cut off his fingers, joint by joint, and then his hand. You'd need the ax for the hand, he said, "and then, ah, well, you have to kill him afterwards." It was the afternoon of July 27th, and he and Rock and a few of the men were sitting around in the new office, talking. He may have been hoping Rock would do it. It's likely that they all were.

Ten

JOHN HAD TOLD Debbie that it was time to "get the hell out of Dodge." It was what he always said when his life took an unpleasant turn. He didn't go to the movies much, and his taste, as he described it to me, was "science fiction," not Westerns. The one movie he had recommended to his men was Fritz Lang's *Metropolis,* although he knew you couldn't call that "fiction" any more than you could call the New World Order fiction. To John, the only difference between Lang's Metropolis and Whatcom County was that it was still a lot easier to leave the county, at least on a day when no one slashed your tires or arrived at your door with a warrant in one hand and a loaded Glock in the other. Perhaps, by July of 1996, Dodge City didn't count as fiction, either—not even his own fiction of the feds careering down Valley Highway in sinister black cars and John the Militiaman placing a

191

few well-aimed shots before he got into his pickup and disappeared, heroic, in a cloud of dust, never looking back, into the kind of sunset that glowed on the free, the just, and the brave. On men like him. John may have been ready to stand his ground in the big battle, the way it told you to do in the Second Amendment of the Constitution of the "true" United States, but when it came to the small battles, the little mutinies of disappointed or misguided men, he preferred to take his potshots, leave Dodge, and save himself.

By then, of course, the people likely to come careering down Valley Highway were a lot more worrisome to John than the agents of the New World Order, and even Debbie allowed that, for once, John was right about Dodge. "Get the hell out of Dodge, John! It's too scary," she told him, straight off, when she drove out to the house to clean a few days after the hot-seat meeting, and discovered him holed up, talking about how his own men were going to kill him. According to Brian, they had taken a vote—the voting was Fred's idea, Brian said; it was the American way—and now the word was definitely out. As Debbie saw things, it was now, "Snuff John!" She packed him off to Bothell on July 15th, and, by her own account, the next thing she knew it was Sunday the 28th and the phone rang and she got the message that John had been arrested at five on Saturday. No one called Maryann Fisher. All *she* knew when the press got to her on Monday was that Fred had left on Saturday for a meeting, and that she hadn't seen or heard from him since then. Fred's meeting turned out to have been a bomb-making class in the new headquarters, and Fred was arrested there, in the company of Marlin, Gary, John Kirk, and two other Seattle Freemen named William Smith and Richard Frank Burton, at the same moment Cathy Fahey was crossing John's lawn. I don't know if anyone thought of calling Judy Carol Kirk, and in the event she was picked up herself that afternoon, at home in Tukwila, and saw her husband at their hearing. The Washington State Militia got a lot of publicity in the course of those first few days, what with the news photos and the television clips of the eight defendants being led, in handcuffs and shackles, into the federal courthouse. But if you believed the gossip at the Bellingham police station, Fred and his friends were *already* in handcuffs when the feds broke into their bomb class, making their showdown something of an anticlimax—less thrilling, certainly, than the militiamen would have wanted. The gossip was that Rock Jackson, hoping to end the class with a small surprise, something he thought might amuse the men, had decided to teach them a trick for getting out of locked handcuffs. The men held out their hands. They weren't suspicious, or even surprised that Rock had thought to bring so many pairs of handcuffs to a class on pipe bombs. Rock always came up with the right ordnance at the right time. Rifles for Gary to work on. Explosives for Marlin to mix. The big new headquarters they were in now. And that, supposedly, was how the feds found them—neatly cuffed and waiting for Rock's instructions. "Arrested without incident," the U.S. Attorney's office said, though it was arguably not without incident to Judy Kirk, who arrived at the holding pen still smarting from the embarrassment of leaving a bomb squad ("hazardous materials team," the papers said) parked on her street in plain view of the neighbors' windows.

Rock himself went to his office, wrote his report, and eventually got a haircut. Rock was a suit. His real name was Michael Eric German, and his credentials as Mike German included a law degree from Northwestern, a decade at the Federal Bureau of Investigation, a talent for impersonation, and a very good track record at the Bureau's Boston headquarters, where he was posted as an undercover agent when he got the assignment to go underground in Whatcom County. As for Ed Mauerer, who had been spirited away at some time during the bust—and was at first thought to be suffering in one of the New World Order's torture chambers—Ed turned out to be no one but himself. Ed was a paid informer, or, as the Bureau called him, a "cooperating witness." He had offered his services to Ramon during a stint in the Whatcom County jail, figuring that the gossip he was picking up from the other prisoners might be worth something, maybe enough to start paying off the money he owed on his bad checks. It was more than enough. After a modest start, informing on the local gangsters (the Lantises and six other suspected "crime ring" members, a militiaman among them, were arrested in a Bellingham police sting that same Saturday), Ed joined the militia, with an eye to extending his benefits. Ed wasn't always accurate. He had a tendency to exaggerate and, given his interest in keeping Ramon happy, to invent, as the feds began to suspect when his descriptions of the "arsenal" in John's garage grew more and more slapdash and extravagant. Eventually, he had to agree to polygraphs to keep the job, but in the end he was $25,000 richer than he had been when Ramon took him on. As Ed saw things, it was a fair exchange.

The militia sting was the biggest news to hit Whatcom County since the environmentalists got the pasture on the Hardys' farm classified as a habitat, and Jerry Hardy had to stop culling his trees and grazing his cows near his own stream. Even John was impressed by the number of people who had spent their time trying to bring him down—not just federal agents and Bellingham policemen but, as the papers said, dozens of men and women from the Bureau of Alcohol, Tobacco, and Firearms, the Puget Sound Violent Crime Task Force, the King County Police Department, the Tukwila Police and Fire Department, the Fort Lewis Army Explosives Ordnance Disposal Unit, and, of course, the Whatcom County sheriff's office (though the orders to Sheriff Brandland seem to have been to stay at his desk and avoid any temptation to try to lend a hand). For a while, John was almost famous. There were so many stories about him in the papers that his sister Sheila pasted them in a scrapbook, just to keep the clips organized. Even Susan, in Bothell, started a scrapbook. The family would leaf through it, like the photograph album from a good vacation, and reminisce about the highlights. John, in shackles, hopping his way to a paddy wagon, after that first hearing at the district courthouse. (He said later that he'd been signaling "kangaroo," as in "kangaroo court.") Debbie, wiping her eyes, and whispering, "I'm worried to death about John." John telling reporters, "Our job is to save lives, not take lives!" You could read about John Pitner in Bellingham, in New York, in London, all over the world. It was sad, of course, that the headline on the front page of the *New York Times* had said "Terrorism . . . Going Homespun," and that the story beneath it called John a "house painter" instead of a Patriot leader and described the case as "like Ozzie and Harriet go to terrorism school." But you had to admit that there was also John's neighbor, Sharon, calling him a family man, "middle class, very clean," right in the first sentence of a page-one story in the house organ of the New World Order. "That kind of got to you, right here," Sheila once said to me, pounding her heart.

John, by law, had been allowed to make one phone call. He couldn't reach Debbie and he couldn't find Rachel, so he dialed a militiaman with a message machine and that was it. There was no war. Whatever John had expected, militias across America did not go on "tac-4 alert." And it was a while before the family even heard from John Trochmann. His brother Dave Trochmann, who was said to be more involved with the Christian Identity church and the Aryan Nations than with the militia movement, eventually made a statement about John Pitner being "a real personable kind of guy," and very involved in helping flood victims. And Trochmann himself did appear in Washington a few weeks later, to speak at a "John Pitner Defense Fund" rally in Wenatchee. But the Militia of Montana didn't march on Seattle in John's defense. Defending John Pitner turned out to be Debbie's job, and she went into action as soon as she heard what happened. She collected Rachel and Sheila and drove them straight to the local news studio, Channel 12, to demand a hearing. She was so angry, so shaken by the injustice of it all, that even the station manager had to tell her, "Hey, you weren't the one arrested!" But he put the family on the news that night, and most of Bellingham saw them, heads high and eyes teary, talking about their faith in John and in John's innocence—which to Debbie's mind helped make up for the humiliation of being turned away at the door when the Bellingham Police held a press conference about the eight arrests, and then of going to her office to find that someone had left the *Herald* propped on her desk, with John's picture on the front page.

It may be that Debbie had found her element, that she was even happy, talking for John without having to listen to John talk to her. She saw to everything. On Sunday, she drove to Bothell with Rachel and, according to Susan, collected an old, locked trailer that John had left in a gulch below her house two weeks earlier. (Susan had wondered what was in it, but John certainly didn't say, and in the event, she figured it would be empty by the time Debbie brought it home.) On Monday, Debbie drove to Seattle for John's first hearing, dismissed his lawyer—the court had appointed him, but according to Debbie he hadn't even seen the charges—and then she got on the phone to find a new lawyer willing to take the case. It helped having such a large family, because the odds were that even one as visibly limited as the Pitners included *somebody* with the name of a lawyer whose Constitution didn't start and stop at the Second Amendment (like the Patriot lawyers Trochmann always recommended), a lawyer who knew something about the First Amendment, and would see that John's best defense was his right to speak his mind freely in the United States and not his right to collect weapons of war in Whatcom County. John, by his own reckoning, had twelve "brothers and sisters"—for family purposes, he always added the Reece siblings to Dick Pitner's brood of children and stepchildren—and sometimes twice that, if he was figuring in the present batch of wives, husbands, and what Debbie called the "fiancés." Ordinarily, the "brother" for Debbie to have asked would have been the policeman in Mountlake Terrace who was married to John's stepsister and who in some ways qualified as the most successful, not to mention best-connected, "Pitner." But it was hard to imagine that a good cop, as he was said to be, was going to want to have anything to do with the man who had

spent the last few years boasting of him as "big-time FBI"—
the brother who was feeding him David Rockefeller's secret
war plans. So Debbie went straight to John's half-brother Joey
Pitner, the youngest of Dick's sons and the one child that he
and Dorothy Two had produced together. Joe, in turn, called
his fiancée, Jackie, an occasional bailiff who served papers for
some of the big Seattle law firms, and the result was that two
days after his arrest, John Pitner found himself represented by
a forty-three-year-old partner in a law firm with offices on the
twenty-first floor of a glass tower, a suitably impressive view
out over Elliott Bay, and nothing more incendiary in its waiting room than a book on Dutch marine painting in the seven-
teenth century. The lawyer's name was James Lobsenz, and
his background was as far as you could get from Whatcom
County: Westport, Connecticut; Andover; Stanford; Berkeley's
Boalt Hall; and a year at Harvard on the way to his law degree. He had been raised as a Quaker by a Congregationalist
mother and a Jewish father who wrote for *Playboy* and the
Reader's Digest. He had made his name with a couple of landmark death-row and gay-rights cases: five death-row cases in
all and one case involving a gay colonel named Margarethe
Cammermeyer, who (as his colleagues told you right away) became the subject of a television movie starring Glenn Close.
And when he took on John as a client he may have been hoping
for another kind of landmark case, one he could argue up to
the Supreme Court, though he told me, in October, that to him
United States v. John Irvin Pitner et al. was just a bread-and-
butter case, a simple matter of "Do you believe the government's proof?" It was the kind of case a criminal lawyer "was
paid to do." He said that the only real question he had about

United States v. John Irvin Pitner et al. was what John meant
by "cluster fuck," a term that had shown up in the tape transcripts. Lobsenz didn't know what a cluster fuck was. He had
thought of looking it up in his *Oxford English Dictionary*, but
he didn't imagine he'd find it, and in any event, whatever it did
mean, he never doubted John's First Amendment right to say
"cluster fuck" whenever it pleased him. "It's sort of a paradox,
me representing the head of the militia," he told me that same
day, referring to the framed American Civil Liberties Union
award hanging behind his desk, and to the Human Rights Day
award from the United Nations Association, and to the eight
pages devoted to one of his cases in a book called *No Contest*,
by Ralph Nader. He meant, of course, that it wasn't a paradox
at all.

Debbie liked Jim Lobsenz. She found him comical—he was
as tall as she was, and rail thin—with his knees and elbows
poking out of rumpled, baggy, blue suits that were really a
little drab when you compared them to John's snappy, speckled
sports jackets. But, as she said later, he was smart. He seemed
to agree with her when she said, "John's nuts, but not *that*
nuts." And he didn't talk much; she liked that, too. She could
see he was "real focused, real deep in thought." He wasn't
interested—not after he'd met them—in getting Patriots like
Brian or Jack or even Doc Ellwanger to appear as witnesses to
John's good character. According to Debbie, he found them
much nuttier than John, and according to Lobsenz himself, his
real concern was keeping John's Patriot friends *out* of court,
since they were not necessarily the sort of people you called on
to impress a jury. They hadn't been charged; there was no evidence against them and, under the law, no just cause to indict

them. But they liked the idea of attention, and it seemed to me that the ones I met that fall and winter were waiting by the phone, feeling, as Doc Ellwanger said, "rejected."

In fact, Jim Lobsenz wasn't much interested in what anyone, even Debbie, had to say about John's character. What interested him was whether the state could prove that John Pitner had sold a machine gun to Gary Kuehnoel (which was one of the charges against John), or that John Pitner had conspired against the government of the United States with Fred Fisher and Marlin Mack (which was another charge), or that he had taken part in the "manufacture and possession of explosive devices." There were nine defendants in *United States v. John Irvin Pitner et al.*, once the prosecutors decided to add the chimney sweep Ted Carter, and six counts of indictment that the government would undoubtedly add to (and did). It was Lobsenz's opinion that John had to be separated, in the jury's mind, from anyone—in or out of jail—who might be guilty of anything worse than an enthusiasm for the kind of language you couldn't find in the *Oxford English Dictionary,* unabridged. John could legitimately claim to have been on leave from the militia since the end of May, and, whatever his involvement still was with the Seattle Freemen, it didn't take more than five minutes in his company to see that if he'd kept on introducing himself in public as the "director of the Washington State Militia"—the way he had at his Seattle debate, a week before the arrest—it was vanity or even fantasy but "not," as he told the family, "my job description anymore."

Of course, it would have been hard for anyone to say what, exactly, John's job description was during those last two months of the militia sting. He never stopped seeing his Seattle Freemen, a group whose own job descriptions were unnerving. John Kirk turned out to be one of the founders of a Snohomish "Justus Township," like the Justus Township in Montana, and before moving south to the Seattle suburbs, he had presided over a "common law court" of the sort that issued bogus sovereign-citizens' liens and judgments against officers of the real courts. (The practice had come to be wildly popular in the Patriot movement, where there were people eager to invest as shareholders in liens that they knew would produce a windfall when the government fell and Patriots took back the United States.) Kirk didn't work—he seems to have had a job years earlier, repairing television sets for J. C. Penney, and he lived on disability checks now—but in other respects he resembled Fred Fisher. He looked a little like Fred, and, like Fred, he had a loyal wife, a couple of doting daughters, and a handful of grandchildren. He also had a record quite similar to Fred's record: a statutory-rape conviction, from 1980, involving his daughters as very young girls. And while neither record was admissible as evidence in *United States v. John Irvin Pitner et al.*, it helped to explain why Kirk, like Fred, harbored a grudge against the government whose definition of Christian family values had proven to be a lot less intimate than his own. On the other hand, not much was known about Kirk's follower and fellow Freeman, Richard Burton, beyond the fact that he had a wife named Caitlin, two children, and a job as a quality-control inspector for Boeing, which was unusual mainly in that it made him the only one of the Freemen who worked. William Smith, whose real name turned out to be Tracy Lee Brown, had been a fugitive since the 1980s, wanted by the police for contempt of a court order to file his income tax forms, and unlikely to reply to that order now, since the only court whose authority he recognized was the common-law court in his own Justus County, in Seattle. Brown—or Smith, or, occasionally, "Stanton"—was a prophet in the manner of John Trochmann. He had the same white beard and hard blue eyes, but not, unhappily for him, the same cash cow of a survival catalog. Brown didn't even have an address; he moved around and carried no papers except his sovereign-citizen papers and a counterfeit driver's license. Nor did he have any known income beyond the pocket money he claimed to have made mowing lawns—though it was certainly possible that somewhere along the way he had cashed in on his title as "administrative trustee" of a fake bank called "the International Commercial Bank of Sweitzerland, Montana," which indeed sold shares in liens against government officials, and a fake "charitable trust" devoted to disaster relief, medical research, and to exposing the Anti-Defamation League of the B'nai B'rith as an agent of the Federal Reserve. What Brown did have was a high reputation on the lunatic fringe. His banking partners had at one time or another been involved with nearly every hate group to emerge in Washington since the war, and according to David Neiwert's book, *In God's Country,* his commentaries on the Bible and the Constitution had been the occasional highlight of Seattle's public-access television hate shows.

Charged in a conspiracy with friends like the Seattle Freemen, John was in some ways a civil libertarian's dream client (though this was not an assumption Lobsenz would ever have admitted to me). His case involved so many complicated and engaging issues: issues of free speech; issues of Second Amendment interpretation; issues of entrapment arising from the indisputable fact that the feds had supplied not only the safe house but a good deal of the matériel that made their sting successful; and issues of conspiracy which, almost by definition, were difficult to prove, or disprove. And the complications were exponential, when you considered that every defendant's brief was going to be different, with Lobsenz very likely making a First Amendment argument, and Marlin's lawyer a Second Amendment one, and Gary's lawyer arguing entrapment and Fred's arguing that there was no conspiracy to begin with —and those were only the four militiamen's lawyers. John Kirk was refusing to agree to a plea, even an innocent plea, with *his* lawyer, on "religious grounds." And Tracy Lee Brown wouldn't even talk to his lawyer. (He'd refused counsel on what he called constitutional grounds, but inasmuch as he'd also refused to speak in his own defense, the court had had to appoint one.) On the other hand, from the prosecutors' perspective there was the issue of "clear and present danger," at least as it applied to a group of Patriot zealots who hadn't actually blown up anything but included the kind of people who kept bombs in the barbecue; zealots who hadn't harmed or killed anybody either but talked about little else and, at the time of their arrest, were discussing how to kill their own leader and maybe even counting on an undercover agent of the FBI to do it for them. What happened to the Washington State Militia was in some ways a classic sting, but if the enticements were a little obvious and the arrests, as it could be argued, a little premature, it could also be argued that you didn't have much choice if you were Mike German and believed you were going to get an offer you could not refuse.

Of course, in August of 1996, not many people in Whatcom County knew much more about the sting than what they read in the paper. No one even knew the name of the militiaman who had fed the FBI its information. The court documents cited Ed Mauerer only as "the cooperating witness" —sometimes it was "the confidential witness"—and while it didn't take long for the men in jail to figure out who that co-operating witness was, if for no reason other than that Ed wasn't in jail with them, it took a defense motion to compel the federal prosecutor's office actually to release his name so that the defense, along with everyone else, could begin to piece together what had happened and, more important, how it happened. The militia, or what was left of it, went under-ground, but the silence was broken and people seemed less uneasy, and a good number of militiamen—they preferred "ex-militiamen"—decided to take their distance, publicly at least, from John. For a while, they kept the local militia watchers busy. Cathy Logg got to begin a special militia series for the *Bellingham Herald;* she said that even her boss, the Gannett stalwart known to his staff for a reluctance to offend or upset anyone who read the paper, had to accept that John Pitner was a big story. Paul de Armond got to stay up all night, every night, digging into the background of a cast of increas-ingly unpleasant characters for the edification of the hun-dreds of other researchers and rights advocates on his e-mail network: there was that much demand. And so many lawyers and investigators and reporters were spotted, parked along Whatcom County's winding roads, maps in hand, trying to locate the house of a militiaman or, for that matter, of some-one, anyone, who knew John Pitner that the people they didn't visit felt neglected. Jack Schleimer had to admit that the visit *he'd* had from John's lawyer gave him a certain stand-ing in Whatcom's Christian circles. Jack called it "our initial confrontation," though it was in fact their only confronta-tion, and when I saw Jack, a month later, he was starting to

wonder why Jim Lobsenz had been so unreceptive to his
views. He thought that Jim had missed a real educational op-
portunity, asking questions that had mainly to do with things
like whether he'd ever seen an "arsenal" of weapons in John's
garage. "Lobsenz [had] seemed like a nice guy," Jack told me.
So nice that Jack had been willing to go to Seattle to testify on
John's behalf—depending, naturally, on "what the circumstances were." Not that he'd forgotten how much John had
hurt him, spreading those rumors about him informing when
all along it was Ed doing the informing. Of course, he was
angry at Ed. He had never suspected Ed. He had even called to
warn Ed as soon as he heard that some of the men were arrested. But he was much angrier at John. Could anyone say for
sure that John Pitner wasn't a federal agent? Had anyone actually seen John Pitner in jail? John hadn't been saved, like
Jack, he didn't have God to guide him, so it wasn't surprising
that he'd had no scruples about confusing the group with his
"Hegelian dialectics," saying one thing one day and another
the next and keeping the men "in a state of paranoia and crisis," primed for the attack that never came. Judie Ellwanger
said pretty much the same thing when I visited *her*. "I saw the
writing on the wall, way back then, yes I did," she told me,
looking as pleased with herself as one of the pretty kittens in
the posters on Doc Ellwanger's waiting room wall. John was
an asshole. If John had listened to Judie, way back when, he
and the boys wouldn't be locked up now, and Judie wouldn't
be left with the responsibility of having to write them letters;
she couldn't see Debbie Pitner writing letters, not even to
John, whose face was always in the papers. She even showed
me her dog-eared copy of the "Rights of Prisoners" handbook. It was an American Civil Liberties Union publication,

but Judie was willing to overlook that if it meant the boys were fed properly and got their exercise time. Judie had to look after them all now, and it was John's fault. "I told him and I told him and I told him, 'Check into [Ed's] background,' " but John had been so busy being "Mr. Leadershit," the guy who could call Seattle and get $5,000 for ammunition, that he took it as a big patriotic gesture when Ed promised him guns, goggles, grenades, whatever he wanted, "at one-millionth of the price." Judie liked to imitate John, listening to Ed talk prices, rubbing his hands and thinking, "Oh boy!" John was definitely an asshole. He was the only one she wasn't looking after, and it had nothing to do with the fact that Jim Lobsenz had called Doc Ellwanger after *their* visit and told him to stay away. She had done her best for Gary, more than her best, since "it took an act of Congress just to get him an undershirt" in jail. She had even done her best for Fred, and that wasn't easy, either. Fred's lawyer had paid them a visit, too— and fled, or, as Judie put it, "couldn't get out of here fast enough." Judie was still determined to get to the bottom of those ridiculous rumors about Fred, including the one that he had "cannibalistic tendencies," just because he'd tried to lighten the mood at his hearing and told the judge that none of the Fisher kids would get on a plane with him, knowing that if it came down to it he'd eat the whole family to survive. Judie knew that Fred was a good person. According to Judie, even his stepdaughter said that what happened when she was seven "was more *her* fault." It was John whom Judie resented; and even Doc Ellwanger, who had something nice to say about everyone, thought that John had made them all look bad. Doc Ellwanger hadn't even tried to visit John, and he was usually so responsible about doing his duty and visiting Patriots in jail. (The day I met Doc, he'd been on his way to the county jail, on the off chance that there was somebody there who needed talk and comfort, or wanted advice about filing a lien against the sheriff who had locked him up, as Doc himself had.)

In the end, the only militiaman who really stood up for John was Brian. Brian wanted me to know that John wouldn't have lifted a finger against anyone, that the best way to describe John Pitner was "like a pacifist." He told me he'd offered to testify for John, but it would have been more accurate to have said that he'd offered to argue the case himself. To Brian's mind, the government had kidnapped John. He knew, even if none of the lawyers did, that "kidnapping people on private property is an act of war," and he didn't believe the evidence the government claimed to have gathered anyway. He had never seen that evidence, but he had "proof" that the government's tapes were doctored, that even the videos it had shot, secretly, in the new headquarters were doctored. "If the military is going to give us anything we need, why would we be playing around with pipe bombs that can blow up in your face?" he asked me. The truth, according to Brian, was that there was no case against John Pitner and his men; *United States v. John Irvin Pitner et al.* was simply a thank-you note from Janet Reno to Ramon Garcia, who Brian believed had "coordinated" for Reno "down in Waco." Brian had warned John, too. He had checked out Ed and knew that Ed was a crook—in the business, he said, of doing "hits and arsons" for bigger crooks (though he couldn't say what hits and arsons). He hadn't been able to check out the man he still called

Rock, not completely, but he was willing to swear that Rock had tried to get *him* to convert his best "sporterized" AK-47 back into an automatic and had even offered him $700 for it. He had had to lay down the law to Rock: "Cease and desist any more illegal activities" was what he'd said. Rock had arrived in Whatcom with so much "stuff"—survival meals, military radios, "anything you can imagine"—and Brian had looked at that stuff and known right away that it was all junk, the kind of surplus the military threw away and then the feds picked up for making stings. He'd gone to a couple of classes at the new headquarters, and it was clear that something fishy was going on, because Ed or Mike—he didn't remember which one—had told him to leave his weapon at the door, in a steel box, and he'd had to remind them that Patriots didn't give orders like that to other Patriots. Patriots trusted one another. "I trust everybody here," Brian had said, "and I expect they trust me not to pull out my gun and kill somebody."

Eleven

JEFF MARGOLIS, at Everybody's Store, came from
Brooklyn, and he took a cautionary view of what he considered my New York attitude. He said that calling people
like John Pitner—or, for that matter, Doc Ellwanger or Ben
Hinkle—crazy, the way I did when I dropped by Everybody's
to talk, was "being a New Yorker," because in Whatcom
County someone like John was "just another local yokel."
Jeff's motto, through twenty-six years of life as the proprietor of a Whatcom County general store, had always been,
"Who's not an asshole? It's not hard to see what the other
guy's up against." And while it seemed to me that the same
thing could also be said of Brooklyn, there was some truth to
his theory that "John Pitner's behavior is the local behavior
writ large." People were all a little weird in Whatcom County,
including, by his own admission, Jeff Margolis. That was the

beauty of the place and, of course, the problem. Jeff put it this way: "People have beliefs, but you have to keep on inter-acting. It's called denial."

Jeff was an opinionated, old-fashioned, generous, Jewish radical, a devotee of Durkheim, Bergson, and Wilhelm Reich, a man who had once offered the farm boys at Whatcom Com-munity College a course in political thought called "Plato to NATO." He liked to say that the reason he referred to himself as the I. F. Stone of Van Zandt was all the lost causes to his credit. He could talk your ear off about everything from or-gone energy (he was for it) to nuclear energy (he was against it) to how to put a little *Gemeinschaft* back into the *Gesell-schaft* that was modern life. When Jeff arrived in the county, in 1970, he was a sometime doctoral student with a master's degree in political philosophy, a thesis on "theories of mass society" to finish, a wife and a small daughter to support, and the stubborn certainty that there were no real academic prospects for a noisy dissident in the America where, as he put it, "Cambodia had happened, Kent State had happened." He owned, by his accounting, the clothes on his back, the money in his pocket, and the old milk truck in which the family had crossed the continent, looking for some better America. When they came to the Bellingham exit of the Interstate 5, they turned right, as much by accident as intention, and saw the snow on the mountains, and the sun on the snow, and of course they kept going and ended up on Valley Highway, not far from the land where John eventually put his house, in front of a ramshackle general store with a "For Sale" sign on the front door and a thousand dollars in groceries on the shelves. They stopped, and stayed. A few mornings after they had the place patched, painted, and scrubbed down, they discovered the words "Fuck you, hippies!" written in excrement on the front wall. Jeff was offended—"I was no hippie, I was a *radical*," he told me—but in his opinion it could have been a lot worse. It could have been "something deep-seated, like 'Fuck you, Jew.' " That was life in Whatcom County: whatever happened, you were grateful that it wasn't worse. The best you could do was exercise a modest caution. When Jeff, inevitably, got into local politics—his first cause was killing the plan for a nuclear power plant, just over the border in Skagit County—he was threatened so convincingly that he "started sleeping with my gun." By the 1980s, with fugitives from The Order rumored to be hiding in Whatcom County, he had three guns, one of them a Magnum, and by the 1990s, with John Pitner on Valley Highway, chasing sunbathers off the south fork beach, he had come to the conclusion that "if everyone's a gunslinger, maybe you're going to be less scared of the guy with a gun."

The first time I saw John after his arrest—on a Sunday morning early in October, during visitors' hours at the Kent jail—he was talking about going home. The court had denied his first bail motion, but that was August, when everything was confused. This time they were ready. Debbie had got their house and their ten acres appraised at $140,000; John had got the papers he needed to quit-claim his half of the property to Debbie at a new hearing; and what with that property and Susan and Betsey's house as collateral, not to mention John's exemplary behavior and recent "promotion" to the jail bakery, there was a good chance that he would soon be released and put under monitored house arrest, pending trial. John was excited, though he didn't really know why he couldn't go home to Valley Highway, or why Debbie, having lived for twenty-two years with John's "little bit of a hero thing," was no longer in the mood for heroes. Debbie told me that every nut in Whatcom County would be at her doorstep if John came home. She didn't want the responsibility and she didn't want the conversation and she didn't want John wandering down to Everybody's and picking a fight with someone about David Rockefeller or the beach association. In the event, Debbie wasn't a promising candidate for the job of John's keeper, since the prosecution had plans to indict her and did indict her, on November 13th, on charges of giving "false testimony" as to whether she had or had not slept through Ted Carter's sparkler-bomb demonstrations. John's father wasn't a promising candidate, either, being old and ill. And, judging from the messages Dick had started posting on the Internet in John's defense, the nuts were already on *his* doorstep. John's brother Richard, in his trailer on Lake Samish, certainly wasn't a candidate. John's sister Sheila, in *her* trailer, wasn't a candidate, despite the print she'd hung—rosebuds with the legend "Sisters are for sharing and caring"—and the enormous flag, "my Fourth of July flag," flying hopefully from her deck "in solidarity with John." Not even Rachel, who had a paying job at a print shop, a real house, and a Juice Man juicer ("for fiber," she said) to recommend her, was likely to inspire confidence at a bail hearing. Rachel adored her father. She would probably have started her own militia to make him happy, though she had some problem with the idea of militia clothes. What she preferred were the "real neat-looking" sequined suits she'd worn for parades when she was in junior high school and twirled batons on the drill team—an experience she described nostalgically as "almost like girls in the army where they twirl their little guns." Then, too, Rachel was already looking after one man, a Bellingham dockworker by the name of John Leonard Smith, who boasted a shaved head, a six-inch red goatee, and, on his shoulder, a large and elaborate tattoo featuring Merlin, the moon, a Chinese dragon, and a crystal ball, which Rachel herself had designed in her capacity as "a creative gal" and which, according to her, he had "passed out twice" receiving. ("He's really different," is the way she described him.) She and John Leonard had been together since high school, and after a couple of postponements having to do with a year she'd spent working the graveyard shift at a South Seattle gas station (her parents thought she was studying graphics at a Seattle art school, and so, apparently, did John Leonard), they were married in early September of 1996, some five weeks after her father went to jail. Everyone said that, except for the jail part, it was a perfect wedding—"a burgundy-and-white theme wedding," just what she'd always wanted. It began with a ceremony at the Smiths' and ended with a reception at Command Central, and it was notable for the abundance of family feeling, you could really say family values, and the tears shed when John began feeding quarters into the Kent jail prisoners' pay phone so he could talk to them all and hear Sheila make "a toast to my brother, who has fathered this vision of loveliness standing before us." Rachel was still upset, just thinking about her father at the pay phone. "She puts up a real brave front, but Auntie knows," Sheila told me. They were all upset, because the family had offered to pay whatever it would have cost to bring John home that day, even if that meant paying for federal marshals and even if John wasn't allowed to stay for more than the few minutes it would take him to walk Rachel down the aisle and deliver her to John Leonard and the preacher they'd hired from

Ferndale. But the judge said no, and John never got to see Rachel in her white gown, carrying a red bouquet ("Burgundy," as she said, the day we looked at her wedding album), or for that matter John Leonard in his white tails, white trousers, and white shoes, accented for the occasion by his red goatee, or the little flower girl in what was certainly a burgundy dress, scattering flowers from a basket. Rachel had written the invitation ("burgundy on cream") inviting her friends to witness "Rachel Louise and John Leonard . . . unite in marriage of forever love and peace." It was a tribute to John Pitner, who wanted everybody to live in love and peace, as he himself said in the epithalamium he wrote in jail, and read that day on the telephone:

> Marriage is like a planting of a garden of love.
> Communication and trust are its fertilizer,
> compassion and understanding its rain. Sharing and
> truth are its sun. The more love you plant and the better
> you care of it, the more you will receive from it over the
> years. May your harvest be rich and plentiful.

THERE WAS REALLY only one person in the family who was both willing to take John in before his trial and at the same time was the sort of person a judge would trust to see that John didn't run, or take up with his old friends, or even, in desperation, rummage under the kitchen sink for something he could hook up to a piece of candlewick and ignite. There was only one person willing to mortgage a house and match the amount of money Debbie could raise, on *her* house, in order to secure a bail bond. Dick Pitner certainly didn't offer, though he was quite put out at everybody else who didn't, including the policeman in Mountlake Terrace. On the other hand, if it embarrassed Dick to see his Patriot son rescued by the liberal, lesbian, "bleeding-heart daughter" he had once stopped speaking to for fifteen years because, as he put it, "I don't approve of her lifestyle," he was too thick-skinned or, possibly, too tight-fisted to admit it. And if it even occurred to him that, by any standards but his own, Susan and her partner, Betsey—who actually owned their house—ranked with the policeman and *his* wife as models of probity in an otherwise questionable clan, he didn't admit that, either. The most that Dick would concede (at least, to me), once Betsey had staked her life's savings in order to be able to take John in, was that, unlike most gay women, Susan and Betsey were "not in your damn face about it." All things considered, he had to say they were respectful. "They're very careful around me in that they don't show any emotional connection," is the way he described his own moderating influence on the Sapphic life. "And I appreciate that, because, you know, that's the way I want it."

John's bail hearing took place on October 16th. Bail was set at $79,000, and paid, and in early November John moved in with Susan and Betsey, wearing the electronic-surveillance ankle bracelet that would keep him connected to the Bothell police station and complaining about the treatment he'd received as a "political prisoner" at the Kent jail. The thin mattresses, the plastic pillows, the terrible Alcoholics Anonymous videos that passed for entertainment, the crackhead roommate who'd kept him awake snoring and shouting in his sleep, the Russian mobster who owed him about eight million dollars from the chess games he'd lost, the two days it had taken the guards to call a doctor when he was having a gall bladder attack and "passing out from pain." Debbie didn't stay. She drove him to Bothell from Pioneer Fellowship, the halfway house where he had spent a week or two of psychological evaluation—adjustment weeks, the court called them—reading the Isaac Asimov book he'd found there, on outer-space mining, and waiting for the bail paperwork to clear. She settled him into Susan's guest room. And then she got back into her new used T-Bird and drove home, leaving John with three big shopping bags of clothes she had scooped up, for $130, on a run through J. C. Penney's on the day she heard that the bond had cleared.

John was plainly disappointed, but it didn't take long for him to see the advantages of house arrest as Susan's favorite brother over house arrest as Debbie's uninvited spouse. And Susan and Betsey were enchanted with John. They hadn't requested copies of the FBI's tape transcripts, and even when they did get transcripts, they refused to read them. They took it on faith that John was being punished for the terrible things other people had done. As Betsey said, he had tried "to raise consciousness about community," and he was so good at it, so smart, so charismatic, that all of those other people had used him. Betsey was a famously kind woman. You could mention her name to someone who had met her only once, and only for a few minutes, and the person would smile, remembering something comforting she had said, some thoughtful or benign gesture she had made. Betsey even looked comforting, plump and bosomy in a flowered blouse or a sparkly T-shirt. She had a scrubbed, pink, muffin face and a halo of white curls winding around it, and at first, it was hard to reconcile the Betsey I met with the highly trained trauma nurse who worked not only as a pediatric clinician at Seattle's Children's Hospital but on a University of Washington research team with a six-year grant, from the National Institutes of Health, to study the effects of ketogenic diet on children with histories of epileptic seizure. But that, in fact, was what Betsey did. She told me that she loved Susan, and she believed in John because Susan believed in John. When John told her that all he had tried to do was "give the people the solutions," she thought he was just like that nice mayor she'd read about in Philadelphia, the one who had taught poor people to rebuild their houses so that they, in turn, could teach other poor people to rebuild *their* houses. She wanted to protect John from fanatics like Jack McLamb and John Trochmann. She had met Trochmann when she drove to Wenatchee with Susan for the John Pitner Defense Fund rally, and found him to be a horrible bigot. She knew it the minute he referred to the attorney general as "Butch Reno." And as for the audience at the rally, she thought they looked like Nazis. "There was nobody there with an IQ over a hundred," she once said, shaking her head at the remarkable coincidence of finding so many stupid people together in the same room. It hadn't been hard for Trochmann to frighten them with his fake drawings of government crematoria and his undocumented seismographic charts. She recognized the problem. "People in that audience weren't educated enough or intelligent enough to evaluate anything," she told me, but of course that wasn't a statement that applied to John.

Betsey cooked John's favorite food. She drove to the deli from work and brought home treats. She pinned a take-out menu from Tai Ho, her favorite Chinese restaurant, to the bulletin board. She kept her small house spotless for John. She emptied his ashtray and did his laundry and was careful to see that his new bathrobe didn't bleed in the washing machine. Susan provided the job and, as she put it, the tough love. "I'm going to chain John to my side," Susan had told me when I drove to Bothell for the first time, about three weeks before John moved into the little upstairs study cum guest room that became his bedroom, and started working on a gardening crew for Susan's landscaping service. "When John gets here, there's ninety-six yards of bark he's got to scoop. He won't have time to play." And he practically *was* chained to Susan, given that his ankle bracelet was programmed to start beeping at the station if he wandered more than twenty feet from the house without her. She told him that her computer was out of bounds, her e-mail address was private, her telephone (which she figured was tapped anyway) was for talking to family and lawyers and no one else. When John Trochmann started calling, she shouted, "Don't call here again, you bloodsucker!" Her view of Patriots like Trochmann was not that different from Betsey's. She said that John had always been in the habit of bringing home strays, and that "this time he brought the fleas with the strays." She didn't know why her brother should have gone to jail when fleas like Trochmann got invited to testify on militia theory to the United States Senate. John was a Patriot, and maybe he had fallen under Trochmann's bad influence, but he wasn't a crook and he wasn't a terrorist, whatever the *New York Times* said about "terrorism going homespun." Even Debbie talked about how hurt he'd been, the time they'd gone to a Halloween costume party on Valley Highway, with John dressed up as "G.I. 'John,' " and a woman looked at him and said, "Jeez, you'd make a great terrorist!" Susan had always liked Debbie. Debbie had tried to be a good influence,

but Susan knew that, to John, Debbie would always be—
Sheila had put it best—"just a baby having a baby." Susan, on
the other hand, was "big sister." She had taken John in that
summer, never stopping to ask why a man who had not spent
more than three hours in her house, not in all the years she'd
lived there, had suddenly called, crying, and had begged to
move in with her and Betsey. She thought his distress had
mainly to do with Rachel's leaving and Debbie's leaving and
the terrible state of American democracy ("First it was Rachel,
then it was Waco," is what she said), and so she had never even
asked why John had arrived in his trailer, and not his car, or
why he had parked in a gulch, instead of in the driveway, or for
that matter why he had disappeared to South Seattle, the first
morning he was there, when she was expecting him to help her
out on a landscaping job.

Susan looked tougher than she was. When you got to know
her, you saw the fragility; it was as if she couldn't really believe that the unhappy girl who had run away at seventeen to
join the air force had come to roost, after all those years, in a
pretty house on a pleasant suburban street, with a companion
like Betsey filling her life with kindness, and neighbors calling
her every day to plant their gardens. Susan was short, solid,
and strong—a chunky woman who somehow managed to look
wiry. She had close-cropped graying hair and a nice, plain,
weathered face, and she was visibly more at ease in her jeans
and a T-shirt than in the pale pants suits and flowered blouses
she wore when she and Betsey went out to celebrate a birthday
or an anniversary or simply their astonishing good luck at
having met each other. "I *am* a survivor," she liked to say. She
had survived Dick Pitner turning her into an indentured servant when she was twelve, and then another kind of indenture

that began when she was seventeen and met a man in the processing line at an air force base in Nebraska, and not much later married him. Her marriage was an experience she described to me once as a downhill run from "Oakland, Nebraska, to Jersey City, New Jersey, where the household bird is a cockroach," but in fact, even in Oakland, at the top of the hill, she and her husband were almost comically incompatible. She was a welder—she liked being a welder—and wore overalls. He was an engineer and wore three-piece suits, played golf, and ran the office that laid coaxial cables for the phone company. And those were the good years. When he retired at fifty, he moved the family to a prissy New Jersey town, and not much later—or, you could say, thirteen years of marriage and two children later—he called up her equally prissy boss and let him know that Susan liked women. She was thirty years old and went, as she put it, "from a Continental to a Datsun B210 in three and a half weeks." When Betsey found her, she was thirty-one, in the middle of a breakdown, and trying to scratch out a living as a nurse's aide in the hospital where Betsey worked. Even Dick Pitner had to admit that it was Betsey who'd saved Susan. It was Betsey who put Susan through nursing school, and Betsey who eased her through the grisly *rite de passage* into the life of a Newark emergency room trauma nurse—Newark, at the time, being a place where the crime of choice involved boiling a pot of grits and lye, flinging it at your neighbor's crotch, and then shooting him between the eyes. Susan didn't love the job, but she was good at it. She worked the emergency room for the next five years. She was "kicked, bitten, stabbed, choked" more often than she was thanked, which may be why, to her mind, the happiest day she ever spent was the day she told Betsey, "We're going to go some place where people wear clean underwear and don't call you motherfucker!" They moved "home" to Washington in 1986. Ten years later—ten years in the course of which Susan lost a kidney, suffered a stroke, damaged her right hand in a freak accident inside a CAT scanner, and installed an oxygen machine, for her sleep apnea, in the bedroom—Susan was still happy. She introduced Betsey to me as "my life partner," saying that because of Betsey her children had a family again. Her son was bartending in Seattle. Her daughter was living in Bothell; in fact, they were landscaping partners. And Susan herself was ready to accept that she'd actually got somewhere in the years since she drove off on her first gardening job, with a spatula for edging, a rake with three missing teeth, and a contract for $339 on the backseat of her old car. Now she had five trucks, a team of contractors, and so many clients that the company was going to gross $147,000 that year. With John's help, maybe more.

John meant to be grateful. True, there were now some subjects you couldn't bring up at dinner. You couldn't convince John that the Thirteenth Amendment in Betsey's encyclopedia wasn't a fake, written by the New World Order, any more than you could convince him that the government didn't have a lab full of dead, extraterrestial creatures hidden somewhere in the Nevada desert. You couldn't even mention the Clintons. John "knew" the truth about the Clintons. He still believed everything he had heard from Ben Hinkle and John Trochmann, and everything he had read on the wacky Patriot Web sites of the Internet, but he didn't believe Betsey's copy of the Constitution—he had the "true" version in his Patriot handbook—or the Federal Reserve charter as published by the Government Printing Office. He acknowledged that Susan and Betsey were smart. Even Dick Pitner acknowledged that, now that he had read an article saying that homosexuals were smarter than "the average person" and—Dick liked this part— that "there are more homosexual millionaires for their group, on an average, than any other group." What was difficult, for John, was that Susan and Betsey weren't smart enough to believe *him*. They didn't think the president had killed Vincent Foster; they didn't think he was running Colombian dope through Little Rock; they didn't even think his philandering was a crime or a conspiracy to cover up the hundreds of other crimes he had committed. Once, when I was at dinner and John started arguing about Clinton and the Federal Reserve— "Not one penny that we pay in federal income tax goes into the United States Treasury," he said, "and if you look at the back of your check that's been cancelled, you'll find out who is getting the money!"—Susan got so exasperated she told him, "John, I can't see the boogieman around every corner, I can't *live* with the boogieman around every corner, it's like knowing the day of your death." But usually, when I was there, she would just give up after a few minutes and head upstairs with whatever book she was reading, saying that she'd leave us alone to talk.

The truth was that in most ways John was his father's son. His view of women was that men knew better. He might have stayed grateful, or at least gracious, in a house with men, because he wouldn't have lasted a week hounding a man the way he started hounding Susan, taking over the household as if he had rights there that she and Betsey did not. The rest of the family dropped away. John's half-brother wouldn't speak to him anymore. His brother Dick came for a visit once, at Thanksgiving. Rachel came twice. Debbie came four times, never for very long, and then she stopped coming. Susan and Betsey didn't blame Debbie—not after her last visit, which ended when John began shouting at her in the middle of a restaurant. (She'd told him that while his ideas were good, perhaps his tactics were wrong.) Thanksgiving had been so bad that Susan's children were now refusing to come home for Christmas if John was there. "If you could have seen our home before this," Susan said, after one difficult day. "It was people coming in and out. We were fat and happy." It didn't help that she sympathized with John. Everyone expected John to be a little stir-crazy, living in a tiny house with two women, never able to go out alone. Everyone understood his tension. It may have been different in jail, where you could complain all day about a snoring roommate or a day room with six chairs for twenty-four prisoners; you were expected to complain in jail, but you weren't expected to complain about a loving sister with a friend who made your favorite chicken and put fresh croutons in your salad. He took it out on them.

At first, Susan refused to believe that anything was wrong. She thought she could make a family out of their uneasy ménage, the way Jeff Margolis had thought he could make a community out of Whatcom County. When she started losing clients, she swore that it wasn't because of John, it was because of all the outrageous and unfair things the papers were saying about John. People knew she was John's sister—she must have had forty calls the day the family appeared on television, outside the Seattle courthouse—and she wasn't surprised that some of those people were a little nervous. She had assumed that once they met John, once he was in their gardens and they saw what an honest, agreeable person he was, everything would change. It never occurred to her that John would start haranguing *them* about the New World Order, or that her crew would quit, one by one, because he was haranguing them, too, giving them orders and calling them stupid or wrong for doing the same good work they'd been doing for years without him (or, as Susan put it, for not doing the work *his* way). In three months' time, Susan lost every gardener she had except her daughter, and close to $40,000 worth of contracts.

When Susan stopped taking John out on jobs, and then, when there weren't any jobs to take him out on, he was home alone. He began to spend his time at the Mac computer on a big oak desk beside the front door. He battled the aliens on Planet Alpha Ceti, in a computer war game called Marathon 2. He blew up "generation stations," zapped monsters, fought his way back to his space teleport. He didn't read, he didn't write. "He just sits and plays the same goddamn computer game, sometimes sixteen hours a day," Susan told me. It wasn't long before he was on the Internet too. He read her e-mail. He decided which letters she and Betsey should get, and erased the rest. They'd come home from work and find "zero megabytes one day, and half a million the next"; they didn't know what to do or how to stop him, and they didn't ask him to stop. They worried that he'd get angry and disappear, which, of course, would mean that they'd lose their house as quickly as they had lost their e-mail. And they began discovering things about John Pitner that they hadn't known, things that involved them. They discovered that he'd been running from a serious death threat, or from something he believed was a serious death threat, during those two weeks he'd spent in Bothell in July, that he'd put them all in danger and hadn't told them why or even warned them. Not even Debbie had warned them. According to Susan, the only thing Debbie had ever said to suggest that John was involved in something dangerous—it happened weeks after his arrest—had to do with her going off with Rachel and dumping stuff in the river and burning papers. Susan hadn't thought much about it then. ("We were *all* paranoid then," she told me. "I burned the Constitution. Think about that. I burned the Constitution.") But thinking about it now, she saw that John had put his own family in danger, too. She said that the first few months with John were like that. Whenever she and Betsey read something about John—in a trial brief or a bail motion or sometimes just in the paper—they learned something they didn't know. They learned that John had been suicidal in Panama, that the army had declared him psychologically unfit for service, and, even then, it was six weeks into the trial before they learned that he'd been court-martialed in Panama, too.

"That's not my brother!" Susan announced one day in February, when we were talking about John. The brother she knew had been "live and let live, enjoy every day." Everybody liked that brother. The Hindu family that had picked John up, hitchiking, when he was sixteen and running away to see New York, had ended up taking him home to Brooklyn. The guys in the gay commune who'd discovered him next, camping in a box over a steam vent on the roof of a building near Washington Square, had taken him home, too, and made him the "mascot" of a big Greenwich Village house. Even those nice people in North Carolina, whose house he broke into—he was hungry—after he'd left New York and was heading south on a stolen bike, determined to see Cocoa Beach and Cape Canaveral, had invited him to live with them. For a long time, it had seemed like the only family to have a problem with John

Pitner was the Pitner family, which perhaps explained why Susan was determined to stick by her brother now. She had agreed to testify on John's behalf, and she wasn't going to let him down, just because he was driving *her* crazy. But she also agreed with Betsey that it was time for John to leave. Early in January, just after learning about the death threats, the women retained a lawyer of their own. The first thing they asked him was how much longer John was likely to be living with them—that is, if he didn't go back to jail or run away. The Pitners were still united, but as Susan described it now: "Our family is united in one thing. We all want this man out of our lives. We will not let this man into our lives again."

Twelve

ON THE MORNING OF January 16, 1997, John
drove into Seattle from Bothell for his trial. Judy
Kirk, the only defendant besides John to have
posted bail, drove in from Tukwila. The other defendants in
United States v. John Irvin Pitner et al. arrived in handcuffs,
from their various jails. By then—with 546 documents filling ten volumes in the case file, and so many superseding indictments that no one was really sure about who would be
charged with what until nine that morning—the defense was
nevertheless down to seven people. The charges against Debbie had been dropped on January 8th. Ten days earlier, Ted
Carter had pleaded guilty to conspiracy and agreed to testify
for the prosecution. Richard Burton had pleaded guilty to one
count of conspiracy, to possession of destructive devices, and
to a charge, filed after his arrest, involving a call he'd made to

his wife, Caitlin, persuading her to withhold or destroy evidence. And Caitlin, who was then arrested herself for withholding or destroying that evidence, had pleaded guilty to obstruction of justice. Outside Bellingham, the Washington State Militia had dropped off the front page. Still, John arrived at the federal courthouse optimistic, expecting to be cheered on by a big crowd of Patriots demonstrating on Union Street and lining the courthouse steps to shake his hand, and if he was disappointed not to find one he tried to be philosophical about it. "We decided to play it quiet," he told me. (In fact, the Patriots didn't have a permit.) The courtroom itself was full. There were five or six reporters and at least as many militia-watchers on one side of the room, which seemed to have split spontaneously, into a kind of trial version of the bride's and groom's sides of a church at a wedding; if you looked across the aisle from the bench the reporters had appropriated—it was halfway back, and for some reason it never changed—you saw what amounted to a rogues' gallery of characters from Seattle's Patriot right, scribbling notes and leafing through papers. They were men mainly, and most of them looked to be too old, or too angry, to hold down jobs that might have kept them away that day. But it was clear that they considered themselves reporters, too, and in a way they were, since if you added up the various newsletters and Web sites those Patriots ran or represented, you would have to acknowledge that they probably had as many readers as their colleagues across the aisle. It was sobering to see them: old men with unsavory histories of their own, sitting together in a court of law, comparing notes, passing out statements, and occasionally whispering among themselves about the size of the liens they'd file against John C. Coughenour, the judge who was going to hear *United States v. John Irvin Pitner et al.,* and the two federal prosecutors who were going to try it. They were a reminder that, however loopy or inept the self-styled Patriots of Whatcom County and a couple of Justus Townships turned out to be, there was very little light at the end of the road those Patriots had taken. Some of the men dated back to the John Birch Society and the Minutemen and the Populists, and even to the Duck Club, a particularly nasty Seattle group devoted to hunting Communists. ("If it walks like a duck, squawks like a duck . . . ," was the definition.) It was said that a few of the old timers in John's bleachers—Paul de Armond and Dave Neiwert pointed them out to me one day—were still under suspicion of having incited a wandering psychopath named David Rice to murder a young, liberal, Seattle lawyer named David Goldmark, Goldmark's wife, and their two small children. The murders themselves dated from the mid-eighties, but the Goldmark family had been an obsession of Washington's lunatic right since the McCarthy days. In the early sixties, Goldmark's father—a Democratic legislator and cattle rancher named John Goldmark—had won a landmark libel case against a group of Okanogan County politicians and newspapermen who had tried, publicly, to destroy him, and for me there was a certain reassuring irony in the fact that the lawyer who had argued that case for Goldmark, William L. Dwyer, was now a colleague of Coughenour's on the Ninth District bench. (Dwyer, who died this winter, had been a brilliant and famously humane civil liberties lawyer, a legend in First Amendment circles. As it turned out, he'd also represented Paul de Armond's father in the early sixties, in a suit against the *Seattle Times,* which had printed a right-wing politician's claim that de Armond was a "Moscow-directed agent.") It was doubtful, of course, that John Pitner knew anything about John Goldmark or about his son David or, for that matter, about Bill Dwyer, hearing another case in a courtroom down the hall. The history of warped patriotism that linked the angry old men glaring at Judge Coughenour from the back benches of a Seattle courtroom to the politicians in the high, dry flatlands of Okanogan County who had first set out to ruin the Goldmark family was not something that figured in what John had called his research. John thought that "McCarthyism" was the term for what David Rockefeller was doing to him.

The trial was slow to start. Tracy Lee Brown was still refusing to speak to his own lawyer. John Kirk was objecting to the gold fringe on the courtroom flag. Neither of the Freemen was inclined to rise, as ordered, when the judge entered, because as far as they were concerned John Coughenour had no authority to ask them to do anything. The judge, who knew what was coming (it arrived in February, in the form of a $176 billion sovereign citizens' lien), sat down looking as if he had a very unpleasant headache. The one time I saw him smile, in nearly a month at the trial, was the morning he respectfully asked the jury to extend its lunch break by a half hour, having just got word that his boat—he loved his boat—was leaking diesel fuel. I never saw the prosecutors smile. The two federal prosecutors, an irritable, overweight woman named Susan Dohrmann, and her deputy, Gene Porter, an anxious, underweight man with a habit of wringing his hands, seemed to me to regard everybody in the courtroom, from the militiamen and their whispering friends to the jury and the journalists, as interlopers. In the event, they refused to talk to me, or even acknowledge me, or answer a phone call or even *The New Yorker*'s phone calls. At first, it was even hard to convince them to release tape transcripts which were already entered in the trial record. John thought that Susan Dohrmann was irritable because her feet hurt, squeezed into the ballet flats she often wore. (He wanted to send her Earth Shoes.) More likely, she was distressed at the prospect of having to go on record herself, at least before the defense did, with the three felony counts against her most important "cooperating witness" ("He made a criminal mistake" was the way she introduced the subject of Ed Mauerer) or the fact that "he did not tell the truth" about a lot of what he heard or saw until he was wearing a wire and found it marginally more difficult to lie. But at the time, I also thought she was suspicious of *me,* because I knew John and often had lunch with him, at the bar of an Italian restaurant called Tulio's, which was across the street from the courthouse and therefore unlikely to set alarms ringing at the police station. And the truth was that a lot of people seemed suspicious of me. It wasn't just the Patriots thinking I was some sort of New World Order secret agent. (Apparently, even Jeff Margolis had begun to wonder if I was FBI, perhaps because he couldn't think of another reason why anyone would keep coming back to Whatcom County.) I wasn't thin-skinned. I'd been a journalist for over thirty years, and at one time or another had found myself hated, feared, avoided, ignored, used, trusted, confided in, and even admired, but I had rarely been suspected of being anything other than what I was. Just a journalist. Now I seemed to have wandered deep into Hofstadter country, though I couldn't really be certain that the style I encountered in Washington was

Hofstadter's paranoid style and not provincialism, or the kind of none-of-your-business heartland xenophobia that put an East Coast (though arguably American) writer somewhere between Stroessner's Paraguay and Mao's China. What *was* certain was that it would have been a lot easier for me to make an appointment with the president, in the other Washington, than it was to get past the door of some of the public servants in the Washington I was in now. On January 16th, Ramon Garcia still hadn't answered any of my calls, either, though he'd briefed some local reporters I knew—the ones *he* knew, too. He hadn't answered my calls that fall, months after the sting was over, and when I met him in court in January, and asked if we could meet for a talk, he gave me a sniffy look, said, "No! Not even for a cup of coffee!" and walked away. By then, I wasn't surprised. Two months earlier in Seattle, I had spent some time with an FBI agent from one of the Bureau's special units. It was a background talk—no names, no quotes, no tape recorders—but I had left convinced he had been taping *me*. It has to be said that the agent was friendly, forthcoming, and had a sense of humor. ("Everybody has a college degree" is the way he described his unit. "This is not the NYPD!") He had the confidence, or maybe the authority, to be critical. And under the circumstances, he was courteous, or courteous enough to let me catch him fiddling with the machine on his belt, which may be why I never invoked the Freedom of Information Act and demanded to see his report.

John, on the other hand, lived in Hofstadter country, and for him the trial was a taste of freedom, like shore leave after months at sea. He sang on the walks he took with Jim Lobsenz. He talked about Lobsenz as "my friend Jim," and was sure it meant something that they both knew all the lyrics to the song that started "Where, oh where, can my baby be?" And he liked sitting at the bar at Tulio's, eating salads and drinking coffee and then joking with the barman about his "nervous stomach." His freedom was illusory, but it gave him a kind of stature among the men in handcuffs. He could take a long, tolerant view of the way they had simply collapsed, without him, and allowed themselves to be led astray. Two months earlier, I had asked him whether he hated those men, given the rumors that they'd planned to kill him, and he had shaken his head and said, "The Christian side of me tries not to, but the other side of me . . ." Now, he forgave them all. He knew that Fred was basically a "good man," who had never really meant to hurt him. (In fact, he'd refused even to acknowledge Fred's presence at the defendants' table until the day their lawyers insisted that, just once, they sit together and try to look like friends.) He knew that "young Marlin" was a good man, too, and would still be home in Bellingham, doing right by his country, if Mike German hadn't picked him out as the impressionable one, the kid to work on. John had never "approved" German for the unit. "He slipped in, excuse me, slicker than snot," he told me. And as for Gary, there was never any doubt in John's mind that Gary was his faithful friend—next to Brian, his best friend. Gary had, after all, gotten into his car and taken the bumpy road to Command Central the morning after the hot-seat meeting. He'd wanted to warn John, and listen to what he had to say. Gary's problem was that he hadn't listened to John earlier, when Ed and Rock got after him to convert some rifles. He had driven over to Command Central that day, too, asking for advice, and John had told him, Don't do it! and assumed that the subject was closed. It wasn't until they all met in the holding cell in Seattle that John learned about Gary giving in and turning a rifle into an automatic. Gary was suffering now. He had never been able to stand or sit for very long, and the pain was much worse after so many months in jail. It was cold in jail. John could vouch for that. He said that, even before the weather changed in September, the pins in Gary's back were pinching, and by then Gary was already shivering so much that he broke the rule about keeping your blanket in your cell; he brought his blanket into the day room and was put in solitary confinement for it. "A guard threw him in the hole," John told me, and said that he'd come out looking so old—so stooped over on his cane and with his hair suddenly so gray—that from that day on the inmates called him "Einstein." By now he was hurting every minute, moving slowly, step by step, and unable to sit at all. His lawyer had had to get a couch moved into the courtroom, just so Gary could make it through the trial. The couch was placed next to the defendants' table, and for six weeks Gary got some rest, lying on his right side, propped on his elbow, with his lawyer in a chair beside him, tapping him gently if he began to snore.

When John was talking about his men, worrying about them all, the way he worried about Gary, he was almost cheerful. He became expansive, and in his own way confidential, though of course it was impossible to tell how much truth any of his confidences carried. He wanted me to know how hard he had tried to convince the men to let me into their secret meetings, which of course they hadn't. Ed had always been against it (that didn't surprise John now), and then "Uriel had a problem with it." Uriel was the man, or men, who in our conversations seemed to have replaced Daiwee as John's adviser—his "plug into Fort Lewis." "Uriel was active military, he was pretty guarded," as John described him. But Uriel was squarely behind John on the matter of need-to-know and the buried ordnance which may or may not have existed, though after a few weeks at Susan's, John had begun to revise that story, too. There wasn't really much ordnance. There was "the *idea*" of ordnance. His men had needed that idea. They had been so frightened by all the intel coming in about the United Nations and the troop deployments inside America that they'd needed the reassurance of weapons, so John, in a manner of speaking, gave them weapons. "They figured, 'We don't have nothing—nothing to protect ourselves with,' " John told me. "So I said, 'You've got hundreds of pounds of dynamite, hand grenades, thousands of rounds of ammunition." They wanted land mines; John told them they already *had* land mines." They wanted claymores; John said claymores. "I lied to them and said, 'Don't worry,' " is how he explained it to me, and very likely to his lawyer, too. Of course, that wasn't the only thing John had lied about to his men. The men thought they had paid for weapons, not for the idea of weapons, and John wasn't going to talk about where their money had gone any more than he was going to talk about where the $5,000 from his benefactor—the windfall that had done so much to establish John's reputation in militia circles—had gone, or, indeed, that it was John himself who'd frightened them with that alarming intel. John wasn't on trial as a confidence man. There was even the possibility that he was lying now about lying. In the end, his most spectacular sleights were sleights of logic. He argued his innocence to *me* by insisting, "If I was truly the person he [Ed] said I was, I'd have had him killed."

When John was in a reminiscing mood, he'd tell me stories about the "good times." He told me about the famous Alaska picnic that Debbie had once described—how he had left Debbie to watch their skiff for five minutes, and Debbie had wandered off with Rachel to look for agates, and he had come back to discover that the skiff was beached, high and dry, and wouldn't start, and what an adventure that was. True, he'd blown up and thrown a rock at Debbie, but it was something they laughed about now, because afterward he'd built a fire on the beach and stood over his "girls" with a stick, all night long, terrified that a grizzly would get them. He told me about the time on Mount Baker when a bear nearly did get them; it wasn't a grizzly but still, he was so scared that time that "I beat Debbie down that fucking mountain, and her legs are twice as long as mine." He told me about the time in Yellowstone, when another bear raided their campsite and ate their steaks and they'd had to hide in the fiberglass canopy on the pickup, trying to keep the dog quiet while the bear scraped and scraped at the back bumper, looking for a way in. He told me about the time he'd scared Susan in her tent, pretending to be a bear, and about the time he'd got the wrong tent and burst in on a couple of perfect strangers. His stories were little Western fables. Bears, boats, wild places, and a joke on the cowboy in the end. Everybody liked them. I did. The barman did. John could even make Susan laugh, at the end of an angry day together in Bothell, by talking about the pretty transvestite who had tried so hard to seduce him in New York when he was sixteen and impressionable and thought that anything in a dress was female, or about Sheila's first husband, the husband who looked like an extra from *The Grapes of Wrath,* trying to club a three-and-a-half-foot salmon he had just caught and getting John's toe instead. John had been so excited about that big fish that he didn't even notice his toe was broken until they got home. The odd thing about John was that the tall stories he told were true, while the stories he had come to believe were true were the ones he'd invented.

It was the unraveling of those inventions, day by day in Judge Coughenour's courtroom, that finally got to John. Nothing else seemed to upset him. He could sit calmly, almost abstracted, during the most humiliating revelations. He could listen to Jim Lobsenz tell the jury that "odd as this might sound to you"—meaning to a fairly reasonable person—John Pitner actually believed that the United States was going to be invaded by the United Nations. He could listen to the courtroom titter because John Pitner thought that his own backwater county was the "first line of defense" against the New World Order and that it was up to him to save it. He could listen to tapes and read transcripts of the terrible threats John Pitner had made, and the terrible threats that people John Pitner had considered friends made against him. He could listen to the shaming things John Pitner had said about his wife, to the lies he'd told, and the language he'd used, and the whining monologues of his self-regard. He could sit through it all, taking copious notes on a piece of paper and occasionally shaking his head, or smirking, or sighing in a knowing way (a little like Al Gore, listening to George W. Bush rattle off the wrong figures). But he could not easily listen to anything suggesting that the men of the Washington State Militia hadn't entirely bought into the hero called John Pitner, that they had told jokes about his stories and, in the end, spent most of their time debating whether *any* of them were true. When he heard their conversations—"Will the real John Pitner *please* stand

up?" one reporter in the courtroom described the tape transcripts—he would turn red and hang his head, and shrink into
his new clothes. You could feel the tension at the defendants'
table.

Sometimes, after a bad moment, Jim Lobsenz would put
his arm around John's shoulder and give it a squeeze, and John
would be reassured. "We're in this together," he once told me,
as if Jim was a Patriot, too, only a little different when it came
to tactics. He liked to think of his lawyer as a kind of courtroom militiaman, working the enemy from its own ranks.
There was never much irony in John. It never really occurred
to him that most of the lawyers sitting beside their clients at
the defendants' table, sorting through piles of transcripts and
documents on those clients' behalf, represented a world he de-
spised: that they were dues-paying American Civil Liberties
Union liberals, two of them Jewish liberals, who would have
defended Communists as willingly as Patriots if the same issues were involved; that they argued issues of free speech and
entrapment and reasonable doubt, but didn't believe that the
New World Order was after John Pitner's militia; that they
thought maybe it was Ramon Garcia, more than David Rockefeller, who had got excited at the prospect of putting them all
away. In fact, when Tom Hillier—the United States public defender and, for the purposes of the trial, John Kirk's lawyer—
suggested that Jesse Helms, warning a president of the United
States not to attempt to enter North Carolina without a body-
guard, was much more dangerous than any of the men on trial
in Judge Coughenour's courtroom, those men tended to side
with Helms. The only defendant who seemed actually to
grasp that their lawyers were paid to be advocates of the law,

not partisans of the cause, was Tracy Lee Brown, the Freeman who refused to speak to *his* lawyer.

None of this made for a gratifying trial. The lawyers who tried to be witty or entertaining or, worse, eloquent drew blank looks all around. It didn't matter if the lawyer was Tom Hillier, who was known for eloquence, or Marlin's lawyer, James Roe, who was known more for grandiloquence and could keep a straight face while describing the Washington State Militia as "that rural task of the yeoman farmer" or referring to Ed Mauerer as "Iago." (With Iago, he had to add "in the words of the immortal bard," and after a minute, "Shakespeare," and even then Marlin shook his head, confused as to whether those names were FBI or Federal Reserve or United Nations.) The lawyers who tried to be clever got cut off. Judge Coughenour had a reputation for impatience. He didn't like long oral argument (the lawyers called him "the Clarence Thomas of the Ninth Circuit"), and he was often exasperated by Gary's young lawyer, David Zuckerman, who like Lobsenz thought they had a shot at arguing *United States v. John Irvin Pitner et al.* up to the Supreme Court. By the time the trial opened, Zuckerman was already studying precedents for his appeal. (His favorite precedent had to do with a decision that denied Second Amendment protection to people with knifes; the implication, he told me, was that people with guns *had* that protection.) Lobsenz, arguably, had the trickiest case, since John's part in the alleged conspiracy had more to do with incitement than action and yet, at the same time, everyone else's actions seemed to lead back to him or to something he'd once suggested. Nobody had seen John sell a machine gun to Ed Mauerer, which was one of the charges against him.

Nobody had taped him delivering a bomb, or filmed him converting a weapon, and, in fact, he hadn't been charged with delivering bombs or converting weapons. Nobody had kept him supplied with explosive powders or spare rifle parts or rented him a big office where he could do incriminating things. Nobody had tried to entrap him, though it was possible to argue that at one point, when he starting showing his house, the FBI had searched it without a warrant. Nobody but the Freemen had even seen much of John Pitner after he took his "leave of absence." But everybody had heard him talk. Everybody had heard him threaten. Even the militia dropouts who appeared, early on, as prosecution witnesses (either because they volunteered, or were subpoenaed, or had made a deal to avoid getting arrested themselves) talked mainly about how scary John had sounded, or how untrustworthy he was thought to be. Lobsenz had moved to separate John's case from the others, claiming that John had dropped out of the militia by the time most of the crimes that figured in the indictments were committed. But the judge had denied the motion, and John's best chance now was a strong First Amendment argument, the way, say, Fred's best chance was a strong challenge of the state's "proof" of conspiracy, or Kirk's was a "testing" argument—an argument to the effect that Kirk was only practicing when he made bombs, not planning to explode them. Lobsenz maintained that you couldn't convict John Pitner for exercising his right to free speech unless you were ready to convict the people who had entered 100,000 pipe bomb sites on the Internet, with instructions it took you less than three minutes to access.

John was counting on his family. Debbie was ready to testify. Rachel, he said, was taking a day off from her job at the

Bellingham print shop to testify. (Lobsenz had told the court she was studying architecture, and no one thought to correct him.) Even Susan still felt obliged to testify for John. None of that mattered to John, though, once he discovered that his "brother" Larry in Mountlake Terrace had refused. It was hard to imagine how John could have believed that the policeman he had reinvented as his Deep Throat (not to mention as an FBI operative who "pretty much" controlled the West Coast) would be overcome by Pitner-family feeling, even assuming the policeman accepted that being the husband of Richard Pitner's second wife's daughter made him John's brother, which it demonstrably did not. But John believed it. John and Susan had a fight about Larry and his wife, Denise, at dinner the night John got the news. Susan begged him to understand that Denise and Larry had worked for years, building a home and a reputation, building a life, she said, and that he couldn't ask them to throw that life away. But that was exactly what John was asking. "I know what *I'd* do," he told Susan. If the tables were turned, he'd do whatever he had to do for Larry—or, for that matter, for Susan herself—"because it's family." And Susan kept saying, "How do you know what you'd do?" She didn't know what *she'd* do. And the end of it all was that John stormed off, reappearing in his best bathrobe to log on to a video game and fight some aliens.

A few weeks later, when the trial was winding down, Debbie testified. The questions were perfunctory. It was established that Debbie had supported John, that she had gotten tired of supporting John, that she had never forgiven John for buying two pairs of expensive, imported night-vision goggles (when one pair was really all he'd needed), that she had left John, and that "Yeah, when this is over," maybe they'd get

back together. Then Rachel testified. It was established that
she was related to John—"I sure am!" she told the jury—and
that at the moment she was actually unemployed and that she
had designed the eagle on the Washington State Militia newsletter. And finally Susan testified. It was established that Susan
had hired John and that he had worked steadily for her until
the trial started and he had to be in court all day. She was on
the witness stand for five minutes, and she said it was easier
than she'd expected. For Susan, the hard part came a couple
of days later when John told her that their father, who'd come
in from Whidbey with Dorothy for the closing statements,
"wasn't behaving" in the courtroom—that he was muttering
things and making faces at the jury. Susan drove back to Seattle the next morning in order to be with him. By then, Dick
Pitner was so upset that he broke down in the courtroom and
started crying. It got worse once the court was adjourned and
the jury began its deliberations and Dick learned that Susan
and Betsey had been granted a return of title to their house.
When John went back to jail, Dick swore that he would never
speak to Betsey again. Rachel stopped speaking to Betsey and
Susan, and Debbie resolved the problem in her own way, by
pretending the women weren't there. "Here we were sitting on
this for four weeks, because we didn't want to do anything to
hurt John's case," Susan told me on the phone, later. Four
weeks of John talking about bolting to Montana—his plan
was to punch John Trochmann in the nose and take it from
there—and Susan and Betsey's lawyer saying, Do it now!
Susan had been determined to wait until the jury was out and
nothing they said or did could prejudice anyone against John.
But it was clear that she couldn't wait much longer than
that—not with mistrial motions going back and forth and the

jury sending out word to the judge that it was undecided and was even having trouble with one member, who'd refused to listen to the others or to follow procedure or even to address some of the charges, let alone vote on them. (I found him in the case files at the King County Courthouse, where he had once been sued by a contractor he'd hired to build what was referred to in the documents as an "Islamic center.") There had been a short hearing. Betsey, requesting a return of title, had been careful not to say anything at all negative, only that the emotional stress of the trial had come to be more than she and Susan could handle, and because of this, Susan was especially bitter about the family's furious reaction. She wrote to her father, asking, Where were you all these months? She called Debbie and Rachel, asking the same thing. No one else besides Debbie had gone to court that fall with the deed to a house in hand, and no one was offering now. No one, not even Debbie, was saying, Let's take over from Susan and Betsey. No one in the entire Pitner family wanted the burden of John Pitner, waiting for a verdict. According to Susan, even Jim Lobsenz seemed unwilling to accept the fact that she was sending her brother back to jail. Susan told me that when she went to see him, saying, "Jim, please do something, I'm going to pull the plug," he had simply got mad and demanded to know why a week or two more with John made such a big difference. After that, he called once and asked her: "How can you do this to John?" It was the last conversation they had.

The jury was out for seven days. They were by all reports exasperating days, because the Muslim juror was still refusing to vote on any charges that involved conspiracy, and the judge had refused a request by the jury foreman to replace him, instructing the jury—or so it was reported later—to "work it out." The defense, for its part, had filed motions to the effect that eleven jurors were guilty of bullying the twelfth, though most people I talked to at the trial suspected he was simply a Muslim version of the Christian Patriot "jury nullifiers" who had been plaguing the system for the past few years. (A jury nullifier is a juror who sets out to sabotage deliberations and prevent a verdict, or prevents it himself by ignoring the judge's instructions, and the Patriots have come up with a handbook on how to be one.) In any case, there was a stalemate, and the result was that on February 28th, the day the verdicts were read, Judge Coughenour had no choice but to declare a mistrial on all of the conspiracy charges—which, in effect, had held the men responsible for one another's crimes and would have made them eligible to serve one another's sentences—as well as on five separate charges involving Gary Kuehnoel and the Kirks. His decision left Fred Fisher, Judy Kirk, and Tracy Lee Brown with no convictions against them; they were released from custody (though Brown, who was still, legally, a fugitive in contempt of court, was arrested again before he could leave the courthouse). Marlin Mack was found guilty on seven counts of "possession of an unregistered destructive device," and returned to jail to await sentencing. John Kirk went back to jail, guilty on one count of the same charge. Gary Kuehnoel was found guilty on one count of "possession of a machine gun," and acquitted on three counts involving possession of unregistered firearms. John Pitner was found guilty on one count of "possession and transfer of a machine gun," and swore he was innocent, because the "automatic" he was said to have offered Ed Mauerer—the jury had heard a blurry tape of their conversation—wasn't an Uzi at all, as the prosecution claimed, but a pickup truck, with automatic transmission. He'd assured me of that on the day the tape was played. He said I could ask anyone who knew him: John Pitner preferred automatic to shift. In the end, it didn't much matter what kind of truck John liked driving. He was in prison for most of the next four years.

A few weeks before John went back to jail, we were at the bar in Tulio's, talking about the New World Order. John wanted me to know that, whatever happened, he bore no grudges, because when you came down to it everyone was a victim. He worried about Susan Dohrmann's swollen feet and John Coughenour's leaky boat and he even worried about the people who walked into the courthouse without a clue that the murals on either side of the courthouse door contained a subliminal message from the New World Order, urging them to accept tyranny in the interests of an orderly state. The trial had taught him something. "I'm not a legal beagle, I'm getting a good education," he said. He had even met a few good people, like David Zuckerman, the lawyer who had represented Gary. Zuckerman was a little man, like John, but he had "a lot of chutzpah." "Chutzpah" was a word that John had picked up in New York, thirty years earlier, and had always remembered, but he knew that chutzpah alone wasn't going to defeat the New World Order. When he thought about all the effort that had been made just to bring him down, all the taxpayers' money that had been spent—right down to the "speech processors" that could cut the words "pickup" and "shift" out of a friendly business conversation—he was more convinced than ever that in the next few months we would be at war. He wanted the good Americans to know that wherever he was then, they were welcome to join him. Racists could join him. Blacks could join him. Even Chicanos—he hadn't liked

Chicanos since one of them stabbed his brother, though he didn't say which brother—could join him. He didn't discriminate. "Getting the message out is more important than my personal differences," he told me, standing up and putting on his black bomber jacket. "If you get a piece of information out to two or three people—that's lifting the rock and letting the sun in."

Afterword

J OHN PITNER LEFT the Federal Detention Center
called Sea-Tac on January 5, 2001, released on time
served and placed under supervision for the next three
years, and went straight to Whidbey Island to see his father.
Dick Pitner, at eighty-one, was by then so ill with metastasiz-
ing cancer that he seemed to have kept himself alive by force
of will, waiting for that day (and, in fact, died not much more
than a year later). John stayed on the island long enough to
make some repairs on Dick and Dorothy's house, and then for
a while he was back in Bellingham, living with his brother
Richard, Richard's wife, and their small son in Autumn Lane
Mobile Park, the trailer park on Lake Samish where he had
once been so unhappy. He found a job and lost it. No one I
talked to knew precisely what the job had been, but it may
have had something to do with construction, since he'd told

people he was fired when his parole officer stopped by and demanded to enter a "secure site," and he'd had no choice except to take him. In the event, he left Bellingham last year, apparently for Mount Vernon. And whatever his life was now, Debbie wasn't part of it; not even Valley Highway was part of it. Debbie had divorced him in February of 1998, while he was still in prison, agreeing to leave him his pickup, his motorcycle, his tools, his computer, and his stereo in exchange for keeping the trailer, the car, and the house with its ten acres—and in the process assuming the debts he'd accumulated on five or six credit cards and the liability for $10,000 of his bill from Jim Lobsenz's law firm. Six days later, she married a man named Grant Gormley (who was not, as it turned out, any of the men John had once suspected of replacing him). By the time John got back to Whatcom County, she had a job, too—at a local company that dealt in sawdust pellets—and what with her new husband and her new job, not many people in the family saw her. Rachel was said to be so angry at her mother for divorcing John that she *refused* to see her. Dick Pitner refused, too. I hadn't seen her myself since the trial—or John, for that matter. The only people in the family I'd kept up with were Susan and Betsey, who had become my friends, though you could say that for a while John had kept up with me, through the Web site called Caged Patriots, which posted his prison letters under the title "Nightmare." The letters comprised, in John's words, "a brief History of Events to the best of my recollection," and he always signed them "In Liberty's name."

Some of John's "recollection" was accurate. There was no doubt that Ed Mauerer had failed a couple of lie detector tests, or that he'd been cashing benefit checks from the state's Department of Labor and Industry at the same time that he was getting paid handsomely by the FBI. There was no doubt that the transcripts of tapes that had been entered in evidence at the trial were transcripts the government had made. There was no doubt that an argument could be made for entrapment and incrimination, if for no reason other than that it *had* been made, in court, and that to some very good legal minds the issue was far from settled. But John's disclaimers—he had been a law-abiding citizen leading a group of law-abiding citizens who, as early as 1995, had even stopped "sharing" the kind of literature that could conceivably fall into some madman's hands and lead to another Oklahoma City—were, if anything, even more unsettling from a distance. They had left me longing for reality. Or maybe I couldn't really believe how I had spent the year.

I had promised myself not to write anything about John and his men until they were out of jail and the first appeals had been decided; I wanted to see for myself what happened. And of course there were appeals—more appeals than I would have predicted. There were appeals filed on the original convictions, and then, because the prosecutors had filed a new conspiracy indictment against John and four of the other defendants, scarcely a month after the trial ended, there were appeals on the indictment itself, on the grounds of double jeopardy. Eventually, those appeals were denied, but it's safe to say that in April of 1997, the men now formally recharged—John, Fred, Marlin, John Kirk, and Tracy Lee Brown—were already beginning to weigh their chances and to think about making their separate deals. For one thing, they were under a certain amount of pressure, since with the exception of Fred they were all in jail, waiting for sentences that couldn't be set unless they *made* deals or went to trial on the new charge. For

another, while the first indictments had been quite complicated, involving as they did four different "objects" of conspiracy, and a score of separate charges, the new indictment
had the alarming advantage of simplicity. (There was only
one object of conspiracy now: the charge was conspiracy "to
make and possess destructive devices," with fifty-four acts
and examples cited, but no separate counts against any of the
men.) And, finally, there was the undeniable fact that Gary—
who had just admitted to having owned an Uzi and to trans-
ferring that Uzi to Ed Mauerer in the sale that John was
convicted for brokering—had been dropped from the new
indictment and would soon be sentenced. Richard Burton,
having done his own bargaining before the first trial, was already serving *his* sentence. Judy Kirk, who was facing a new
charge of "possession and transfer of a destructive device,"
had never, as far as I knew, been considered for the conspiracy
indictment. And by the time the new case came to jury trial,
in November of 2000—three years after the indictment was
handed down—Fred, Marlin, and even John Kirk had made
their arrangements with the prosecution. Marlin had been out
of prison for eight months, having entered a plea of guilty in
exchange for a sentence of time served and an eventual appearance in court as a prosecution witness—an appearance
he would commemorate by apologizing so profusely to Judge
Coughenour that the judge told him: Be careful what you say.
You might talk me out of it. Kirk had agreed to plead guilty in
a simple exchange for time served. And Fred, who held out
until September that year, had gone to "bench trial," meaning that he had agreed to the "stipulated facts" of a conspiracy and had then appeared before Judge Coughenour, been
found guilty, and been sentenced to three years' probation and

to the seven months he had already spent in jail when the first trial finished in 1997. In the end, it was down to *United States v. John Irvin Pitner and Tracy Lee Brown,* and it was over quickly. The trial began just before Thanksgiving and, after a holiday break, ended the following week with convictions for both men. John was released with a sentence of time served (and appealed on procedural grounds; a decision was still pending at the end of February this year). Brown was sentenced to time served and an additional six months, which kept him in prison till summer. He was the last man freed.

By the fall of 2001, the Seattle Freemen had gone to ground. Brown, who had always refused to state his age but, by some estimates, was now in his middle sixties, claimed to be living with his parents in Port Ludlow, Washington. The Burtons had dropped out of sight, left their house, and then resurfaced at a new address in Seattle. As for the Kirks, not even Tom Hillier, the federal defender who'd represented Kirk, knew where to find them. The last phone number and address they'd put on a court document turned out to be false, so it wasn't surprising that none of the old militiamen claimed to have seen them, or heard from them—though in all likelihood some had. Gary was back in Whatcom County, living alone at his father's place. His father had died of cancer in 1998, while Gary was serving time, and his sister, who'd inherited the farm, was letting him stay there. He sent me a message in September, through a Bellingham researcher I'd asked to find him, saying that he'd been beaten and "tortured" in the Texas prison where—I never knew why—he had served his sentence, and that because of those beatings his back was now too painful for him to go out at all, let alone to a political meeting. It wasn't as if his views had changed; he was clear about that. It was just that he could only keep up with the movement now by listening to the Patriot stations on shortwave radio. Fred, for his part, was apparently not keeping up at all, at least not publicly. The last time anyone had spotted Fred at a Patriot meeting— it was a Citizens for Liberty meeting—was in 1997, not long after he got out of jail and came home to Bellingham to revive Fred Fisher Masonry. Marlin was said to be living with his father in eastern Washington, out of contact and repentant. Ted Carter was doing what he had always done—sweeping chimneys. He was said to have come full circle from sparkler bomber to government witness to ardent Patriot, and by all reports was now quite taken with the idea that, of all the important Patriots, the government had chosen *him* to frame. Brian claimed to be working at a heavy-machine shop in Mount Vernon. (Nesbit's, where he'd been working when I met him, had long since closed.) If Brian was in a militia now, it wasn't one with what John would call a public face, and the same could probably be said of anyone who had ever showed up at Alpha One. The militiaman called Mark was by all accounts a model citizen; so was the militiaman Dan. Even the militiaman who'd been arrested in Bellingham's crime ring bust was known now as "a man who keeps his nose clean." He had pleaded guilty, served ninety days, and by the end of 1996 was already at home, paying his court fines and even his share of the restitution. (Ike Lantis himself was never tried; the charges against him were dismissed "without prejudice" after he was diagnosed with congestive heart failure, and so were the charges against his son Donald, who was involved in a car crash that left him comatose and, in less than a year, killed him.)

Officially, the Washington State Militia had disbanded. No

one I knew who was in it, or who had ever been in it or in any way connected to it, had been charged with any crime since John, Fred, and Marlin were indicted for conspiracy in 1997. Jack Schleimer, who'd quit so early, suspecting the group was infiltrated, said that he wouldn't even *think* about getting active in anything political now: "Not with the way those guys can infiltrate groups." Ben Hinkle—who could still be seen handing out leaflets at the Bellingham Farmers' Market, and was in fact enjoying a certain renewed attention as the first Whatcom County Patriot to publicly swear off celebrating the Fourth of July until America left the United Nations—still told everyone that he was never really in the militia, only an adviser. Ben's friend Doc Ellwanger had died quietly in 1997. Judie Ellwanger, who'd inherited her husband's debts to the IRS and, it seems, his sovereign-citizen principles, was mainly occupied with filing refusals to pay. Most of the people who once used John's open meetings for publicity or making speeches had moved on. Sharon Pietila and her husband had moved to Oregon, away from her wayward son, to raise her grandchild. Chuck Cushman was busy organizing in Alaska. Skip Richards had been born again as an environmentalist, and was helping the Nooksack Indians save their salmon. As for the people pitted against John by David Rockefeller, John Coughenour was still hearing cases on the Ninth Federal Circuit, and was now not only its resident expert on Freemen—having gone from the Seattle Freemen to the Montana Freemen, whose trial he presided over in 1998—but could probably claim to have been served with more wacky sovereign citizens' documents than the rest of his colleagues put together. Susan Dohrmann remained an assistant United States attorney on the Ninth Circuit; Gene Porter, her partner at

John's first trial, had been transferred to Kansas City, Missouri, by the time John was tried again. Ramon Garcia was in Ottawa, on loan to a joint anti-terrorism task force. (It wasn't difficult to find him, though the information officer at the Bureau's Seattle office had refused to release that information, or, rather, had said that he'd spoken to Ramon and that Ramon refused.) His old partner Cathy Fahey was now working out of the Milwaukee office, and Mike German had been posted to southern headquarters, in Atlanta. John's old mentor, John Trochmann, was himself said to be so absorbed in the white supremacist "theology" called Christian Identity that his own militia had been reduced to a warehouse. MOM was known in the Patriot movement now as "the mail-order militia," although the truth is Trochmann did so well after September 11th—selling out an enormous stock of gas masks and survival gear—that he announced he'd be raising prices as soon as a new shipment arrived. (He blamed his "Israeli supplier," saying that *he* was the one charging more.) None of this, of course, meant that militias had disappeared from Whatcom County. It meant that whoever was left was serious.

Nothing about hate has changed. The Patriots who inspired Timothy McVeigh and Terry Nichols to kill 168 people in Oklahoma City in 1995 still have most of the same enemies Osama bin Laden had when he organized the murder of 3,061 people in New York, Virginia, and Pennsylvania six years later, and if you open their Web sites you'll find that most of them still say so. Psychiatrists claim that groups like the Washington State Militia can have, at least in theory, a socializing function, that they can discipline paranoia, and by extension paranoiacs, by focusing on a delusion everyone in the group shares, that they can set perimeters on delusion and thus permit some otherwise dangerously capricious people to live the rest of their lives as useful and harmless citizens. Maybe. John, of course, had told me the same thing. I used to wonder if John was right—if apart from his own evident delusion he was actually quite shrewd. The question that haunts me now, in a very changed world, is this: Was it the militia that kept John from terrorism, or simply the fact that he wasn't shrewd enough or smart enough or organized enough or rich enough to do the things he dreamed of?

Sometimes, writing about John, I would think of Sharon, whom I liked enormously and disagreed with about almost everything, telling me how she had been born again as a Christian. It was the 1970s, and Sharon was down and out in Whatcom County, living in a house full of hippies on Valley Highway, right by Everybody's Store (her cousin Maeve, who never stopped being a hippie, still lives there), and wondering if she'd ever again have the money to buy drugs and get stoned. Then she remembered that the Pentecostalists in the church down the road claimed to be getting stoned, in a manner of speaking, every week at their Sunday service. So she went to church and "got high on the Holy Spirit," and of course she went back the next week, and got high all over again, and in no time her life had changed. Sharon's story was the most interesting story I heard in a year of traveling to Whatcom County, and in any case it's the one that still reminds me of how many people have sat in the woods there over the last century, down and out and matching wits with their own cravings. I knew, or thought I knew, what Christians like Sharon craved, but I have no notion at all of what John and his militiamen craved—violence, or the idea of violence, or the "discipline" of enemies, or even the discipline of punishment. All I do know is that they got stoned just talking about their war, and that they thought of it as a holy war, and never mind if, as Paul de Armond once said, you could take them out with a group of Girl Scouts, or if they never got stoned enough to think of themselves as weapons.

Susan said that "the saddest part" of John's brief history as a hero was that "the only person who believed him was the FBI." But, to me, the saddest part was that the people who believed him were Susan and Betsey. It was their life, the life they had put together against so many odds, that in the end changed. They bought a new house in a new town and started over, and told everyone how much they liked it; there were so many different kinds of people there. But then Betsey lost one of her jobs, and a year later the other, and in January last year, the month John got out of prison, Susan had a second stroke. And it's hard to avoid the conclusion that a few years of believing John had something to do with the struggle they have had since then—Susan was back in the hospital two weeks after her father died—and the family that still talks more about the day Susan and Betsey "sent John back to jail" than about anything John himself did. I think of those women now as the real patriots in John's life, maybe because they picked themselves up and started over a third time, the way Americans are supposed to do. Betsey went back to college to learn how to run a business. She took on their landscaping jobs, and even got slim, digging up flower beds and laying grass and swinging thirty-pound sacks of fertilizer over her shoulder. By the fall of 2001, Susan was back, frail and gritty, and they were working together. When I wrote for news then, they said they had ten new clients, a new young partner—Susan's daughter had moved to Portland—and a wonderful new rock, from a neighbor who'd been to China, for their collection. In a few weeks, with the gardening season over and the flu season starting, they'd be driving through eastern Washington on a visiting nurse program, Betsey giving the shots and Susan registering the patients. They didn't know what John would be doing. "We are no longer innocent," they said.

—March 1, 2002

Author's Note

As I was not allowed to attend any of the Washington State Militia's secret squad meetings, and was obviously not party to any of the members' private phone calls or conversations (beyond, of course, their conversations with me), I have relied mainly on government transcripts of the FBI tapes of those meetings, phone calls, and conversations. Most of the transcripts from which I've quoted were made from tape recordings and video tapes, or portions of tape recordings and video tapes, which were entered in evidence in the trial referred to in this book as *United States v. John Irvin Pitner et al.*, in January and February of 1996, and were played at that trial; the relevant transcripts were provided to the press in court. A few of the transcripts I've used involve both portions of tapes that were entered in evidence and portions that were not entered in evidence but were provided to the defendants' attorneys, some of whom provided them to me. Susan B. Dohrmann, the assistant U.S. attorney who led the prosecution team in both the 1996 trial and in John Pitner's subsequent conspiracy trial in 2000, has emphasized that it is the FBI tapes themselves, and not the transcripts of those tapes, that constitute the evidence of what was, or was not, said.

About the Author

JANE KRAMER is *The New Yorker*'s European correspondent. She is the author of eight books, including *The Last Cowboy, Europeans,* and *The Politics of Memory.* Jane Kramer lives in Europe and New York.